THE DREYFUS AFFAIR
IN FRENCH SOCIETY AND POLITICS

For Jonathan

THE DREYFUS AFFAIR
IN FRENCH SOCIETY AND POLITICS

ERIC CAHM

Longman
London and New York

Longman Group Limited,
Longman House, Burnt Mill,
Harlow, Essex CM20 2JE, England
and Associated Companies throughout the world.

*Published in the United States of America
by Longman Publishing, New York*

Originally published as
L'Affaire Dreyfus by
Le Livre de Poche 1994

© Librairie Général Française, 1994
English translation and adaptation © Eric Cahm 1966

This edition first published 1966

First published 1996

Transferred to digital print on demand 2001

ISBN 0 582 276780 PPR

British Library Cataloguing-in-Publication Data

A catalogue record for this book is
available from the British Library

Library of Congress Cataloging-in-Publication Data

Cahm, Eric.
  [Affaire Dreyfus.   English]
  The Dreyfus affair in French society and politics / Eric Cahm.
     p.   cm.
  Includes bibliographical references and index.
  ISBN 0–582–27679–9 (csd). — ISBN 0–582–27678–0 (ppr)
     1. Dreyfus, Alfred, 1859–1935—Influence. 2. Trials (Treason)–
–France—Political aspects. 3. France—Politics and
government—19th century—Social aspects. 4. Antisemitism—France–
–History—19th century. 5. Intellectuals—France—Political
activity. I. Title.
  DC354.8.C3413   1996
  944.081′2′092—dc20   95–40520
                                                           CIP

Printed and bound by Antony Rowe Ltd, Eastbourne

CONTENTS

PREFACE

That there is nothing new to be said about the Dreyfus Affair is an almost universal illusion in France. 'Surely it has all been said already?': this opening gambit seems to have become commonplace. So that when I was invited to produce, in French, a short paperback on the subject for students and general readers, I did not only want to seize the opportunity to re-tell the familiar story as clearly and concisely as I could, giving due weight to all the events, the larger-than-life characters and the locations of the Affair, and synthesizing the findings of the most recent research. I also wanted to demonstrate that there is still much awaiting discovery about one of the Third Republic's most profound crises, even after a century's study, which has produced a veritable mountain of books and articles.

The illusion that everything has been said already is fostered precisely by this terrifying weight of existing work, as well as by the undoubted fact that everything worth saying has indeed been said about the whodunnit side of the subject and the role of the General Staff, notably by Marcel Thomas in *L'Affaire sans Dreyfus* (1961). However, in the last three decades, the attention of serious scholars has shifted to the political, social and cultural dimensions of the Affair, and work continues apace in these areas. The publications of 1994–95, coinciding with the centenary of Dreyfus's first trial, have now shown that the international impact of the Affair is only today, for the first time, being seriously tackled on a world-wide basis (*see* p. 193).

The present book, by its title and its contents, aims to take account, therefore, of the research of recent decades, bearing notably on the reception of the Affair in France by individuals, social classes, religious denominations and the political parties, and the forms of its interaction with society and politics.

I have summarized, too, in the Prelude and the first chapter, some of the findings of my own research, centring on the Affair and public opinion in 1894–95, which was based on an exhaustive study of the

Paris daily press from November 1894 to January 1895 (over 40 titles). (*See La première affaire Dreyfus. L'affaire Dreyfus et l'opinion publique en 1894–1895* (1993), 230pp., unpublished. A copy is available for consultation at the Institute Français de Presse, 92, rue d'Assas, 75006 Paris).

I have been and remain convinced that the mass of under-exploited press and archival material on the Affair and its role in French society and politics is so enormous that the only possible strategy for the individual scholar is to try to cover *all* the sources for a strictly limited period.

My research, and many years spent teaching the Affair, starting at Portsmouth Polytechnic, have led me to two significant conclusions. The first of these is that there is a crucial distinction to be drawn between the extremist anti-Dreyfusism of the nationalists and antisemites on the one hand, and, on the other, the moderate anti-Dreyfusism of successive governments from 1894 to 1898, of the whole of official France and much of the bourgeoisie (*see* pp. 486–88). This distinction has until now been largely overlooked, although it was noted by Joseph Reinach, and also emerges from Janine Ponty's ground-breaking work on the press in 1898 and 1899. It draws attention to the whole governmental position in these years, which has also rarely been characterized in detail.

The second conclusion, relating to the socio-political dynamics of the Affair, is that the extent of the mobilization for and against Dreyfus was due in large measure to the fact that the Affair offered a golden opportunity to a variety of discontented social and political groups – from the intellectuals to the nationalists and the old ruling classes – to assert themselves against France's new rulers, what may be called the contented classes: the governing centre Republicans, placeholders of all kinds and the mass of the bourgeoisie. To the latter, the Dreyfus Affair was disruptive and unwelcome; they preferred to behave as if, in the celebrated words of the Prime Minister Méline, there was 'no Dreyfus Affair' (*see* pp. 104–8). Apart from these major conclusions, I have been able to document from the press the way Rochefort and Drumont successfully blackmailed General Mercier in November 1894 into using the famous secret file not shown to the defence, so as to ensure Dreyfus's conviction, and how, when he capitulated, they switched overnight from being his slanderous opponents to being his most ardent champions (pp. 19–20). I have drawn attention for the first time to Madame Bodson's sensational interview of 6th November 1894; to the fact that it was precisely after Bernard-Lazare sought in 1897 to present the Affair as a Jewish issue that he was silenced by the Dreyfusards; to the fact that the story of Dreyfus's escape from Devil's Island, usually attributed to the *South Wales Argus*, was actually first told in the London *Daily Chronicle* and was only 'confirmed' by the Welsh paper afterwards; and the odd fact that Dreyfus was tried in 1894 in the very room in which Victor Hugo's wedding feast took place in 1822. I was excited to discover that there was actually ample documentation on the location of the 1894 trial in the rue du Cherche-Midi, including plans and photographs of the old Hôtel des Conseils de Guerre, which hardly gets a mention in any book on the Affair. The press coverage of the 1894 trial itself is full of fascinating detail.

In short, there is still plenty awaiting discovery, even on the most familiar episodes of the story, let alone on its socio-political and international context.

This edition of *L'Affaire Dreyfus* (published by the Livre de Poche in 1994), has been entirely re-written in English, revised and some-what augmented, e.g. with regard to the 1898 elections and to the role of women and feminists. The Epilogue has been extended to include the echos of the Affair in the france of today; a Prelude sets the scene with a sketch of France in 1894. Finally, the book has been provided with a much fuller bibliography, so as to take account of the variety of useful material in English. There are some remarkable pieces of forgotten eye-witness reporting by such English contempor-aries of the Affair as George Barlow and G. W. Steevens.

The translations of the extracts from Zola, Jaurès, Maurras, Barrès and others are my own: I have tried to give a flavour in English of the passionate rhetoric of 1898–99.

I owe, like all students of the Affair, an enormous debt to Joseph Reinach's monumental six volumes, which remain an inexhaustible mine of information on every aspect of the Affair. I have often found that his exact words still provide the best account – sometimes the only account – of certain moments of the Affair, and the best picture of some of the characters. His testimony remains irreplaceable.

Tours, August 1995

ACKNOWLEDGEMENTS

The French original owes much to the support and encouragement of my colleagues at Tours University, Pierre Citti, Gérald Chaix and Michel Simonin, director of the 'Références' collection, and to the understanding of Dominique Goust, of Le Livre de Poche. Madeleine Rebérioux, whose knowledge of the Affair is unrivalled, and whose friendship and support I have valued over many years, read the whole manuscript and helped me to avoid a number of historical blunders.

This English version has also benefited from the advice of Nelly Wilson (Bristol University) on Bernard-Lazare, of Michael Burns (Mount Holyoke College) on Dreyfus's religious views and of Máire Cross (University of Northumbria) on women and feminists. Helen Trouille (University of Bradford) gave generously of her time to guide me through the minefield of French legal terminology and Paul Redman and Mary Poku, barristers in London, suggested some elusive courtroom equivalents. Staff at Longman suggested a number of useful additions, notably the Prelude.

Joy Harwood typed the original French text from a not always legible manuscript. Finally, my research assistant, Joanna Loughlin, has been a faithful helper from the beginning, and her skilled eye has enabled me to eliminate a large number of infelicities in the translation and in my English.

My warmest thanks are due to all these people: the responsibility for any remaining errors and shortcomings is, of course, entirely my own.

NOTE ON REFERENCING

It has not proved practicable for reasons of space to reference every single quotation, but a great many will be very familiar to those who have previously worked on the Affair; a number frequently recur in anthologies. For an English version of Zola's *J'Accuse . . .!* see that by Snyder; the full French text can be found in that by Colette Becker (see 'Further Reading'). The source of practically all the quotations can in any case be readily established either from the date, in the case of a newspaper article, or from the place in the narrative. Direct quotations from trial proceedings are either taken from the official records of the Zola trial, the Rennes trial or from the Leblois anthology. Quotations attributed to Reinach, Léon Blum, Mathieu Dreyfus or Maurice Paléologue are all from the works appearing in the 'Further Reading' section. The footnotes in each chapter are to sources not previously quoted in works on the Affair, and to one or two recent works of scholarship to which my debts are evident.

PRELUDE

When, on 1 November 1894, the French public learned that a Jewish artillery officer, Alfred Dreyfus, on attachment for training with the General Staff, had recently been arrested on a charge of high treason, they naturally reacted with horror and indignation. If a French officer was actually guilty of treason, this must surely be the worst scandal in the French army for many years. And, seven weeks later, Alfred Dreyfus was duly tried by court-martial and unanimously found guilty of communicating with a foreign power. Only a monster, it seemed, could have committed such a crime against France's beloved army. Dreyfus only escaped execution because such a sentence was impossible in peacetime: he was transported to Devil's Island early in 1895 and France soon forgot about him. Outside his family, only a handful of people at first believed he was innocent. Although in 1894 France had been deeply shocked by the affair, which was serious enough in all conscience, no one yet had any idea that it would develop, in 1897–99, into one of the gravest crises of the Third Republic, and that it would become one of the most celebrated miscarriages of justice in modern times.

In France, a campaign to clear Dreyfus's name grew month by month from the autumn of 1897. Families, religious communities and political parties became increasingly divided by it. Dreyfus's supporters argued that his case must be re-opened out of respect for Truth, Justice and the rights of the individual, while his opponents, beginning with the government and the whole of official France, stood by the decisions of the courts, and held that to campaign in favour of a retrial was to impugn the honour of the army. The General Staff and some anti-Dreyfusards even said that it was against the national interest to review his case at all, and they appealed to the notion of raison d'Etat. A twelve-year campaign was also waged among extreme anti-Dreyfusards against the prominent position middle-class Jews had attained, not only in the army, but in many areas of French state and society.

Normal life was suspended for two years in 1897–99 while a

passionate debate raged on these and other issues, issues which went far beyond the fate of a single individual. The social and political ramifications of the Dreyfus case became so extensive that it set one social group against another, Catholic against Jew. It ranged anticlericals against the Church, Republicans against nationalists, and it eventually aligned the whole of the Republican Left with the pro-Dreyfus camp, in opposition to an anti-Dreyfusard Right and extreme Right.

The pardon of Dreyfus after his second court-martial in 1899 coincided with a political victory by the Dreyfusard Left, after a winter and spring during which the Republic itself seemed threatened by an extreme right-wing coup: the Affair had put the loyalty of the army under the most severe strain, as the nationalists of the extreme Right called on it to help overturn the Republic.

But there was no coup, and the immediate effect of the Affair, as it came to be called, was to bring the Left to power in France for a decade after 1899, to consolidate the Republic, and to relaunch the Left on its course of secularization of French society. The anti-Dreyfusard activities of certain religious orders during the Affair, notably the Assumptionists, gave the Left an opportunity to restart its campaign against them and against the Catholic Church in general, seen as having been hostile to Dreyfus; the new campaign culminated in 1905 in the Separation of Church and State.

During the turmoil of the Affair, long-standing friendships were to be destroyed and lifelong political and ideological commitments abandoned in favour of new loyalties, which would be decisive for 20th-century France. Writers and intellectuals who supported Dreyfus were to become committed to the cause of social justice and of socialism. Socialists were to become divided for decades between revolutionaries and reformists over the issue of participation in bourgeois governments, which they came up against for the first time in 1899 as a result of the Affair. In the other camp, the Affair gave a political and ideological impetus to new forms of nationalism on the extreme Right, in particular that of the Action Française of Charles Maurras. The impact of the Affair on France, both in the short and the long term, has been such that the shock waves can still be felt today, for example in the attitude of the far Right and a minority of the French public towards the Jews, and in the army's continuing sensitivity about anything concerned with the Affair.

Outside France, the Affair attracted widespread attention from the beginning, being followed with close, sometimes passionate, attention, from the United States to the depths of Russia. The personal fate of Alfred Dreyfus aroused sympathy everywhere, and the issues raised stirred consciences all over the world. Dreyfus's second conviction at Rennes in 1899 sparked off world-wide protests, and threats to boycott the Paris International Exhibition of 1900. Meanwhile, foreign observers had been watching with anxiety or hope to see whether the Republic would survive the onslaught of forces which seemed for a time to threaten its very existence and the survival in France of the principles of the 1789 Revolution, which she had long ago given to the world.

But of all this, as has been indicated, the French in 1894 suspected nothing. The Republic seemed well and truly in control. It had successfully weathered the crises of Boulangism and Panama. And it had now at last begun to believe that its victory over the monarchists was complete. The latter no longer felt able to campaign as such, and simply called themselves conservatives.

The main threat to the stability of the Republic, since the beginning of the 1890s, had been the upsurge of socialism and syndicalism, and the wave of anarchist bomb outrages from 1892 to 1894. The Republicans now suddenly felt threatened politically and socially on their left flank, at the very time when they were beginning to feel their victory over the monarchist Right was irreversible. The danger now seemed to come from the Left.

At Fourmies, in the Nord, the army had fired on working-class demonstrators on 1 May 1891; nine people were killed. A wave of public sympathy followed, there were more and more strikes, trade union branches sprouted, and politicians, notably Jaurès, stood for Parliament to represent the interests of the workers. At the 1893 parliamentary elections, Socialist representation leapt to around 50. The Republicans, for whom the workers had up to then been junior partners in the fight against the Church, took fright. So as to defend society and the rights of private property, they began, in the spring of 1894, to make advances to the Catholics with the aim of making common cause with them against the socialists.

This shift in alliances had been made easier by a papal encyclical of 1892, which enjoined Catholics in France to accept the legitimacy of the Republican regime. While few Catholics in France actually went over to the Republic, the Republicans, at the beginning of the Affair, continued to court them, declaring that the great battle with the Church was over. In this situation, the Republicans' chief message in the autumn of 1894 was one of peace and reconciliation, now that the anarchist threat had been removed by repressive legislation in the summer. For them, it was time to forget the old political and religious quarrels: simply the socialist threat must be lifted, by refuting the new doctrine and weaning the workers away from it by concessions to the underprivileged. All the French people were invited to rally round a Republic wedded to 'progress'. The governing Republican party now actually called themselves Progressists. When Dreyfus's arrest was revealed to the French public in November 1894, there had been a certain return to peace and quiet after the fright to the bourgeoisie from the anarchist bombers. In October, just before the re-opening of Parliament, the political commentator of the establishment journal *La Revue des Deux Mondes*, wrote that though very lively debates were to be expected in the new session, 'the general state of public opinion is very quiet'.

Normal political life was returning after the anarchist bombings, and the only problem on the horizon was the likely disruptive behaviour of the socialists in Parliament. Since the 1893 elections, they represented a significant parliamentary force, and they were now expected to launch a campaign of vehement speeches and obstructionism in the Chamber. 'The holidays are over,' complained the *Revue des Deux Mondes*, 'and we can expect a hail of parliamentary questions such as has never been seen before.' The radicals were little less militant than the socialists in their opposition to the ruling Republicans: they had joined them in a violent campaign against the new President of the Republic, Casimir-Périer, elected to replace Carnot who had been assassinated by an anarchist in June: as a big industrialist he seemed to the Left to epitomize the identification of the Republic with the capitalist class. Hostility was thus increasing in the autumn of 1894 between the governmental Republicans and the socialists and radicals on the extreme Left.

As to the syndicalist movement, it came out at its Nantes congress in favour of the revolutionary general strike.

Thus, though terrorism had abated, bourgeois society in France still felt threatened by an extreme Left and by a trade union movement whose violence, though it remained at the verbal level, still gave rise to anxiety: it seemed likely that France was at least in for a stormy parliamentary session.

This said, what concerned the majority of Frenchmen more than anything else in October 1894 was actually the illness of the Russian Tsar Alexander III. Interest in all other events, wrote the *Revue des Deux Mondes*, had been eclipsed by the serious state of the Tsar's health. 'After Russia, it was France that felt the deepest emotion on hearing of Alexander III's illness. From one end of the country to another, in towns and villages, in châteaux and cottages, the feeling was unanimous; we have never met one that was so general.'

The reason the French showed such a universal attachment to a Tsar who ruled a police state was that he had finally, after much hesitation, agreed late in 1893 to sign a military convention with France that had delivered her from 20 years of diplomatic isolation. A wave of Russophilia had been engineered by the French authorities, and the Tsar had become an immensely popular figure in France. 'The Tsar has become popular in himself in France,' explained *La Revue des Deux Mondes*, 'simply because of the good he has done to France. A quarter of a century ago, we were cruelly unhappy; since then our feeling of ill fortune has weighed heavily upon us ... The joyous cannon of Kronstadt [during the French fleet's visit] resounded throughout Europe and was heard in the remotest hamlets of France ... France trembled with joy. It was he [Alexander III] who gave us, after such a long and bitter time of waiting, the feeling, so infinitely sweet to a great nation, that we were appreciated at our true worth, spiritually and materially ... How should we not have been grateful? From that day, the Russian Emperor has been associated in our hearts with all that we hold most dear.' The news of the Tsar's eventual death actually coincided with the revelation of Dreyfus's arrest, and the shock to the French was such that for a day or two it almost drove the case of the treacherous artillery captain from the newspapers.

Such then was the climate in which the Dreyfus Affair began. But though the case only came to public attention on 1 November, the fact that a French officer had committed treason had first been brought to the attention of the authorities at the end of September 1894. The whole Affair, which was almost to turn France upside down, began with some torn strips of paper.

1 THE FIRST DREYFUS AFFAIR: DREYFUS IS TRIED AND CONVICTED OF TREASON

A BORDEREAU

The date was 27 September 1894. In a low room in the Paris War Ministry in the rue Saint-Dominique, a massively-built officer with a moustache showed his comrades in the counter-espionage service a document proving that a French officer had committed treason.

'Just look at what has come into my hands! This is really strong stuff and I hope we shall nab him!'

This is what the author of the unsigned document had written:

Though I have no news to indicate that you wish to see me, nevertheless, Sir, I am sending you some interesting items of information:
1. A note on the hydraulic buffer of the 120 and on the way this piece behaved.
2. A note on the covering troops (some changes will be made under the new plan).
3. A note on a change in the artillery formations.
4. A note relating to Madagascar.
5. The draft Field Artillery Firing Manual (14th March 1894).
This last document is extremely difficult to obtain and I can only have it at my disposal for a very few days. The War Minister has sent a fixed number of copies to the army corps, and the corps are responsible for them. Each officer in possession of one must return it after manoeuvres. If, then, you would like to extract what interests you from it and keep it for me afterwards I shall obtain one – unless you would like me to have it copied out in full, and then to send you the copy.
I am going to leave for manoeuvres.

MAJOR HENRY

Who was the officer who had obtained this incontrovertible evidence of treason, and how had it reached him? It was Major Henry, a man of 48, a ranker who had become the dominant figure in the counter-espionage service. He was 'bullet-headed, with a low forehead and an upturned nose above a short, heavy moustache; his eyes were small and protruding'. From a peasant background, intelligent and wily, but uncultured and ignorant of foreign languages, he had owed his first appointment to the department – known for security reasons as the 'Statistical Department' – to the patronage of General Miribel, who was anxious to be seen to be 'democratizing' the War Ministry. In 1894, it was Major Henry's task to sort the documents arriving in the department and, if they were in French, to reconstitute them. This is what he had done in the present case, by sticking together the torn pieces. He was efficient at what were essentially police duties; these also included the preparation of forgeries intended to deceive foreign powers.

The latest document, which came to be known as the *bordereau*, or covering note, had been handed over to him by Marie Bastian, a French agent employed as a domestic servant at the German Embassy. Being thought of as a stupid woman, she had never aroused the suspicions of her employers. Once or twice a month, she would deliver to Henry or one of his emissaries the documents she had quietly removed from the embassy waste-paper baskets. These meetings, straight out of a cheap novel, took place at dusk, in a nearby church, usually the basilica of Sainte-Clotilde, which was directly opposite the War Ministry and set back less than a hundred yards from the rue Saint-Dominique.

Henry immediately submitted the *bordereau* to his departmental chief, Colonel Sandherr, an Alsatian and a great patriot, who prided himself on having bombarded the German general staff with false information for years. All the officers in the Ministry who saw the *bordereau* on the first day were sure the author was one of their own number: his language, they thought, was so much the same as that which they used themselves. They did not trouble to notice the incorrect terms he had used.

As a result, they all became suspect at once. Their apprehension was only heightened by the atmosphere of spy-mania that prevailed in the Ministry, and in the country at large. The German press found it only too easy to mock the French propensity to discover spies at every street corner.

The *bordereau* was then submitted to the top officials: it even reached the office of the Minister, General Mercier. But for several days the enquiry got nowhere. It was then decided to put a photograph of the *bordereau* to the four Bureau chiefs and to the directorate of artillery.

Those at the top were already convinced that the traitor was someone in the Ministry, and, because of the references to artillery matters in the *bordereau*, they also believed that he was a gunner. But no one could recognize the handwriting.

On 6 October, they were ready to consider the matter closed. However, it was just at this moment that the head of the Fourth Bureau, Colonel Fabre, showed the photograph to his new second-in-command, Lieutenant-Colonel d'Aboville, who had just taken up his duties. The latter responded that it would not be difficult to identify the author of the document. 'If I were asked, I think I should manage it.'

'How?'

'Obviously the author is an officer extremely well versed in technical matters.'

Then, wishing to draw attention to himself in his new position, d'Aboville explained that the author of the document must have been in contact with the First, the Second and the Third Bureaux, and that only a staff trainee could have had such opportunities.

Fabre could think of no reply. He looked through the list of trainees on attachment to the General Staff and his eye fell on the name of Alfred Dreyfus, to whom he had given a poor training report: 'This officer is not fully competent. While he is intelligent and very gifted, he is pretentious and does not fulfil, in regard to his character, his conscientiousness and the execution of his duties, the necessary conditions for employment on the General Staff of the army.' D'Aboville went further, adding: 'His character was underhand, he was not liked by his comrades and everyone noticed his indiscreet curiosity.'

A captain in the artillery, Alfred Dreyfus had so far had a brilliant career. He was already a General Staff trainee at 35. He belonged to a family of Jewish industrialists from Alsace, which had been incorporated into the German Empire after the Franco-Prussian War. From the day in 1871 when, as a boy of 12, he had watched German troops marching into Mulhouse (his 'first sadness'), he had harboured feelings of hostility and resentment towards Germany. These had been a major factor in his decision to take up a military career. The whole family, apart from one of his brothers, had opted for French nationality in 1872. Until now, Alfred had been considered by practically all his superiors to be a keen and intelligent soldier. He had had an exceptional education, and set out to master the most difficult problems. His future looked rosy, and he could even hope to rise to the rank of general. Furthermore, he was wealthy, having married Lucie Hadamard, the daughter of a Paris diamond merchant. He lived with her and their two children in an apartment in the smart 16th arrondissement, at the bottom of the Avenue du Trocadéro (now the Avenue du Président-Wilson.

But it was true that he was not liked by his fellow-officers. One who had known him at the Ecole de Guerre drew this unflattering picture of him:

> Physically he was not well-endowed but he seemed unaware of it as he had such a high opinion of himself. Medium-sized, with red hair and eyes level with his face, his head set deep between his shoulders, he was excessively short-sighted. He was very intelligent and not at all dissolute: those in his year had more confidence in his integrity than sympathy towards his personality.
>
> He was overproud by nature, which inclined him to constant and universal ostentation. He took great pride in his wealth and his connections, and had a room at the Ecole where he lived alone.[1]

There was no doubt that Dreyfus's wealth cut him off from the other officers, many of whom had to live entirely on their meagre pay. Also, he did not belong to the same artistocratic milieu as a number of his comrades. He represented a new type of officer, who owed his promotion solely to his technical ability. However, his isolation, his unpopularity and his excessive curiosity were not enough to provide Fabre and d'Aboville with proof of his treason. There was still the handwriting question. But, as ill luck would have it, his handwriting bore a superficial resemblance to that of the *bordereau*. As soon as the two officers found a sample, they saw a 'striking similarity'. They immediately made known their discovery to General Gonse, the second-in-command, and to General de Boisdeffre, the Chief of Staff.

When Sandherr, the antisemitic head of the Statistical Department, learned the suspect's name, he exclaimed: 'I should have known!' But, as Marcel Thomas has pointed out, the fact that neither he nor the other officers had made the connection before shows that it was not Dreyfus's Jewish background which first made him a suspect.

1 'Un traître', *Le Matin*, 3 November 1898.

JEWISH OFFICERS

Before the Dreyfus Affair, Jewish officers had been able to rise to the highest ranks in the French army without meeting any official obstacles as Jews. Republican policy was to treat all officers equally, regardless of religion. Twenty-five Jews were to become generals under the Third Republic: Dreyfus himself had only had one occasion to complain when he received a poor report at the Ecole de Guerre from General Bonnefond, who declared he wanted no Jews on the General Staff. General Dionne wrote, 'I have seen many Jewish officers at the Ecole de Guerre. I can state that none of them met with any animosity from their superior officers or their comrades. If this was not so for the honourable M. Dreyfus, this was because of his revolting character, his intemperate language and his undignified private life, and in no way because of his religion.' It was only from the time of the Dreyfus Affair that Jewish officers began to find the progress of their careers hampered by the fact that they were Jewish.[2]

During the first days of the Affair, Dreyfus's origins simply made his treason seem less surprising in the eyes of certain of his fellow-officers. He was suspected initially because of a similarity of hand-writing. This similarity immediately struck General Mercier, the War Minister. Mercier was 'a tall, slim man of 60, with sallow skin and harsh features'; he had a grey moustache and eyes that always seemed half-closed. When he was informed by the Chief of Staff that Dreyfus was under suspicion, he experienced, he said, 'a terrible feeling. At first sight, there appeared to be no doubt.' He believed at once that Dreyfus was guilty. Mercier had the reputation of sticking obstinately to his first impressions: he had taken to remarking that he never went back on an order. From the outset, he was thus to remain unshakeably convinced, not only, like his subordinates, that the traitor was to be found within the Ministry, but that the guilty man was indeed Dreyfus. He ordered an enquiry: 'Make a search! Find the man!' But he was in no doubt about the result.

From his point of view, the matter was urgent and the enquiry must be brought to a rapid conclusion. For he was politically in a highly vulnerable position. He had a reputation as a Republican, but after a very promising start in office, and some easy parliamentary successes, he had become over-confident and had committed two blunders. Firstly, he had refused to see the inventor Turpin, who had

2 Pierre Birnbaum, *Les fous de la République. Histoire politique des Juifs d'Etat de Gambetta à Vichy* (Paris, 1992), p. 244.

already sold an explosive to the French government. This had earned him a reproof in Parliament, after a debate in which he had provoked general mirth by referring to his 'gunner's flair'. He had then ordered the early release of 60,000 conscripts, which had depleted the army garrisons. Since the spring of 1894, he had upset the army chiefs, Parliament and the entire press. The nationalist papers constantly made fun of his 'gunner's flair'. He was being threatened in Parliament with an appearance before the army committee, and the other members of the government were already thinking that he would have to be dropped. An unresolved case of treason would deal the final blow to his ministerial career.

In this critical situation for the Minister, the assistant Chief of Staff, General Gonse, decided to call in the help of Major du Paty de Clam, who was seen as one of the rising stars in the Ministry. Du Paty was a marquis, proud of his noble rank, a figure representative of those scions of the nobility who, under the Third Republic, no longer shunned the army, as they had done in the democratic days of the Revolution and Napoleon, and, graduating from Saint-Cyr in ever-greater numbers, now took their place again in the upper ranks of the army, which still preserved so many vestiges of the Ancien Régime: one in nine officers was now from the nobility. They felt that in the army they could maintain their traditions of service to France even though they detested her Republican regime. Their only thought was to exclude from the upper echelons Republicans, Protestants and Jews, all those who, like Dreyfus, did not owe their promotion to their noble birth. Of course, Dreyfus was not only a Jew, but one of the new technical elite, and he was a bourgeois upstart and a *nouveau riche* into the bargain.[3]

The army of the 1890s had thus not been wholly republicanized, despite the efforts of Gambetta and his successors. For the opponents of the regime, it still remained the possible instrument of a political come-back. It was thus an officer of noble birth, hostile to Dreyfus and his kind, who was put in charge of the initial enquiry and the first handwriting comparison. Du Paty prided himself on his talents as a graphologist, but he was in no way an expert. He was in fact so short-sighted that he walked awkwardly without eyeglasses: he was too vain to wear them. His conclusion was that, despite the differences between the two handwritings, there were enough similarities to warrant calling in an official expert.

---

3 Ibid., ch. 12, and Jérôme Hélie, 'L'arche sainte fracturée', in Pierre Birnbaum, ed., *La France de l'affaire Dreyfus* (Paris, 1994), pp. 231ff.

Mercier did not need any convincing. An official expert's report was obviously a legal requirement, but he saw this as a mere formality as his mind was already made up. He sought the name of an expert from his colleague Guérin of the Justice Ministry; the latter recommended Gobert, the graphologist employed by the Banque de France.

MERCIER TAKES ACTION

By 9 October, Mercier had thus involved himself personally in the Dreyfus case for the first time. Thinking, however, that he could not act entirely on his own initiative, he went the next day to inform Casimir-Périer, the President of the Republic, explaining that the *bordereau* was the work of a General Staff officer and that the treason 'appeared proven'. He also stated that the documents that had been communicated to a foreign power were of 'little importance'. From the Elysée Palace, he hurried to see the Prime Minister, Charles Dupuy. Dupuy decided that it was necessary to act with the utmost discretion. He called a restricted cabinet meeting involving only those ministers directly concerned. At this meeting, held on 11 October, Mercier announced the discovery of the *bordereau*, explaininig that it had been found in the waste-paper basket of the German military attaché, and that it had been torn into pieces, reconstituted, and photographed. From the handwriting comparisons, he said he had concluded that the guilty officer was on the General Staff, but he refused to name him.

Gabriel Hanotaux, the Foreign Minister, objected that without more proof it would be impossible to prosecute. He was afraid of a diplomatic incident if the German Embassy were to be implicated publicly in a spy case. He extracted a promise from Mercier not to pursue the matter if no other proof could be found. That same evening, he insisted on the same point again in a private discussion with Mercier. The latter obstinately replied that he had sufficient presumptive evidence, and that he was legally obliged to pursue his enquiries. In any case, as the matter had become known to a number of officers, he was afraid of a scandal from the opposite direction: 'We should be accused of making a pact with espionage.' In fact, despite his promise to the other ministers, Mercier had already decided on Dreyfus's arrest. The Chief of Staff, de Boisdeffre, announced to du Paty that he had been made responsible for the arrest and would be in charge of the judicial enquiry to follow.

In the meantime, Mercier ordered another handwriting report

from Alphonse Bertillon. Bertillon was not a graphologist either, but the head of Criminal Records at the Prefecture of Police.

HANDWRITING REPORTS

Gobert's was the first report to arrive. Alas! it was not conclusive. Although he found 'fairly significant analogies' between the two hand-writings, he also found 'numerous and important differences', and he concluded that the letter in question 'might be from a person other than the one under suspicion'. Bertillon wrote: 'If we eliminate the hypothesis of a document forged with the utmost care, it appears quite evident to me from a comparison of the two documents that it was the same person who wrote the letter and the documents I have received.' They did not agree. But this was not crucial for Mercier: he went ahead and confirmed to du Paty on 13 October the order to arrest Dreyfus; to cover himself, he claimed to be acting on the authority of Casimir-Périer and Dupuy.

THE ARREST

The scene of the arrest was prepared by du Paty in minute detail and suggested he had read too many novels. Dreyfus was ordered to attend a general inspection at the Ministry, in civilian clothes, at 9 a.m. on 15 October in the office of the Chief of Staff.

When he arrived, du Paty dictated to him a letter containing the main words contained in the *bordereau*. If his hand were to shake, this would be, for du Paty, the proof of his treason. A mirror was so placed that he could study the changes in Dreyfus's expression, and a loaded revolver was placed on the table . . .

During the dictation, du Paty said sharply: 'Your hand is shaking!' 'My hand was not shaking,' wrote Dreyfus in his memoirs. 'This vehement remark surprised me greatly, as did the hostile attitude of Major du Paty. But as any suspicion was far from my mind I supposed he was finding fault with my handwriting . . . As I continued to write without appearing flustered, du Paty tried again, calling out violently: "Pay attention, this is a serious business!".' Deciding it was useless to continue the experiment, du Paty then put his hand on Dreyfus's shoulder and exclaimed: 'I arrest you in the name of the law: you are accused of the crime of high treason!' Dreyfus protested: 'Take my keys, open up everything in my house, I am innocent!' He refused to commit suicide. He was escorted by Henry to the military prison in the rue du Cherche-Midi and incarcerated in conditions of complete secrecy.

Du Paty immediately rushed to see Lucie Dreyfus and searched the apartment: he could find nothing compromising. He told the distracted Lucie, who thought her husband was dead, that he had been arrested, and forbade her to tell anyone about it: 'One single word, and there will be a war!' In reply to her questions, he would only say, with an air of mystery: 'Think of the Man in the Iron Mask!', adding in a hostile tone: 'Your husband is a coward and a scoundrel.'

When he agreed to see Dreyfus's nephew, du Paty accused the captain of leading a double life and deceiving his wife. His vivid imagination also led him to inflict senseless exercises on his prisoner, such as ten consecutive dictations . . . He showed him one line of a photograph of the *bordereau* by the light of a lamp. Day after day, his interrogation went on.

Not knowing the exact charges and failing to understand du Paty's questions, Dreyfus became more and more disorientated: after ten days, according to the prison governor, Forzinetti, he was on the verge of madness. Du Paty's enquiry had produced no result, and he was forced to admit sensibly to Boisdeffre that Dreyfus was not going to confess and that in view of the flimsy nature of the concrete evidence, which might lead to an acquittal, 'there might be good reason to abandon the prosecution'. On 31 October, in his report to the Minister, he refused to offer any conclusion and left it to Mercier to decide how to pursue the affair.

What was Mercier to do? The new handwriting reports he had ordered were once again contradictory. Bertillon had put forward the first of his bizarre theories, which were later to become more and more incomprehensible: according to him, the author of the *bordereau*, without really trying to disguise his handwriting, had merely modified certain details so as to be able to claim the document was a forgery: 'Proof has been established, conclusively. You know what my belief has been, from the very first day. I am now absolutely certain of it, without the slightest reservation.' For Charavay, the similarities outweighed the differences. He and Teyssonnières concluded that the handwritings were identical, and both saw signs that that of the *bordereau* had been disguised. Pelletier, on the other hand, found that it was normal, that the detailed analogies were 'trivial' and that there were important differences. In short, he did not feel he had any grounds to attribute the *bordereau* to the 'suspected persons'.

9

What avenues were open to Mercier? If he thought of retreat, which seems out of the question in view of his own convictions, the press left him no alternative but to advance. On the very day du Paty submitted his report, 31 October, *L'Eclair* confirmed the rumours already circulating to the effect that an officer had been arrested. The officer in question 'was not, however, a superior officer'. *Le Soir* and *La Patrie* even revealed Dreyfus's name. In a panic, Mercier had to have the Havas newsagency publish an official press statement at 10 p.m. at night. In it, he continued, as ever, to minimize the affair so as to protect himself, and he avoided mentioning Dreyfus by name: 'Grave presumptive evidence has led to the temporary arrest of a French army officer suspected of having communicated some unimportant but confidential documents to foreign individuals. The preliminary legal investigation is being conducted with the discretion usual in such matters and a solution will be reached very shortly.'

A STREAM OF REVELATIONS

But it was too late. The next morning, the *Libre Parole*, the antisemitic daily run by Edouard Drumont, printed a huge front-page article under the sensational headline: 'HIGH TREASON. THE JEWISH TRAITOR ALFRED DREYFUS ARRESTED'. Drumont stated that Dreyfus had made a 'complete confession', that there was 'absolute proof he had sold our secrets to Germany', and above all that 'the affair will be hushed up because the officer is a Jew'. As if a signal had been given, the news was reproduced all over the French press, generally with the inaccurate details which Drumont had put into circulation – Dreyfus's confession, the certainty of his guilt – and the fact that the German Empire was implicated. From this first day, Dreyfus was overwhelmed by lies and condemned without any evidence. Thanks to Drumont, the antisemitic campaign against him had begun. Only *Le Temps*, the unofficial government organ, and *Le Figaro*, which had recently gone over from Orleanism to the Republic, were still reluctant to name Dreyfus and present him as being guilty.

In Paris, according to *Le Voltaire*, 'the news spread like wildfire along the boulevards, from one café to another, the crowds stopping for a moment in amazement, dazzled by a thousand flickering lights'. The entire country was stunned. The shock was deeply felt: the newspapers expressed their horror and their indignation.

Several ministers, including Raymond Poincaré, first learned of the news from their morning papers. Surprised and indignant, Poincaré telephoned the Prime Minister Dupuy to demand an immediate government discussion of the affair. Although it was All Saints' Day, the cabinet met at once at the Interior Ministry in the Place Beauvau.

Poincaré, Barthou, Leygues and Delcassé began by complaining that they had not been informed earlier. The explanations Mercier felt bound to give them were interspersed by their barbed remarks. Some of them saw him as an incompetent, because of the blunders he had committed as a minister. But they did not question his words when he affirmed that the documents mentioned in the *bordereau* 'could only have been communicated by Dreyfus', that 'only he had known of them; only he had had them in his possession; only he could have sold them'. Mercier recounted the scene of the dictation, describing how the face of the scoundrel 'looked highly disturbed when the documents in the *bordereau* were enumerated' and how his hand and his writing were shaking. Mercier attributed the crime to disappointed ambition. His tone was fiercely affirmative as he proferred these threadbare arguments. He had not a shred more evidence than the previous day, but the voice of Drumont had spoken. He must convince his colleagues at all costs.

Hanotaux maintained his objection to legal proceedings based on a document purloined from a foreign embassy. But the members of the government were only too happy to leave this new affair to the blunderer Mercier: they wanted as little to do with it as possible, and they voted unanimously to start legal proceedings.

Thus the antisemite Drumont had intervened decisively in the Dreyfus affair. It would not be the last time.

ANTISEMITISM IN FRANCE

By seizing in this way on the arrest of a Jewish officer accused of high treason, Drumont hoped to be able to exploit the affair to the hilt so that French antisemitism could at last make its decisive political breakthrough. He was a 'bitter, violent man, with a biblical face and bushy black hair. His obsessed black eyes glittered from behind glasses.' He had become the prophet of antisemitism in France since the days in 1886 when his book *La France Juive*, a recapitulation of every known argument against the Jews, had become a record bestseller. Drumont and his supporters nursed the ambition of capitalizing on the current of antisemitism within French society and turning it into a political movement. The 1880s had turned out to be a propitious moment for the development, side-by-side with the old theological antijudaism of the Catholics, of a new economic and social form of antisemitism which could take root in politics. Since the

11

eighteenth century, the centre of gravity of French Jewry had shifted from Alsace to Paris, and in the space of only two or three generations many Jews had assimilated into bourgeois French society and some had risen to great wealth or come to occupy important positions within the Republican state structure. Drumont could hope to unite against them all the malcontents in France: the resentment of workers made unemployed by the economic crisis could be turned against the Jews, usually identified with capitalism, whilst Jewish competition could be blamed for the ruin which now threatened small traders; at the same time, conservatives and Catholics equally faced Jewish competition in finance, and had actually been forced out of the state structures which were now open to Jews and Protestants. The failure of a Catholic bank, the Union Générale, in 1882, was blamed on the Jews, and it was easy to present the Jewish financier or the Jewish prefect as the embodiment of a 'Jewish invasion' which was dispossessing the French of their own country. 'France for the French!' was the cry.

Furthermore, the arrival in the same period of poor Jewish refugees fleeing the pogroms in Eastern Europe after 1881, Jews who spoke Yiddish and clung to their religion and customs, provided a more clearly-defined target than the Frenchified bourgeois Jews for antisemitic prejudice against the 'filthy Jew'.

By holding the Jews responsible for all France's ills, Drumont could hope to create a political coalition of elements of the Left and Right who were hostile to the Republic.

The political development of antisemitism had had its ups and downs with the ebb and flow of events, and it had been handicapped precisely by its political incoherence. There had been a wave of public indignation in the spring of 1892, when a Jewish captain, Armand Mayer, was killed in a duel by the marquis de Morès, the protector of the *Libre Parole*, after the paper ran a campaign against the position of Jewish officers in the army. If Drumont's new daily the *Libre Parole* had taken off later in 1892, with a circulation of 200,000 copies, thanks to the Panama scandal, in which Jews had been implicated, at the time the Dreyfus affair began, the attempts to found an antisemitic movement seemed to have failed. Drumont himself had had to take refuge in Brussels because of a contempt case. Dreyfus's arrest in 1894 represented a heaven-sent opportunity to relaunch the movement. An act of treason by a Jewish officer on the General Staff seemed to offer a perfect illustration of the antisemitic idea that the Jew was a traitor by his very nature.

GERMANY ON THE ALERT

Drumont's revelations on 1 November had a further effect: they immediately attracted the attention of Germany, directly implicated, as we have seen. At the same time, most of the French papers presented Dreyfus as having been in the pay of Italy.

The two Great Powers, allied with Austria within the Triple Alliance since 1882, could not help feeling concerned when the French press attempted to implicate them in a serious case of espionage. For Europe in the 1890s was in a permanent state of jitters, and even the slightest diplomatic incident could be seen as a threat to peace, particularly since war-mongering nationalists in each country did as much as they could to inflate their importance.

The Great Powers had been engaged since the 1880s in a state of unrelenting competition, not only economic competition, but also competition for territory, notably in Africa. To sustain this, they constantly needed fresh allies and stronger armament. France, whom Bismarck had kept isolated in face of the Triple Alliance, had at last coaxed Russia into a military convention at the end of 1893 and this had ended her isolation. But the European situation had not been stablized and the arms race continued, as did the domination of the continent by Germany. Europe was on the way to being divided into two armed camps. French defence and mobilization plans were in a constant state of flux, and espionage flourished.

The anxious General Staff in Berlin telegraphed the German military attachés in Paris, Rome, Berne and Brussels. They all replied that they had never heard of Dreyfus before. The Italian military attaché in Paris, Panizzardi, then sent a telegram to Rome in cipher: 'If Captain Dreyfus has not been in contact with you, it would be appropriate to ask the ambassador to publish an official dementi in order to avoid adverse comment in the press.' This telegram was intercepted by the French post office. Deciphering it took several days, and the cryptographers first suggested a reading which ended with the words 'our emissary warned'. Sandherr saw in this another proof of Dreyfus's guilt. But when he saw the definitive version he attached no further importance to it.

The telegram did prove, however, that Dreyfus had not been in contact with Italy, for it dated from after his arrest. If Panizzardi was not telling the truth he could expect to be given the lie immediately. This meant that the French government could be sure that only Germany was involved.

The fateful 1 November was also marked by the arrival in Paris

13

of Mathieu Dreyfus, Alfred's elder brother, who was now in charge of the family cotton mills in Mulhouse. Du Paty de Clam had at last allowed Lucie to call him to Paris.

Mathieu was tall and fair with blue eyes and a naturally sunny temperament, but the news of the charge against his brother came as a great blow to him. 'For a few moments I was struck down and incapable of thinking . . . I could not understand . . . I never doubted for a single moment his complete, his total innocence. I knew his complete honesty, his character, his good and his bad qualities, his liking for hard work and his passion for the soldier's profession.' Mathieu had been more than a brother to Alfred: according to Joseph Reinach, 'he was his chosen friend, the closest to his heart. Never was there a closer intimacy.' Sharing with Alfred the characteristic French patriotism of the Jews of Alsace, protesters against German rule, he had, like Alfred, dreamed of a military career. But after failing at the first attempt he had had to resign himself to entering the family firm. During the Dreyfus Affair, he supported his brother from the very first.

When he arrived in Paris he immediately sought an interview with du Paty. The latter presented his brother as a monster and a womanizer. Mathieu affirmed his belief in Alfred's innocence, asking what the motive of the crime could be, and explaining to du Paty that nothing about his brother's life so far had suggested that he might be a monster. 'You are not just a monster for 24 hours, you are a monster all the time.' When Mathieu suggested to du Paty that he should put the question of his guilt to Alfred on the quiet, the latter replied: 'Never, never! One word and we shall have a European war.' 'He must be a madman,' Mathieu decided. But du Paty, aware that proceedings against Dreyfus had already been initiated, added: 'Tomorrow your brother will be sent before a court-martial.'

So it was. On 3 November, the military governor of Paris, General Saussier, ordered proceedings to begin against Dreyfus. Major d'Ormescheville, rapporteur to the first Court-Martial of Paris, was put in charge of the preliminary investigation. Saussier had to act against his own personal judgement in this, as he had from the beginning been hostile to any proceedings; he had even advised Mercier to have Dreyfus posted to Africa where he could get killed, which would have avoided the embarrassment of a trial. Saussier was the most senior officer in the French army. According to Marcel Thomas, he was 'as level-headed, diplomatic and realistic as Mercier was authoritarian and abrupt. Well-known for his obesity, he had towards things and people the somewhat disenchanted attitude of a bon viveur who was often irritated by Mercier's curt and peremptory ways.' It was public knowledge that the two generals did not see eye to eye. In December, while on a hunt at Marly, Saussier would remark to the President of the Republic: 'Dreyfus is not guilty. That idiot Mercier has dropped another clanger.' On 3 November, however, Saussier had no choice but to open proceedings.

All that Mathieu could now do was to find his brother a lawyer. He was recommended Maître Waldeck-Rousseau, the most prominent business lawyer in Paris. Waldeck-Rousseau asked for time to think over the request. The time of waiting was to be painful for Mathieu: throughout the first week in November, a flood of articles in the press proclaimed his brother's guilt. Many newspapers would hear of nothing but the death penalty: popular feeling could not conceive of any other punishment for a traitor. After a high civil servant explained in the semi-official newspaper *Le Temps* that Dreyfus had simply betrayed his country for money, a series of fanciful stories appeared in the press: Dreyfus, it was claimed, had allowed himself to be used as spy bait; he had sold the secrets of French mobilization plans, sold documents to Italy, betrayed the names of officers on secret missions and so on. His crime could be explained by his links with a 'beautiful noblewoman' he had met in Nice. All these stories were of course complete inventions and none of them survived for more than a few days. But in the absence of any official denials, they had time to produce their effect. 'It was a flood we could do nothing to stem,' wrote Mathieu in his memoirs. 'We could not put out a single line of protest against the slanders being propagated.' It is true that *Le Temps* somewhat corrected its stance by publishing an interview with Madame Hadamard, Dreyfus's mother-in-law, in which she stressed his patriotism and the fact that he had no financial worries. But the storm raged on. Mathieu's feeling of impotence is entirely understandable.

While the first reaction of all the papers had been to take it for granted that Dreyfus was guilty, since the War Minister would surely not have had him arrested without serious evidence, several of them began to recall the need to respect the presumption of innocence. These were essentially the Republican papers.

In fact a survey of the Parisian press of November 1894 shows that attitudes towards Dreyfus's arrest varied enormously according to the type of paper.

THE DAILY PRESS AND THE GOVERNMENT IN 1894

The four largest dailies, *Le Petit Journal, Le Petit Parisien, Le Journal* and *Le Matin*, were aimed at the general public, and, so as to maintain as high a circulation as possible, they concentrated on news, avoided polemics and put on a veneer of political neutrality. They remained restrained in their attitude to the beginnings of the Dreyfus Affair, although the *Petit Journal* did publish one article which came near to antisemitism.

As for the political press, reactions varied totally from one paper to another. *Le Temps, Le Figaro* and the *Journal des Débats*, which were the main organs of the governing Republican bourgeoisie, carried on the political debate in a courteous and rational manner. They reflected the official policy of saying as little as possible about the Dreyfus Affair, which was an embarrassment to the entire government, and not only to Mercier. For the main priority of the centre Republicans governing France in 1894 was political and social stability. That stability had been threatened, since the beginning of the decade, by the upsurge of socialism and syndicalism, and by the wave of anarchist bomb outrages from 1892 to 1894.

The arrest of a Jewish officer on a charge of high treason, which could revive religious hostilities, seemed like a particularly unwelcome addition to the Republicans' troubles, obsessed as they were with the socialist threat. There was also, of course, the risk of diplomatic incidents with Germany. For both these reasons, from 1894 to 1898, successive French governments, as well as the centre Republican press, did everything in their power to minimize the Dreyfus Affair, preferring if possible not to mention it at all. With some exceptions, the socialist and radical press also hardly mentioned Dreyfus before his first trial, though not for the same reasons.

The nationalist and antisemitic press, on the other hand, made as much as they could of the Dreyfus case: in *L'Autorité* (Bonapartist), *La Patrie*, and above all in Drumont's *Libre Parole* and the *Intransigeant*, in which the redoubtable old polemicist Henri Rochefort, famous since the Second Empire, continued his vituperative opposition to the regime. Rochefort was also an antisemite. For all these papers, the Dreyfus Affair offered a heaven-sent opportunity to attack the government: Drumont and Rochefort for their part launched a massive campaign against the Jews.

These newspapers were aimed at ordinary people and workers. They pandered to their lowest instincts. Their columns were filled day by day with expressions of passion and prejudice, the polemics reach-

16

ing levels of violence which would be inconceivable today. the difficulty of bringing libel actions under the Press Law of 1881 gave them almost total immunity.

At this time, however, the Paris press varied from the execrable to the outstanding: and side by side with nationalist and antisemitic mudslinging, one could also find the work of one or two remarkable journalists who began to ask some highly pertinent questions. Edmond Magnier, who ran the very well-informed radical paper *L'Evénement*, wrote about Dreyfus:

> This officer is a son of Alsace. His family stock is that of the big industrialists of Mulhouse, whose name he has borne honourably until today. He is thus doubly French. He is highly educated. He is from the élite of the Grandes Ecoles. At 35, he is an artillery captain at the top of his grade. His past is satisfactory, his present is smiling, and his future full of hope. His superiors have always found in him exemplary obedience as well as a keenness only waiting for employment, and for the confrontation with danger. Married to a wife who is herself from the most respectable of families, he has two children whom he adores. His personal wealth, combined with that of his wife, and added to his pay, guarantees him a style of life consonant with and even above that of his rank. There is nothing to prevent him from having the highest ambitions, no height to which he cannot aspire. And this is the soldier who has suddenly turned into a spy, a renegade and a traitor? What a nightmare![4]

Magnier was quite right; and the absence of any plausible motive for his presumed treason was to continue to preoccupy all those who took an objective view of Dreyfus.

And what is one to make, too, of the spectacular interview given by Madame Bodson to *Le Journal* on 6 November? She asserted that of all the officers she entertained in her salon when Dreyfus was at the Ecole de Guerre, it was he who was the most patriotic, the most chauvinistic even; she revealed that he had actually broken off their relationship because of her contacts with a German officer![5] In the same paper, Emile Bergerat courageously demanded for Dreyfus 'the right to be innocent'.

But the handful of articles favourable to Dreyfus became obscured for contemporaries, and have remained so in the eyes of history, by the flood of violence and untruth which threatened to overwhelm him even before he had been tried. It is true that the Republican press kept a sense of proportion when it came to the penalty. If the nationalists and antisemites called for the death penalty – and they were not

4 Edmond Magnier, 'Le traître', *L'Evénement*, 5 November 1894.
5 'Chez Mme. B.', *Le Journal*, 6 November 1894.

17

alone in this – the Republican papers began a learned but confused legal debate on the issue, concluding in the end that Dreyfus's alleged crime came under article 76 of the penal code, but that he would avoid execution, the death penalty having been abolished for political crimes by the revolution of 1848.

Inevitably, the question on which the divergence was most flagrant was that of antisemitism. The Republican papers severely condemned the use of antisemitic arguments against Dreyfus: they did so both on the basis of their Republican principles of religious neutrality, and because of their wish for peace and quiet. Drumont however deployed his antisemitism with a fierce delight. For him, the Dreyfus Affair was 'just another episode in Jewish history'. The Jews had always been traitors. 'With this type of person, treason is inevitable: it is the curse of their race.' He brandished threats:

> If France is defeated, these words '*The Jews! It is the Jews!*' will once more regain the true meaning they used to have for the French. They will sum up all their indignation, and justify their every impulse. Perhaps a few innocent people will be caught up among the cowardly criminals who have abused the most naïve and also the most generous of hospitalities . . . We have been called forth from within the people . . . to predict to the invaders from Judea the fearful punishment that awaits them![6]

But it was not enough for Drumont to foreshadow the persecutions to come: he turned the weapon of antisemitism against General Mercier. Dreyfus had been arrested on 15 October. 'What was the Minister waiting for? Why the delay in opening his investigation?' Mercier had, according to Drumont, only one thought in his head: to hush up the affair. Untiringly, throughout the first week of November, Drumont repeated that Mercier had been slow to act on account of Jewish pressure. All the ministers knew. 'They are all as guilty as one another.'

For Rochefort, too, Jews like Dreyfus were merely cogs in the machinery of the great Jewish Plot; he too linked his antisemitism to his attacks on Mercier.

The use of antisemitic arguments even extended to the Catholic papers: to *L'Univers*, a veritable mouthpiece of the Catholic party, and to *La Croix*, the newspaper of the religious order of the Assumptionists. For them, the Jews remained a nation of deicides – this was the traditional Catholic theological argument. But furthermore they could not be trusted with the secrets of France's national defence, for

---

6 Edouard Drumont, 'L'espionnage juif', *La Libre Parole*, 3 November 1894.

they were not genuine Frenchmen. These newspapers were thus now espousing more political arguments, bringing them closer to Drumont.

His and Rochefort's campaign against Mercier reached its height just before Le Hérissé was due to intervene in Parliament, on 6 October, to raise the War Minister's early release of the conscripts. Drumont called the Ministry a 'sewer', while Rochefort denounced Mercier's 'negligence, stupidity and bad faith', which made him practically an accomplice of the traitor. He called him 'the Soft-head of the War Office', and exclaimed: 'In any other country by the name of France, that man Mercier . . . would have been taken by the scruff of his neck several days ago, and kicked as hard as possible down the backstairs of his own ministry.'

Mercier was on the verge of disaster. Le Hérissé was loudly applauded in Parliament, whereas the beleaguered Minister met with a stony silence as he spoke. He was about to be censured when the Prime Minister had to rescue him at the last moment by a vote of next business. When he left the Chamber, Mercier was a mere shadow of himself.

MERCIER SURRENDERS TO BLACKMAIL

To save his ministerial position, he now gave in to Drumont's and Rochefort's blackmail in the press: he consented to see to it that Dreyfus would be found guilty come what may, and in spite of the flimsy nature of the evidence he held against him. It was the only way to save his job. This is how he came to use, at Dreyfus's trial, a secret file not shown to the defence.

What proves this is Drumont and Rochefort's spectacular volte-face towards him. As early as 8 November, Rochefort was writing: 'If anyone had predicted that we should find ourselves one day on the same side as Mercier, our surprise would have bordered on the most total incredulity.' According to Rochefort, Mercier had declared at a cabinet meeting that 'he had decided to go right through with it, that is to condemn Dreyfus to death and execute him'.[7] While there is no evidence that Mercier ever said this, nonetheless, as if by magic, Drumont and Rochefort's attacks stopped abruptly overnight, and the two polemicists at once became his most ardent champions, even defending him *against* the other members of the government. Mercier had clearly given them assurances about his intention to have

7 Henri Rochefort, 'Les coulisses de la trahison', *L'Intransigeant*, 9 November 1894.

Dreyfus found guilty at all costs. He obviously had not revealed the mechanism of the crime to them, but he gave them to understand that he had other evidence besides the *bordereau*. This point was hammered home several times in the *Libre Parole*.

But what other evidence was there? The need to find some was urgent. However, happily for Mercier, the officers of the Statistical Department had realized the fact already. Under Sandherr's direction, they had adopted their quite normal practice of searching through their old files to see if they could lay their hands on any document which might throw the slightest light on their current enquiry. According to Marcel Thomas, they had already worked out a case against Dreyfus: the leaks which had been happening at the Ministry had been to foreign military attachés, and their informant had been none other than him.

To support their argument, they first chose a note signed *Alexandrine*, that the German military attaché Schwartzkoppen had sent his Italian counterpart Panizzardi. This note, which had been intercepted in the spring, began: 'My dear fellow, I am sorry I did not see you before I left. In any case, I shall [misspelt] be back in a week's time. Herewith [misspelt] five large-scale plans of Nice that that scoundrel D. gave me for you.'

For the officers in the Statistical Department the initial D. stood for Dreyfus, despite the fact that it was most improbable that the first letter of his name would have been used to refer to him. Apart from this, the large-scale plans were worth only 10 francs a sheet and would plainly have been of no interest to Dreyfus.

Next there was a note in Schwartzkoppen's handwriting, made up from torn scraps of paper of which the order was uncertain: 'Doubts . . . Evidence . . . Official letter . . . Dangerous situation for me with a French officer . . . Not to conduct negotiations in person . . . To bring what he has . . . *Absolute Ge* [in German] . . . Intelligence Bureau . . . No connections with army corps . . . Importance only emanating from the Ministry . . . Already elsewhere.'

This letter was supposedly explained by a 'Davignon letter' from Panizzardi to Schwartzkoppen on a non-confidential matter, a letter which ended as follows: 'it must never [misspelt] be made known that one attaché is helping another out [misspelt]'. To these documents were added some reports forged by Guénée, a dubious agent of the Statistical Department, who inserted into an old report which had been made by one of his informants, Val Carlos, and which dated from the spring of 1894, a statement to the effect that there was a traitor on the General Staff.

20

And it was on the basis of these references to a traitor on the General Staff, references so vague as to be almost meaningless, that the officers of the Statistical Department set up the celebrated secret file which was to play such a decisive role in Dreyfus's first trial in December. Once again, Drumont and Rochefort had decisively influenced the course of the Affair; they had forced Mercier into crime.

Sandherr also put Guénée in charge of an enquiry about Dreyfus with the aim of finding a motive for his treason. Without any evidence, Guénée accused him in his report of frequenting no less than four gaming clubs, including the Cercle Washington, the Betting-Club, and the Fencing Club, and of having lost 20,000 francs at the latter establishment. The story went that his wife's family had paid off huge debts for him. Guénée also accused Dreyfus of having had several mistresses, including Mme Bodson, whom we have already encountered. His report was later contradicted by an enquiry made by the Prefecture of Police: it was based on a mistaken identity. But by then it had had time to infect the press.

Meanwhile, d'Ormescheville's preliminary investigation was making almost no progress. From the accounts he had collected it emerged only that Dreyfus was not liked by his comrades.

DEMANGE, THE DEFENCE COUNSEL

However, Mathieu had found his brother a lawyer, after Waldeck-Rousseau had declined, explaining that he was now going to take on only civil cases. Waldeck-Rousseau gave him the name of Edgar Demange, a Catholic barrister who was passionately keen on military matters. At 53, Demange belonged to what was already an older generation in his profession; he had been nurtured in the great traditions of the French bar. He had already brilliantly defended in a series of criminal cases and nothing, for him, was more sacred than the rights of the defence.

Mathieu went to see him, and explained everything he knew: his brother's life, and his own absolute conviction of his innocence. Touched by Mathieu, Demange replied in a solemn tone: 'I accept the brief with the following reservations: I shall be the first to judge your brother, and if I find any evidence to make me doubt his innocence, I shall refuse to defend him. What I am suggesting is extremely serious. The moment the public learns I have refused to defend him, he will be irretrievably undone.' Mathieu accepted this condition. Demange added that he would put the same condition to the accused when he

21

was allowed to see him; for the moment, he was barred from doing so by the secrecy of the preliminary investigation.

The news that Demange had accepted the brief appeared in all the newspapers. He gave an important interview to the daily *La Presse*, in an attempt to stop the spread of fanciful stories. He described them as 'inaccuracies'. He made clear that the motive of the crime remained a mystery, and that the whole trial would turn on the handwriting question. Dreyfus denied authorship, and he, Demange, would oppose a trial in camera 'in the most energetic fashion'. The Bonapartist Cassagnac declared in *L'Autorité*, after this move by Demange: 'I, for one, would not be prepared to agree to having a French officer shot on the report of a handwriting expert, even if he was strongly suspected of being guilty.' Like Demange, he called for a public hearing. Thereupon, the majority of the newspapers followed suit. 'Public opinion unanimously demands the truth, the whole truth,' wrote the old radical Ranc. Cassagnac, in his article, had gone so far as to say that one must be prepared for anything, even 'the innocence of the accused'. The fact that Demange had accepted the defence was indeed food for thought.

La Presse did, however, report the seizure of some letters from Dreyfus to Schwartzkoppen. The German ambassador, Count von Münster, then immediately published a very firm dementi in *Le Figaro*: Schwartzkoppen 'had never been in contact with Dreyfus, either directly or indirectly . . . If this officer is guilty of the crime of which he stands accused, the German embassy has nothing to do with the affair.' The attaché had convinced his ambassador that he knew nothing of Dreyfus. But he had avoided mentioning his connection with the real traitor. In this way he had exploited the gullibility of Münster, who was an upright old aristocrat completely without guile. The French press naturally treated the ambassador's denials with scepticism: it was obvious that he was covering up for his attaché.

By the middle of November, press comment on the Dreyfus affair had died down. But there was still some impatience at the delays to the preliminary investigation. According to *La Lanterne*, it was 'time to have done with the affair . . . It is unacceptable to let public opinion become so overheated.'

In the face of this impatience and the emergence of the idea that Dreyfus might be innocent, Mercier referred in interviews in three dailies[8] to the notes 'proving' that an officer had passed on infor-

---

8 Notably in *Le Journal*: see H. Barthélémy, 'Le crime de trahison. Chez le ministre de la guerre', 17 November 1894.

mation to a foreign power, and asserting his conviction that the officer in question was Captain Dreyfus. He was forced to admit, however, that there had been no confession, and he added that if Dreyfus was found guilty and sentenced, 'it would be to transportation for life'.

On 28 November he returned to the attack, talking in *Le Figaro* of 'glaring evidence' of Dreyfus's treason. The officer's guilt was 'absolutely certain' and the General Staff knew 'from equally cast-iron sources that Dreyfus had been in touch for three years with agents of a foreign government, which was neither that of Italy nor that of Austria-Hungary'.[9]

These words of Mercier were an infringement of the independence of the judiciary. Among lawyers at the Paris Law Courts, the reaction was one of surprise; at Demange's request, Waldeck-Rousseau made an immediate protest to the Prime Minister. There was also strong feeling in the Chamber of Deputies. Joseph Reinach, a Jewish deputy and a prominent Republican, who had had an inkling of Dreyfus's innocence, also added his protest. Mercier issued a denial of the interview, but the journalist on *Le Figaro* insisted that his account of a meeting which had lasted over an hour and a half was an accurate one. The *Libre Parole* was practically the only newspaper to defend Mercier; most of the press thought he had said too much.

But this was not all: Mercier had also sparked of a new protest from Germany by the thinly disguised way in which he had implicated her. Münster, without attacking him head on, reacted by protesting against a series of articles which had appeared in *Le Matin*. These articles were directed against foreign military attachés; in them, the German embassy was presented as the headquarters of German espionage in France. The ambassador demanded effective measures of protection by the French government. The subsequent French statement that there was no intention of abolishing the institution of military attachés did not satisfy him. All in all, Mercier's two interviews had only stirred up fresh criticism of him and they had fuelled the persistent dissatisfaction of the German embassy.

On 3 December, his preliminary investigation completed, d'Ormescheville submitted his report, which concluded that Dreyfus should be committed for trial. The only foundations it offered for the charge of high treason were the resemblance in handwriting (no account was taken of Gobert's report, seen as null and void), Dreyfus's 'indiscreet' attitude, his affairs with women, and his knowledge of foreign languages . . . This was all that fifteen days of interviews and enquiries

---

9 Charles Leser, 'L'espionnage militaire', *Le Figaro*, 28 November 1894.

had produced. Now, at long last, Demange was able to learn how worthless the case against his client was. Explaining it to Mathieu and Lucie, he declared in a tone of deep emotion: 'If Captain Dreyfus was not a Jew he would not be in the Cherche-Midi prison today.' He had never seen a case like it. He said to the prison governor Forzinetti: 'I have been taking cases for 30 years, and this is the first innocent man I have ever had to defend.' He told Dreyfus he did not doubt his innocence and that he would plead his case.

Almost all the newspapers were still calling for a public trial. Demange asked Waldeck-Rousseau to make an appeal to the President of the Republic on this point, but the latter, being bound by the constitution, replied that his hands were tied.

Mercier now had two weapons in his hands: a trial held in camera and the use of the secret file. Though he was attacked once again in the Republican press, Saint-Genest declaring in *Le Figaro* that he should not be kept in office on account of the Dreyfus Affair,[10] the wind was beginning to turn somewhat in his favour.

THE TRIAL OF 1894

The trial was due to begin on 19 December, in an old mansion on the rue du Cherche-Midi, directly opposite the military prison. It was the Courts-Martial Building, which had been familiar to Victor Hugo when he was a young man, the building where his wedding-feast had taken place in 1822, in the very same courtroom where Dreyfus was to be tried![11]

That morning, the feeling outside in the street was that the Minister had been right to carry on with the prosecution. 'It will be the death sentence, won't it?' asked a workman. The usual crowd which turned up for major trials had stayed away, so sure was everyone that the trial would be held in camera.

The hearings were due to begin at noon, in the courtroom on the first floor, a plain room of 60 square metres, 'bare, cold and severe'. The only signs of decoration were a huge painting of the Crucifixion and a wall-clock of the kind found in run-of-the-mill cafés. A monumental stove in the centre of the court gave off a suffocating heat.

10 Saint-Genest, 'Pas d'équivoque. Le général Mercier', *Le Figaro*, 12 December 1894.
11 At 37, rue du Cherche-Midi: see P. Fromageot, *La rue du Cherche-Midi et ses habitants depuis ses origines jusqu'à nos jours* (Paris, 1915), p. 557 and passim.

Mathieu Dreyfus was there, suffering from pangs of anxiety and with perspiration on his forehead.

'Bring in the accused!' ordered Colonel Maurel, the president of the court-martial. Alfred Dreyfus was brought in. All eyes turned to look at this short-sighted officer with his pince-nez. Alas! He was not the tragic figure everyone expected.

'I could see nothing, hear nothing,' Dreyfus recalled in his memoirs. 'I was aware of nothing of what was going on around me. My mind was completely absorbed by the frightful nightmare that had weighed down upon me for so many long weeks, by the monstrous accusation of treason, the inanity, the emptiness of which I was about to demonstrate. I could only distinguish at the back, on the platform, the judges of the court-martial, officers like myself, comrades before whom I was at last going to prove my innocence completely . . . Behind them were the deputies, and then Colonel Picquart, the War Ministry delegate, and M. Lépine, the Prefect of Police. Opposite me were Major Brisset, the military prosecutor, and Valecalle, the clerk to the court.'

As soon as Dreyfus had given his identity, Brisset rose to call for a hearing in camera. Demange then began to read the submission he had prepared in support of his request for a public trial. But when he reached the words 'the only document', Maurel interrupted him: 'The court forbids you to enter in any way into the facts of the case.' 'Yes or no, is my submission accepted?' demanded Demange. Brisset: 'Lay your submission before the court without reading it.' 'But I must read it in the interests of the defence.' Brisset: 'There are other interests at stake in this trial than those of the defence and the prosecution.'

Maurel ordered the court-martial to retire. Fifteen minutes later came the decision to hold the trial in camera. The court was cleared. Dreyfus and his counsel Demange were now left alone to face Brisset and the seven judges; the only spectators were Picquart and Lépine, who witnessed the entire trial.

The clerk read out the bill of indictment drawn up by d'Ormescheville. The emptiness of the document struck Freystätter, one of the judges.[12] Replying to the charges, Dreyfus denied everything. He spoke clearly and precisely, without any sign of emotion. He refused to make any appeal to compassion in his judges: even if he had wanted to he could not have done so, for, though a very emotional person, he always had great difficulty in expressing his feelings. 'There was

---

12 For Freystätter's reactions, see his MS note to Joseph Reinach of July 1900, Bibliothèque Nationale, papiers Reinach, Naf 24896.

nothing about his attitude to arouse one's sympathy,' (Lépine). He did, however, protest vehemently that his whole life spoke out against the charge of high treason.

The prosecution witnesses then followed, including Gonse and Henry. The chief of these was du Paty. He was confounded over his dictation to Dreyfus. Demange showed it to the judges: there was no sign of any shaking in the handwriting. Though Dreyfus had not moved the court on this first day, he had undermined their convictions.

The next day, his comrades repeated the tales about him which d'Ormescheville had already collected from them. They did not produce, according to Freystätter, 'any fact worth accepting as evidence'. The trial was about to collapse. It was time to react. Henry, who was representing Sandherr, had not lost his peasant ways, and he was devoted to his superiors. He decided to strike a blow on their behalf. Recalled to the stand, he asserted that since March a most honourable person had been warning the Statistical Department that an officer at the War Office was guilty of treason. Dreyfus leapt to his feet in protest, demanding to be confronted with the honourable person. Henry: 'When an officer has a secret in his head he does not share it even with his kepi.'

He then turned to Dreyfus, exclaiming: 'There is the traitor!' This theatrical scene impressed the judges deeply. And Lépine recalled: 'I can still remember the Major's gesture and his stance. He was the righter of wrongs who had appeared on the scene.' Judge Freystätter could not conceive that an officer representing his superiors might not be telling the truth.

Up to this point, according to Lépine, the hearing had gone on 'in the dull, colourless atmosphere of a trivial affair'. Henry transformed an everyday spy case into a drama.

Now it was the turn of the handwriting experts, who repeated once again their contradictory evidence (*see* above, pp. 8–9). On the third day, Bertillon expatiated for three hours on his scheme of interpretation based on the idea that Dreyfus had forged his own handwriting, amassing more and more tedious and incomprehensible details. The judges could not understand anything except that he thought the *bordereau* was the work of Dreyfus.

Finally came the defence witnesses: several from Alsace, the Paris chief rabbi, Lévy-Brühl the philosopher, who was a cousin of Dreyfus, and five courageous fellow officers. But the judges listened as if they were not concerned.

Brisset's closing speech for the prosecution was brief, and it was 'devoid of any facts', according to Lépine. He simply repeated d'Ormescheville's indictment. The trial was making no headway; an acquittal was in the offing. Demange said as much to Mathieu Dreyfus.

At the final session, Demange's closing speech for the defence lasted three hours. He showed that the *bordereau* could not have been the work of Dreyfus; he challenged the scraps of gossip from his comrades; and he asked: where was the motive?

But he did not have the knack of handling a court-martial. His method was to set out to sow doubt in the minds of the judges. But they were soldiers who had no time for nuances: they knew that the General Staff thought Dreyfus guilty, that the War Minister had loudly proclaimed his guilt in public, and they had had wind of a secret file. The accused had not even aroused any sympathy in them.

Brisset, in his reply, had nonetheless to drop all the secondary counts, and restrict himself entirely to the *bordereau* as evidence. 'Though I can offer no motive for this crime, the most heinous that can be committed, though I have no other evidence than the letter, this evidence remains overwhelming. Pick up your magnifying-glasses, you will see that Dreyfus wrote it.'

The Prefect of Police, still convinced there would be an acquittal, issued orders in case Dreyfus was in need of protection when he left the court. The judges retired. One of them later revealed: 'Though we were not fully aware of the facts when we went into the retiring room, we all were when certain documents came to us.'[13] The secret file, handed to them 'on Mercier's orders and with his fullest moral authority', reversed the situation-legally, he was not entitled to present them evidence not shown to the defence.

Maurel, the president, began reading the documents in the file, which were those recovered from the old files of the Statistical Department (*see* above, p. 20), accompanied by a commentary by du Paty. All the judges were struck by the 'scoundrel D.' note. In the face of this secret file, and after Henry's speech, they could not doubt the good faith of their superiors. They voted unanimously for Dreyfus to be transported for life to a fortified place. The death sentence, as we have seen, was impossible in peacetime. 'We had only one word on our lips', one of them revealed later: 'The maximum!'[13]

Maurel read out the sentence in open court. Demange broke into tears. The prisoner was not allowed to be present at this point. In the rue du Cherche-Midi, 'the feeling that prevailed was a sort of disappointment that the laws of 1848 and 1850 had allowed such a

13 'Autour de l'Affaire Dreyfus', *Le Gaulois*, 3 November 1897.

great criminal to escape the death penalty. Ordinary people, who are simplistic, cannot understand legal red tape.' (*Le Figaro*)

At nightfall, Dreyfus, waiting in the sickroom, was brought to the entrance hall of the court building. The clerk then read out the sentence to him by the light of a candelabrum. 'You are by law allowed 24 hours to exercise your right of appeal,' said Brisset. Dreyfus maintained his composure during the reading of the sentence, then broke into tears. Maître Demange took his hand. 'Keep up your courage! We shall see how the appeal goes.'

When he returned to his cell, Dreyfus gave way to despair. He wished for death, throwing his head against the wall. He asked three times for a revolver. 'My despair was intense; the night which followed my condemnation was one of the most tragic in my tragic existence.' Outside on the boulevards, people scrambled for the newspapers. They continued to discuss the penalty, and the excitement went on until late in the night.

From the President downward, a great many were relieved at the unanimous verdict. 'This unanimity is quite enough,' wrote Cornély in *Le Matin*, 'to ease those consciences which are still undecided.' *Le Temps* declared: 'If there had been a single divergence of opinion, the public conscience would have been disturbed, particularly since a hearing in camera, recognized as necessary, made any direct clarification impossible.' Already during the trial, the unofficial government mouthpiece had written: 'There are not seven officers in the French army capable of condemning an innocent man, or of acquitting a traitor.'[14] This was a proclamation of the official position which would be maintained for four years: the court-martial was infallible. The entire Republican press fell into line.

Even the socialists, despite their antimilitarism, dared not question a unanimous verdict. Nor could they themselves open again to the oft-repeated charge of antipatriotism.

The nationalists and antisemites gave Mercier a triumph. His portfolio was safe for the moment. 'Has not everything I wrote been justified by events?' asked Drumont. 'Out with the Jews! France for the French!'

Antisemitic agitation revived. Public meetings called for measures of exclusion against the Jews. The Catholic press continued to echo Drumont: without going so far as to call for exclusion, it repeated that the Jews were not proper Frenchmen.

14 'La condamnation', *Le Temps*, 23 December 1894 and 'Le procès de trahison', ibid., 21 December 1894.

28

The Jews themselves showed little reaction. According to Léon Blum, they generally accepted Dreyfus's conviction as being just and final. As faithful Republicans and ardent French patriots, they did not want to make themselves conspicuous. For the most part, they were to continue henceforward to take refuge in silence, hoping thereby to avoid offering a target to their opponents.

What was the attitude of the press to Dreyfus himself? Since the motive of his crime had still not been elucidated, he appeared to be a monster. 'How could a man carry out such an act?' asked Clemenceau. 'He must have no relatives, no children, no love for anything, no link with humanity.'

But the most persistent note throughout the press was annoyance that he had avoided the death penalty so many thought he had deserved, when a private soldier faced it merely for striking a superior officer. Mercier had hurriedly to bring in a bill to Parliament to restore the death penalty for treason even in peacetime. Jaurès, on the other hand, proposed a bill abolishing the death penalty for soldiers guilty of an act of violence against a superior. In Parliament, he accused the government of trading on patriotism, and was temporarily barred from the Chamber. But now the trial was over, the newspapers of every shade of opinion declared that it was time to drop the subject. Dreyfus's appeal was dismissed on 31 December 1894.

THE DEGRADATION CEREMONY

The degradation ceremony took place on 5 January 1895 in the courtyard of the Ecole Militaire, which was lined by detachments of troops from all over Paris. This space, with the semi-circle of the Place de Fontenoy was separated from it only by a railing, formed a vast amphitheatre. It was a freezing winter's morning, but thousands of Parisians had turned out, and were pressed tight beyond the railing.

Nine o'clock struck, and General Darras pronounced the ritual words as the convicted man stood alone in the centre of the courtyard: 'Alfred Dreyfus, you are unworthy to bear arms. In the name of the French people, I degrade you.' Dreyfus cried out: 'Soldiers, they are degrading an innocent man! Long live France! Long live the army!' 'An adjutant of the Republican guard came up to me and rapidly tore the buttons from my coat, the stripes from my trousers and the marks of my rank from my cap and coat-sleeves,' Dreyfus recalled. 'He broke my sword across his knee . . . I saw all these emblems of honour fall at my feet. Then, in the midst of my agony, but with head erect,

I shouted again and again to the soldiers and the assembled people, "I am innocent!" '

The parade continued. Dreyfus was marched round the entire square in front of the soldiers, while the crowd bayed for his blood, howling: 'Kill him! Kill him!' 'I heard the howls of a deluded mob; I could sense the shudder they felt as they looked upon me in the belief that the condemned man they saw was a traitor to his country, and I made a superhuman effort to create in their hearts the commiseration due to an innocent man unjustly condemned.' The voice of Dreyfus was not wholly stifled. He had made his protest heard.

After the degradation and these cries of innocence, doubts began to arise again in the minds of one or two of the celebrities who witnessed the ceremony: Theodore Herzl and Sarah Bernhardt, as well as a number of journalists and the politician Joseph Reinach. But now there was only silence, a silence in line with Government instructions: the Dreyfus case was dangerous; it was better that it should be forgotten.

2 THE BEGINNINGS OF THE DREYFUSARD CAMPAIGN

THE MYTH THAT DREYFUS HAD CONFESSED

The degradation ceremony was hardly over when rumours began to circulate that Dreyfus had confessed his guilt. Several newspapers, including *Le Temps*, reported that he had said to Captain Lebrun-Renault, his escort to the Ecole Militaire: 'I am innocent; if I passed on any documents to a foreign power it was as bait, in order to obtain more important ones in return; in three years' time, the truth will be known, and the Minister will take up my case again.'

The truth was that Lebrun-Renault had gossiped too freely after the ceremony; he had certainly misheard or misunderstood what Dreyfus had said. The rumours surprised the War Ministry, where every attempt to extract a confession from him after his trial had failed; and they contradicted all available information. Lebrun was hurriedly taken to see the Prime Minister and the President of the Republic; he did not dare repeat his gossip and an official denial followed.

This incident would not have been significant if the General Staff, feeling there was a lack of evidence against Dreyfus, had not seized on it in 1897, and from 1898, so as to spread the myth of a confession.

Also, Lebrun-Renault's lack of discretion had given the government another cause for anxiety: it was feared he had revealed that the *bordereau* had originated from the German Embassy.

A DIPLOMATIC INCIDENT

For it was actually on the very day of the ceremony that Ambassador Münster had handed the Prime Minister a stiff note from the German Chancellor Hohenlohe, to the effect that the Emperor himself wished the French President to be informed that His Majesty hoped the French government would offer a confirmation, should it be proven that the German Embassy had never been implicated in the Dreyfus affair. This clearly called for a reply from Casimir-Périer himself.

He summoned Münster the next day and explained that the

31

bordereau had been found within his embassy. 'Oh! It is quite impossible for an important document to have gone astray in this way in
the embassy,' exclaimed Münster. But, with a view to being concili-
atory, he added: 'How can we settle this incident?' The French President replied that he was not implicating the embassy, since there was
nothing to show they had requested the document, and he could not
hold them responsible for every piece of paper they might receive. He
and Münster then came to an agreement that a French note would
clear all the foreign embassies.

In this ingenious way, Casimir-Périer successfully reduced the
slight diplomatic tension which had arisen. But, once again, the incident would hardly have mattered if General Mercier had not
attempted, improperly, at the time of the Rennes trial in 1899, to
turn it into a 'historic' night, when France and Germany were on the
brink of war (*see* below, p. 170).

In view of the dubious circumstances of Dreyfus's trial – not to
mention the persistent complications his case had created – it was
regarded as urgent in government circles that the matter be closed as
rapidly as possible. Mercier took the secret file from Sandherr and
burnt du Paty's commentary, which he regarded as his personal property. He then ordered Sandherr to remove all the other items from
the file and replace them where they belonged. But Sandherr did not
obey; instead he got Henry to lock the file away in a metal cabinet
in the Statistical Department. In this way, the evidence of the crime
was preserved for the future.

During this time, on the night of 18 January, Dreyfus had been
taken in irons to La Rochelle, en route for the Ile de Ré. Soon he
would be forgotten.

In top government circles, some suspected there had been an
error. As we have seen, doubts had also crept back into the minds
of some important personalities when they heard Dreyfus's cries of
innocence at the degradation ceremony. But no one had spoken out
in the press, except the socialist Maurice Charnay of the Allemanist
party. Demange, Dreyfus's counsel, and Major Forzinetti were the
only others who continued to assert publicly their conviction that
Dreyfus was innocent.

In Paris, as the Government wished, the subject had been dropped, even among the Jews. According to Léon Blum, they avoided it:
'A great misfortune had fallen on Israel. They accepted it without a
word of protest, in the hope that time and silence would wipe out its
effects.' The Dreyfus family was completely isolated, Mathieu
recalled: 'Silence, a deathly silence, hung over us.'

All the members of the family, however cast down they were by the catastrophe which had overtaken them, came to an agreement that Mathieu should take charge of the family campaign. 'I understood my task in this way,' he recalled: 'I should start a personal propaganda campaign in all the circles I could reach, untiringly, and without allowing myself to be discouraged by anything; I should recruit people, then ask these recruits, and all our friends, to work within their own circles, to make active propaganda, and finally to search out the culprit.'

After more than a month spent at the Ile de Ré, and a 'terrible voyage', Alfred Dreyfus landed on 12 March 1895 at the Iles du Salut, a small archipelago about 12 miles off the coast of French Guyana.

ON DEVIL'S ISLAND

On 13 April he was transferred from the prison on the Ile Royale to Devil's Island. There, a prison hut had been built specially for him, at the end of the rocky volcanic islet. No more than 900 metres long, Devil's Island had formerly been used to confine lepers. Near the beach, where there was a grove of about twenty coconut palms, there now stood the hut. It 'was built of stone', according to Dreyfus, 'and measured four metres square. The windows were barred; the door was a lattice-work of simple iron bars. This door opened onto an entrance two metres square, which was attached to the front of the hut; the entrance was closed by a solid wooden door.' The warders had orders not to lose sight of the prisoner by day or night. A lamp burned through the night, attracting a horde of insects.

Dreyfus was forbidden to speak to anyone. Whenever he left the hut, he was escorted by an armed warder. 'By day I was allowed to go about only in that part of the island comprised between the landing-stage and the little valley where the lepers' camp had been, a space extending for about two hundred metres and completely bare.' 'What a dreary island it was!' he noted: 'Just a few banana trees and coconut palms, and everywhere basalt rocks showing through the arid soil.'

'At the beginning, my rations were those of a soldier in the colonies, but with no wine. I had to cook for myself, and indeed do everything for myself.' The tropical heat burnt down from ten in the morning. In July, it became terrible. One day, he noted that the temperature had reached 45°.

But the days passed somehow, he noted, 'because of the countless material preoccupations of my daily life'. The appalling part was the sleepless nights:

> As soon as I lie down, however exhausted I may be, my nerves get the better of me and my brain begins to work. I think of my wife, and of the sufferings that she must be enduring: I think of my children, and of their gay and thoughtless prattling. All night there is an endless toing and froing among the warders, the constant sound of doors being opened suddenly then barred again . . . these constant comings and goings, and the sound of locks squeaking, take on, as it were, fantastic forms in my nightmares.

Day followed day, night followed night, in what he called the 'struggle for life', as he constantly waited for his mail, which always arrived after a long delay. But he did not resign himself to the situation, either mentally or physically. 'I shall fight back,' he wrote, 'I shall struggle against my own body. I will live until I see the end of all this.' Despite his insomnia, despite fever and colic, and by sheer willpower, he got down to the study of English. He read Shakespeare and the Russian classics.

He began, for his wife, a diary which allows us to follow his sufferings and his defiance. 'Physical pain is nothing,' he wrote in it, 'compared with the pains of the heart . . . Those of the heart are atrocious.'

But he hardly ever spoke in his diary of being Jewish and he never mentioned God, except to remark that he constantly recalled the saying of Schopenhauer: 'If God created the world, I would rather not have been God.' Suffering such as his argued against the idea of Divine intervention. For him, as an assimilated Jew, it was his Frenchness and his patriotism which counted above all. Religious belief was for the uneducated. On Bastille Day, he wrote: 'I have gazed at the tricolour flag floating everywhere on the island, the flag I have served with honour and loyalty. My grief is so great that my pen falls from my hand; there are feelings that cannot be expressed in words.'

The basic principles to which he appealed were truth, justice and his own honour. 'I must get at the truth, the absolute truth must be brought to light about this obscure affair.' Describing himself as 'a man who placed honour above all else', he wrote that it was his honour, more than anything, which had been impugned. 'If there is any justice in this world, my honour must be restored.'

He constantly called for justice. But as a military man, disciplined to the last, he never questioned the good faith of his superiors. He did, however, write respectfully to the President of the Republic to plead for justice, 'and that justice for which I turn to you, with all the strength of my heart, with all my soul, my hands joined in an ultimate prayer, that justice would consist in finding out the truth about this tragic story and so ending the terrible martyrdom of a soldier and a family'. He received no reply.

For four years, in his letters, he continued to encourage his wife to 'appeal for every help'. But he was to continue, on his sun-scorched island, to remain immured in silence, and in total ignorance about his own affair.

THE ADMIRABLE BROTHER

He could not know that, from the very first, even before his arrival at the Iles du Salut, his brother Mathieu, with great energy and devotion, was making approaches in every direction on his behalf. Mathieu aimed to act with the utmost discretion, to avoid any public initiative. But he knocked on every door. While certain journalists and a few politicians received him with sympathy, none of them were prepared to break the silence. 'The current of opinion against your brother is so strong, so powerful,' said the ex-minister Guyot, 'that only the discovery of the culprit could turn it around. You must discover the culprit.' But who *had* written the *bordereau*? The question haunted Mathieu. He could discover no real lead.

However, he did come by one crucial piece of information. He learned that Dr Gibert, of Le Havre, believed his brother was innocent, and that a medium, Léonie, on whom the doctor had been experimenting, claimed that the guilty man was an officer in the War Ministry. Though he was sceptical at first, Mathieu went to Le Havre. There, without revealing the name of the officer, Léonie provided him with enough convincing details to give him a certain degree of confidence in her.

At the beginning of February, she said one day, at the start of her seance: 'What are those documents they are showing the judges in secret, do not do that, it is not right. If M. Alfred and Maître Demange saw them, they would ruin their effect.' Mathieu did not understand Léonie's words, but the explanation was given to Dr Gibert on 21 February in an audience with Félix Faure, the new President of the Republic. Dr Gibert had been Félix Faure's doctor in Le Havre. Faure, a wealthy bourgeois known chiefly for his great elegance and his success with women, had replaced Casimir-Périer on 17 January. The President said to Gibert: 'Dreyfus was not convicted on the strength of the *bordereau* or of incidents during the hearings. He was convicted on the strength of documents passed to the judges in the retiring room, documents which could not, for reasons of State, be shown to the defendant or his counsel.' This, then, was the explanation of what Léonie had said. The same information reached Demange two months later.

However, with no supporters in journalistic or political circles, Mathieu was unable to make use of what he had learned. It was a young Jewish literary critic, Bernard-Lazare, who was the first to offer his support. Bernard-Lazare was to become the first Dreyfusard, 'the one from whom almost all the rest stemmed', as Léon Blum put it. A pugnacious man, attracted by symbolism, to which he gave expression in *Les Entretiens politiques et littéraires*, the little magazine he had founded with some friends, he was already, at 30, the leading critic of his generation. He also thought that art must have a social conscience: he was attracted to anarchism. And finally, in response to the campaigns of Drumont, he had published a remarkable study entitled *L'antisémitisme, son histoire et ses causes*. In November 1894, he had taken note of the revival of antisemitism sparked off by the arrest of Dreyfus, but he had refused to take up the captain's case. 'I do not know him, or his family. Yes! If he was only a poor devil, I should immediately have been worried for him, but they say Dreyfus and his family are very wealthy: they will be able to sort things out without me, particularly if he is innocent.'

After Dreyfus's conviction, he continued to concern himself solely with the problem of antisemitism in general; however, by the second half of February, he had met Alfred and Mathieu's brother-in-law, Joseph Valabrègue, who had asked to see him. He now declared that the campaign had opened his eyes and the certainty had dawned on him that the Dreyfus Affair was the result of an antisemitic plot.

He received Mathieu Dreyfus, who passed on all he knew, and asked the young critic to write and sign a pamphlet based on the notes and information he now had, and to campaign in support of his brother in press and literary circles. Bernard-Lazare wrote his pamphlet, but Mathieu would not agree to immediate publication. 'I think,' he recalled, 'I should have gone ahead sooner if Mathieu had not been held back by Maître Demange. He thought that an initiative purely on behalf of the family would not have carried conviction.' From August 1895 to August 1896 Bernard-Lazare waited impatiently: 'We could make no headway.'

PICQUART'S DISCOVERIES

However, at the War Ministry, the Dreyfus Affair had been put in the hands of Colonel Picquart, who had, on 1 July 1895, replaced Sandherr, now a very sick man, as Head of the Statistical Department. The matter was still worrying Boisdeffre. He said to Picquart: 'The Dreyfus Affair is not over. It has only just begun.' He told Picquart to bolster up the case by further research, particularly on the question of motive.

Marie-Georges Picquart was, at 41, the youngest lieutenant-colonel in the French army and, in the eyes of his superiors, one of its most up-and-coming officers. As a result of their very high esteem, he had already held posts as professor at the Ecole de Guerre and Head of Intelligence on the staff of General Galliffet. He was endowed with courage, according to Joseph Reinach, and 'a very wide-ranging intelligence, solid and perceptive, though he was without imagination. He was served by a faultless memory.' Being an Alsatian, he spoke perfect German and had a reading knowledge of English, Italian and Spanish. Handsome and slightly aesthetic-looking, he lived quietly as a bachelor. When off duty, he devoted himself to books and art. He did not open up easily and Boisdeffre thought he had too high an opinion of himself.

During the 1894 trial, at which he had officially represented Mercier and Boisdeffre, he had not been particularly sympathetic to Dreyfus. He shared indeed the prejudices of many Alsatians against the Jews. But, having been unimpressed by Henry's intervention, he had thought there would probably be an acquittal. After the sentence, his belief in Dreyfus's guilt rested solely on the secret file, which he had never seen.

Up to March 1896, all the information he had gleaned on the Dreyfus case had been worthless. One day, however, a *petit bleu* or local express-letter on blue paper, which had been found in Schwartz-koppen's waste-paper basket, came into his possession. It ran: 'I am waiting above all for a more detailed explanation than the one you gave me the other day in regard to the question at issue. In consequence, I beg you to give it to me in writing, so that I may judge if I can continue my relations with the firm of R. or not.'

This *petit bleu* was addressed to 'Major Esterhazy, 27, rue de la Bienfaisance.'

THE REAL CULPRIT

Who was Esterhazy? Marie-Charles-Ferdinand Walsin-Esterhazy, aged 48, was the son of a French general: his grandfather was descended illegitimately from a noble family from central Europe which could be traced back to the Middle Ages. He was a man of medium height and slight build, with a crop of grey hair and a long greying moustache. His eyes were deep-set and dark and his expression hard and melancholy.

His military career had been undistinguished. He had reached the rank of captain in 1881, after a period of three years spent in the Statistical Department. But he detested both the army and France. He was an adventurer, avid for pleasure, money and social esteem. He had done his utmost to remain within easy reach of Paris, where he pursued women, speculated on the Stock Exchange and gradually fell into debt. He would stop at nothing to extricate himself: lies, intrigue, even diamond robbery. For he made no distinction between right and wrong, or between the truth and the extravagant products of his own imagination. He was a mythomaniac who firmly believed every word of his own stories. The philosopher William James called him 'a fantastic scoundrel . . . a regular Shakespearean type of villain, with an insane exuberance of rhetoric and fancy about his vanities and hatreds that literature has never yet equalled'.

He was, however, an unhappy man. Suffering from tuberculosis and highly-strung, he could hardly sleep; and to his hatred for the army and for France were added contempt for his wealthy and aristocratic wife, who had not kept him from ruin. He felt persecuted by everyone around him. At the same time, he had succeeded in earning the constant high regard of his superiors, and he had not given up hope of very high-level patronage. For he was also a charmer: 'The blazing passion of his language, his furious mimickry, his intensity of life, the communicative frenzy of this astonishing play-actor had an endless fascination,' wrote Reinach. And he had a certain talent as a journalist, even as a writer. He could produce articles on military subjects and was a regular informant of the newspapers' military correspondents, most notably Major Biot of the *Libre Parole*.

If therefore all his funds were exhausted in 1894, it seemed almost the obvious thing for him to offer his military information to Schwartzkoppen, in exchange for the substantial sums of money he needed. The latter, not without a certain hesitation, had accepted, on orders from Berlin. It was in this context that Esterhazy wrote the *bordereau.* He was the real traitor, always supposing the items of information he offered were actually State secrets.

In the first instance, Picquart thought he was a second traitor, or a mere accomplice to Dreyfus. An old friend from the same regiment revealed to Picquart his dissolute way of life and his incessant curiosity about artillery matters. Picquart had him followed for four months without success. A renegade German agent, Richard Cuers, then revealed that the German War Ministry was being supplied with artillery information by a French officer of about 45, but he would not give his name. This was not enough for Picquart.

It was Esterhazy who in the end gave himself away during an audacious attempt to arrange that he should be posted to the War Ministry. He had managed to obtain a letter of support not only from General Saussier's aide-de-camp, but also from several deputies and two generals ... But on 27 August, one of his letters fell into the hands of Picquart. Picquart saw at once that the writing was the same as that of the *bordereau*, and, what is more, that that document could well apply to him. 'I resolved to consult the secret file,' he testified later, 'so as to see what share in the treason could still fall to Dreyfus ... I must confess I was seized by astonishment when I read the secret file. I was expecting to find grave matters in it, but all I found was a document which could apply to Esterhazy just as much as to Dreyfus, another insignificant document (referring to Davignon), one document it seemed absurd to link with Dreyfus (the one referring to the 'scoundrel D.'), and one where I recognized Guénée's handwriting in an attached report, and which seemed equally insignificant.'

There was nothing left to incriminate Dreyfus. Immediately, Picquart explained his discovery to General de Boisdeffre, asserting that it was important to correct the mistake that had been made in 1894. Boisdeffre listened in silence until the secret file was mentioned, then said: 'Why wasn't it burned as we had agreed?'

Mistrusting Picquart's lack of experience, Boisdeffre at first played for time, and told him to go and seek the advice of General Gonse. 'I see, we made a mistake,' said Gonse. 'The two affairs must be dealt with separately.'

In this way, a gulf began to open up between the young Picquart, who was aiming straight for the objective suggested to him by his intelligence, and his superiors, who were more familiar with the ways of men and of the world, and who understood the complications that would be caused by a review of the 1894 trial; such a review would inevitably bring to light the illegality which had been committed by Mercier.

And, as if to underline the dangerous nature of the situation, a newspaper article now broke the silence the government had sought to impose on the Dreyfus case. An English journalist, Clifford Millage, who had been recommended to Mathieu Dreyfus, suggested they should put out a false report that Dreyfus had escaped, in order to arouse public opinion in England, and, if possible, in France. Mathieu agreed, on condition that the story was made so improbable that it would immediately be denied.

THE FALSE REPORT OF DREYFUS'S ESCAPE

On 3 September 1896, Millage therefore placed an article in his paper, the London *Daily Chronicle*, reporting that according to the *South Wales Argus* of Newport, Monmouthshire, a certain Captain Hunter, on landing at Newport, had recounted Dreyfus's escape on board an American schooner, which had managed to slip past the French government cutter. The Havas newsagency published the report the next morning in Paris, and it was reproduced all over the French press. But, after telegraphing the governor of Cayenne, the French government issued an immediate denial on the very same day. So that when, on 4 September, the *South Wales Argus* mentioned its own – purely mythical – article for the first time, the initial report was already about to be denied in Paris.

In his island prison, Dreyfus was now placed in double irons. Two U-shaped pieces were fixed by their lower end to his bed. To these irons, another bar was fastened to which two rings were attached: when his legs were put through the rings at night, he was unable to move. 'The torture was horrible, especially on these sultry nights. Very soon these rings, tightly fastened round my ankles, began to chafe and give me sore places.' This went on for forty-five nights. 'Putting in irons, a security measure!' wrote Dreyfus. 'It is a measure of hatred and torture, ordered from Paris by those who, being unable to strike at a family, are striking at an innocent man, because neither he nor his family will or should bow their heads and submit to the most frightful judicial error that has ever been committed.'

Meanwhile, in Paris, the operation had succeeded: an article favourable to Dreyfus, by Gaston Calmette, appeared in *Le Figaro*. *Le Jour* mentioned him, and Paul de Cassagnac, in *L'Autorité*, once again voiced his doubts about his guilt. Thereupon, the nationalist deputy Castelin announced he was going to put down a question in Parliament on the government's indifference towards the activities of Dreyfus and his supporters.

Mathieu now thought the time had come to let Bernard-Lazare publish his pamphlet. But on 15 September a long article appeared in *L'Eclair*, which included a detailed account of Dreyfus's arrest and trial. *L'Eclair*, which had taken upon itself the role of spokesman for the General Staff, claimed it was making up for the government's reticence by offering the general public incontrovertible evidence of Dreyfus's guilt. It repeated the General Staff line, worked out in 1894, to the effect that Dreyfus's guilt was proven by the 'scoundrel D.' document. But in this version by *L'Eclair*, the words 'that scoundrel D.' were replaced by the sentence: 'That lout Dreyfus is really becoming too demanding.'

The article also contained an inaccurate summary of the *bordereau*, as well as the crucial admission that the secret file had not been submitted to the defence. The illegality of 1894 was thus proclaimed openly to all and sundry. According to Joseph Reinach, the *Eclair* article was reproduced throughout the press.

> It appeared convincing... and as no official denial followed, people concluded not only that these astonishing revelations were true, but that they had been prompted by the government, which had had them published so as to cut short a detestable campaign before it became too dangerous... This version of the crime, obviously authentic, since it had been confirmed by the approving silence of the authorities, carried conviction, seeped into people's consciousness, and became crystallized there. It was to dominate the mind of the French people for two years.

After the publication of this article, which he was tempted to attribute to the Dreyfus family, Picquart thought it was more urgent than ever to act. 'If we wait any longer,' he wrote to Gonse, 'things will get the better of us, we shall be trapped in an inextricable situation, and we shall have no means of defence or of finding out the real truth,' Gonse continued to stall, and to recommend prudence.

THE MEETING OF GONSE AND PICQUART

On 15 September, however, according to Picquart, he finally reacted, and, when he saw Picquart, said to him: 'But why should you care if this Jew stays on Devil's Island?'

'But, General, he is innocent.'

'This is an affair that must not be re-opened: General Mercier and General Saussier are involved.'

'But I am telling you he is innocent.'

Gonse shrugged his shoulders: 'That does not matter; those are not considerations we have to take into account.'

Picquart then mentioned the Dreyfus family's tactics:

'How will it look for us if they succeed in discovering the real culprit?'

'If you say nothing no one will ever know.'

'What you are saying there is abominable, General. I do not know what I shall do, but I know I shall not let my secret die with me!'

(Gonse always denied the terms of this conversation, but it was in line with the position he constantly maintained.)

Three days later, Lucie Dreyfus submitted a petition for a review of the 1894 trial to the Chamber of Deputies, in an attempt to take advantage of the press agitation which had been started. It was rejected.

For the time being, Picquart was able to continue his surveillance of Esterhazy, but he soon began to be aware that he no longer enjoyed the confidence of those at the top. The wind was turning against him too at the Statistical Department. Henry and his fellow-officers were beginning to look back regretfully to the days of Sandherr, when everything was done 'within the family'. If their young chief succeeded in getting the Dreyfus case reviewed, it would be a disaster for them. After all, Henry had proclaimed Dreyfus's guilt at the 1894 trial without producing any evidence.

Henry convinced Boisdeffre and Gonse that he was right to mistrust Picquart. Boisdeffre then suggested to Billot, the War Minister, that Picquart should be sent to Indo-China to keep him away from Paris. But Billot did not want to inflict a black mark on such a good officer. He finally sent him on an assignment in eastern and southeastern France, on 26 October.

It was now that Henry took it upon himself once again to act, so as to avert the danger of the review Picquart wanted. If adequate evidence against Dreyfus was lacking, why not fabricate some? This after all seemed a normal procedure to Henry; he had had to forge many documents to mislead the Germans. The interests of his superiors seemed to him to call once again for decisive action.

On 1 November 1896, between the authentic heading and signature of a note from Panizzardi to Schwartzkoppen, he stuck the following text, which he wrote himself in blue pencil, imitating as best he could Panizzardi's style and handwriting:

My dear fellow, I have read that a deputy is going to ask a question about Dreyfus in Parliament. If Rome demands fresh explanations I shall say I did never have anything to do with that Jew. Agreed then! If they ask you, say it like that. For no one must ever know what happened with him.

Unfortunately, in view of what was to happen later, Henry did not notice that the cross-ruling on the original paper, and that on the paper he had used for his forgery, were not the same colour. This was to be his undoing.

For the moment, his document, which became known as the Henry forgery, delighted Boisdeffre, Gonse and Billot. At last they had crushing proof against Dreyfus.

During this time, Bernard-Lazare had rewritten his 1895 pamphlet to take account of the *Eclair* article. He had 3,500 copies printed in Brussels, and sent them on 6 November to every deputy and senator, and to all those who might be interested in the Dreyfus case. 'I wish to establish,' he wrote, 'that Dreyfus's guilt has never been demonstrated.' He refuted one by one the allegations of *L'Eclair*. He gave the correct text of the *bordereau* and, insisting on the illegality of 1894, declared that the secret document on which Dreyfus had been convicted did not include his name. 'Captain Dreyfus is an innocent man,' he concluded, 'whose conviction was obtained by illegal means: I demand a review of the case.'[1]

Fearing his pamphlet would be smothered, he made a great many approaches to the press. But in the climate created by the *Eclair* article he had a hostile reception. For who, in Paris, could be expected to take the word of a Jew and an anarchist rather than believe an article which seemed to originate from an official source? Everywhere he met with abuse and insults.

Even the Jews themselves were no more sympathetic. For Bernard-Lazare had broken with their fearful and passive attitude. And, taking upon himself the mantle of a prophet of Israel – which is how Péguy described him in *Notre jeunesse* – he was to set out to defend in Dreyfus the whole of the Jewish people. He made this explicit in the second edition of his pamphlet in 1897: 'It was because he was a Jew that he was arrested, it was because he was a Jew that he was tried, it was because he was a Jew that he was found guilty, and it is because he is a Jew that the voice of truth and justice is not allowed to speak out on his behalf.'[2]

But the Dreyfusards did not want to go into battle on the Jewish issue, any more than did the Jews themselves. Soon after this, Bernard-

1 Bernard-Lazare, *Une erreur judiciaire. L'Affaire Dreyfus* (Brussels, 1896).
2 Idem, *Une erreur judiciaire. L'Affaire Dreyfus* (Paris, 1993) (= his second pamphlet, 1897), p. 6.

Lazare was to be forced into silence on the Dreyfus affair by the Dreyfusards, after suffering among the Jews the common fate of the prophet. He embraced Zionism and was to die in obscurity in 1903, remaining thereafter in oblivion. For many years he was only known through the magnificent pages Péguy wrote about him in *Notre jeunesse*. But his long-term influence on the Dreyfusards was not inconsiderable. Blum wrote of him in 1935: 'There was within him a Jew from the line of great Jews, from the prophetic line, from the line that spoke of "a just man" where others said "a saint".'

What seemed clear to Mathieu, in the immediate, in November 1896, was that the essential, the key event was not the publication of Bernard-Lazare's pamphlet, which had fallen flat, but the appearance, four days later, in *Le Matin*, of a facsimile of the *bordereau*. This allowed him to spread leaflets round Paris showing the facsimile side by side with samples of Esterhazy's handwriting. 'Little by little,' he recalled, 'thanks to this constant visual propaganda, which was more effective than arguments and assertions, the scope of our action grew from day to day.' So much, then, for Bernard-Lazare: to Mathieu, he had never been more than a hired pamphleteer, said Péguy.

On 18 November came the parliamentary debate on the nationalist Castelin's *interpellation*, i.e. his question to the government. The loose grouping of nationalists, made up of elements stemming from the extreme Right and the extreme Left of the old Boulangist movement, did not at this stage call itself by that name. But, like the antisemites, its members were already making use of the Dreyfus affair to harass the Republicans on both flanks. The text of the Castelin *interpellation* called on the government to repress the activities of those who were in favour of rehabilitating Dreyfus.

Opening the debate, the War Minister Billot, knowing he now had up his sleeve the decisive proof against Dreyfus which Henry had just submitted to him, boldly cut the ground from under Castelin's feet:

> This sorry affair was set off two years ago by one of my predecessors at the War Ministry. Justice was then done. The preliminary investigation of the case, the hearing and the judgment were all conducted in accordance with the rules of military procedure . . . It is therefore a matter of *res judicata*, and no one has any right to go back on these proceedings.

At the end of the debate, the government did have to accept Castelin's motion calling on it to seek out, if appropriate, where responsibilities lay in the Dreyfus Affair, but in reality it had been shelved once again. No one in the Chamber of Deputies was interested.

The War Ministry felt relieved. However, so as to be quite certain, moves were begun against Picquart, which soon developed into a full-scale campaign. Henry forged more letters, purporting to show he was implicated in a Jewish plot, and an attempt was made to pin leaks on him, notably the passing of a copy of the *bordereau* to *Le Matin*. Gonse set out at the same time to make life unbearable for him, posting him from corps to corps. And finally a new Henry forgery, a letter signed Speranza, which arrived at the Ministry on 15 December, gave it to be understood he was in touch, for the sake of the cause he was pursuing, with an enigmatic female figure. This was enough for Henry to be able to convince Gonse that Picquart must be sent to Tunisia. The trouble-maker's career seemed to be over.

But would his secret die with him? After receiving a highly threatening letter from Henry, accusing him of plotting against Esterhazy, he eventually decided, after some months, to pass on his discoveries about Esterhazy to his lawyer, Louis Leblois, who was an old friend and a member of the Paris bar. He left with him a will in the form of a letter, to be submitted to the President of the Republic only in the event of his death. At the same time, however, he forbade Leblois to enter into contact with the Dreyfus family or Demange, or to reveal Esterhazy's name to them.

However, fortunately for Dreyfus's supporters, they were in fact able to gain knowledge of Picquart's discoveries. For, on 13 July 1897, swearing him to secrecy, Leblois revealed what Picquart had told him to a leading figure of state, Auguste Scheurer-Kestner, vice-president of the Senate. It so happened that Charles Risler, mayor of the 7th *arrondissement* of Paris, with whom Leblois worked as assistant mayor, was the senator's nephew. Leblois had learned from Risler that he was very concerned about the Dreyfus Affair, and so he resolved to speak to him.

SCHEURER-KESTNER

Scheurer-Kestner was one of the founding fathers of the Republic; he had been one of the associates of Gambetta. Born in 1833, he was a scientist from one of the great protestant families of Mulhouse. A Republican militant at the time of the Second Empire, he was a man whose patriotism was beyond question: he had been one of the last deputies to have represented Alsace in the French Parliament before its annexation by Germany, and he therefore still seemed to personify the lost provinces. He had become a life senator in 1875 and was universally respected in Parliament for his proverbial honesty.

The conviction of Dreyfus in 1894 had disturbed him. Being familiar with the element of Mulhouse society from which Dreyfus came, he had at first found his crime inexplicable.

Like so many others, he had been reassured by the unanimity of the verdict of 1894. But Joseph Reinach and the old radical Arthur Ranc began trying to make him share their doubts after they heard Dreyfus's cries of innocence at his degradation. And from then on, Scheurer had tried to obtain information on several occasions. But his scrupulous scientific mind was not convinced by the explanations of his colleagues Casimir-Périer or Freycinet. Billot, the defender of the *res judicata* in Parliament, and who had been a childhood friend, had firmly advised him not to concern himself with Dreyfus.

Scheurer had received Mathieu Dreyfus in February 1895, and had felt 'such intense pity' that he was swayed by the encounter. Was not he the defender of all Alsatians who were in need of help? He encouraged Mathieu, though without offering any direct support.

Now, two years later, still tormented by the question of Dreyfus, he decided to seek out the truth more actively. At a dinner-party with some friends, he let out the exclamation: 'Oh! I wish I could be enlightened about Dreyfus's guilt!' An officer then assured the guests that it was easy to demonstrate: Dreyfus had been able to buy a house in Paris with the money he had acquired through spying. Scheurer learned that this was pure hearsay. According to his own account, he found such thoughtlessness frightening in an officer who had been involved in the preliminary investigation: all his splendid confidence in the officers of the army was shaken.

> I swore that from now on I would shrink from nothing, whenever the occasion arose, in order to form an opinion on the case of Captain Dreyfus – setting aside his family, which I did not wish to involve in my investigations – with a view to making my own wholly personal enquiry, quietly, and in such a way that I could not be suspected of yielding to any influences outside myself. There must be no sentimentality, I said to myself! No prior commiseration! I must make my own preliminary investigation; no doubt my official position will provide the means to this end. I must make use of my position for the sake of Truth and Justice. If Dreyfus is guilty, I shall find out about it, and if not, I shall save him. It is not acceptable in the nineteenth century, under a Republican regime, and a government based on freedom and open discussion, that iniquities should arise worthy of an absolutist regime from past centuries.

The man of science was here already using typically Dreyfusard language.

And so, when Leblois entrusted him, on 13 July 1897, with Picquart's revelations on the role of Esterhazy, and the General Staff's campaign to ruin him, he was 'staggered'. 'But,' he added, 'I still needed something else to make me totally convinced: I still needed an actual document.' Leblois then showed him Gonse's letters to Picquart, which went on counselling prudence, even after his discoveries about Esterhazy. Scheurer was 'absolutely floored'. The next day, at the Senate, he asserted in the presence of his Republican colleagues his conviction that Dreyfus was innocent.

Throughout the summer, he made this conviction known in political and literary circles. He informed Lucie Dreyfus he had proof of her husband's innocence, and that he intended, when Parliament reassembled, to set about having his trial reviewed.

Mathieu Dreyfus had thus now at last found a major supporter, with enough weight to influence the government and the politicians. But alas! because of his promise not to bring Picquart's testimony into the open, Scheurer would never be able to produce decisive evidence in public. This gravely hampered his action, and the nationalist press had no compunction in greeting the great Republican figure with a hail of derision.

LUCIEN HERR

However, the Dreyfusard camp was now gradually beginning to gather. One of the first to become involved was Lucien Herr, a man of 33 who had been librarian at the Ecole Normale Supérieure since 1888 and was an active socialist. He had set himself the aim of using his influence over the younger generation to direct them towards science and rationalism, and wean them away from nationalism. His role in converting them to socialism was to become legendary. Herr had been convinced of Dreyfus's innocence by Lucien Lévy-Brühl, who was a philosophy professor and the convicted man's cousin. The latter had been converted to the cause by Bernard-Lazare.[3]

By August 1897, these first Dreyfusards had in their hands, apart from Leblois's confidences to Scheurer, the makings of some very substantial evidence: not only the facsimile of the *bordereau*, but a further series of handwriting reports which had been ordered from

3 Daniel Lindenberg and Pierre-André Meyer, *Lucien Herr. Le socialisme et son destin* (Paris, 1977), pp. 55–7, 142.

experts by Bernard-Lazare. But there were still only a handful of Dreyfus supporters gathered around Herr and Lévy-Brühl: they included Gabriel Monod, a Protestant historian and the acknowledged master of the historical method, and just three politicians: Scheurer, Ranc and Joseph Reinach. The latter had also been converted to the cause by Bernard-Lazare.

RANC AND REINACH

Ranc, born in 1833, and, like Scheurer, one of the great figures of the Republic, was universally respected on the Left for his courageous past and his strength of character. Transported to Lambèse by the Second Empire, he had been elected a member of the Paris Commune, but then resigned. Having become one of Gambetta's close associates, he later followed him in his move to a more moderate radicalism. He was elected as a deputy in 1881 and as a senator in 1891. He had been one of the great opponents of Boulanger.

In 1894, he had protested against Dreyfus being tried in camera, and had been the first politician to issue a warning about the revival of antisemitism.[4] From 1895, he had joined Reinach in all the steps he took in favour of Dreyfus. He was later, from 1898, to become one of the chief architects of the Dreyfusard movement's shift to anticlericalism.

However, Joseph Reinach was undoubtedly the leading Dreyfusard in the political class; before even the dust had settled, he was to write his monumental history of the Affair, to which all historians are so much indebted, including the present author.

Born in 1856, he had long been a highly influential member of the Republican party. First noticed by Gambetta, who put him in charge of his private office, he had replaced the latter after his death as the director of his newspaper, *La République Française*. He was also an opponent of Boulangism and had been triumphantly elected at Digne in 1889, defeating the Boulangist candidate. A great patriot, and very hostile to socialism, he was rather a loudmouth and spoke frequently in the Chamber of Deputies. He was also the most prominent Jew in the French Parliament. But he thought of himself as a Frenchman first and foremost and not so much as a Jew; for him, the Dreyfusard campaign was essentially Republican in character and was not a campaign to defend the Jewish people as such. Unfortunately

4 'Pas de huis clos', *Paris*, 13 November 1894, and 'La politique. L'Edit de Nantes', *La Dépêche de Toulouse*, 10 November 1894.

for him, though, it so happened that he was also both the nephew and son-in-law of Baron Jacques de Reinach, who had been implicated in the Panama scandal and had then committed suicide. This had not prevented him from being re-elected at Digne in 1893.

LÉON BLUM

To this tiny nucleus of Dreyfusards, committed from the start, was now added, in September 1897, the young literary critic Léon Blum. Born in 1872, he had been made to leave the Ecole Normale for 'insufficient work', but had remained one of Herr's followers. A young aesthete with anarchist leanings, he wrote for several avant-garde journals, notably the *Revue Blanche*. He was a great admirer of Clemenceau, Barrès and Disraeli (but *see* below, pp. 58–9). This young rebel who sympathized with the poor and the oppressed had been converted to socialism by Herr.[5]

And it was Herr who said to him point-blank, one day in September 1897: 'Did you know that Dreyfus is innocent?' Blum was immediately won over. 'Herr's strength, his incredible, quite unique strength . . . lay essentially,' he recalled, 'in this: that in him, conviction became a kind of self-evidence. He had such tranquil confidence in the truth that it was conveyed effortlessly to those he spoke to, almost as if it were a matter of course. The very possibility of any discussion seemed to be ruled out.'

Armed with the evidence they had begun to collect, and not anticipating any resistance from the General Staff, these first Dreyfusards expected an early victory. 'In the face of such an array of facts and documents,' Blum wrote, 'not a shadow of a doubt lingered in our minds. Our certainty was unmarred, complete, well-founded, and we were convinced it would be spontaneously shared by the entire world once the world came to know what we ourselves had learned.'

JAURÈS

From the end of the summer break of 1897, Herr got down to the task of converting his immediate circle, beginning with the lecturers and students at the Ecole Normale. All through the autumn, too, with Lévy-Brühl, he worked to convince Jean Jaurès, one of the leading figures among the new parliamentary socialists, or Independents. Born in 1859, Jaurès had begun his career as a professor of philosophy,

5 Lindenberg and Meyer, *Lucien Herr*, pp. 136ff.

but had been elected as a deputy for the Tarn department in 1885. With his beard, his short, thick-set figure and his heavy step, he had something of the peasant about him: he liked to say of himself that he was a 'cultured peasant'. But in his speeches and articles he dazzled his contemporaries by his rhetorical powers and his prodigious culture. His carelessness about his attire was proverbial and a symptom of his totally disinterested devotion to socialism. He had actually begun his political career as a left-of-centre Republican, but had gradually become disenchanted with the policy of the Opportunists. He then moved in the direction of socialism. The miners' strike at Carmaux finally led him into active commitment, and he was elected as a socialist deputy in 1893 with working-class votes. For him, the Republic naturally led on to socialism, and the economic emancipation of the workers was the logical consequence of their political and social emancipation.

He hesitated for a long time over the question of Dreyfus's innocence; he had as yet no certainty. Besides, Dreyfus's first champions were staunch opponents of socialism, upper-middle-class figures like Scheurer-Kestner. And could socialists ally themselves with Reinach and politicians tainted by Panama? Throughout the autumn, Jaurès confined himself to asking the government, in the columns of the socialist daily paper, the *Petite République*, why no enquiry had been made about several disturbing questions, particularly the irregularities in the 1894 trial.

What was the attitude of the authorities to the birth of the Dreyfusard movement? Scheurer's statements disturbed Billot, the government and the General Staff, and their first concern was to find out what evidence he had. Their enquiry on this point was unsuccessful.

At the same time, Gonse, fearing that Esterhazy would be denounced, or would take to flight – which would have been tantamount to a confession – launched du Paty into action again. His job was to pass on a warning to Esterhazy. A letter was dispatched to him, about 16 October, signed Espérance, which explained the dangers surrounding him. Seized by panic, he threatened suicide and was only dissuaded from this by his mistress. The General Staff then decided to calm him down and offer him reassurances, at a comic opera meeting arranged in the Parc Montsouris in southern Paris with du Paty and Gribelin, the Statistical Section archivist: the one wore a false beard and the other dark-tinted blue spectacles. They told him he would enjoy protection so long as he kept to the instructions he would be given. This protection of Esterhazy by the General Staff was to be long-lasting.

Furthermore, a new set of charges against Dreyfus was prepared at the Statistical Department, based first of all on his alleged confession to Lebrun-Renault (*see* above, p. 31), then on a series of exhibits, both new and old, forming the basis of a new secret file.

On 22 October, Scheurer asked to see Félix Faure, the President of the Republic. Showing impatience, Faure said that because of his constitutional position he could only offer his 'benevolent neutrality'.

Esterhazy had taken advantage of the protection he was enjoying to write a letter to the President in characteristic style, making reference to the Espérance letter: 'I am the person designated in that letter as the chosen victim . . . my family is illustrious enough in the annals of French history and of great European causes for my government to have a care that my name should not be dragged through the mud.' He asked for justice, otherwise he would appeal to the German Emperor, the head of his house and suzerain of the Esterhazy family. 'An Esterhazy fears nothing and no one but God.'

Scheurer was invited to lunch on 30 October by his old friend Billot, who asserted to him that Dreyfus was guilty and had confessed. 'That's wrong!' Scheurer exclaimed. Billot then gave him a vague promise to pursue his enquiries. In exchange, Scheurer agreed to do nothing more for another fortnight. The nationalist newspapers, some of them prompted by the General Staff, went on showering him with insults, accusing him of undermining the honour of the army.

The next day, Esterhazy went on the offensive, complaining in a second letter to the President that no support had been forthcoming after his first one. 'I am driven to use all the means in my power.' He resorted to threats: on the basis of information supplied by Henry and the Espérance letter, he invented a 'veiled lady', who was communicating with him via letters written in a disguised hand. 'The generous lady who has warned me of the horrible plot hatched against me by the friends of Dreyfus, with the assistance of Colonel Piquart', he wrote, 'has since been able to procure, among other documents, the photograph of a paper that she succeeded in coaxing out of this officer. This paper, stolen from a foreign legation by Colonel Picquart, is most compromising for certain diplomatic personalities. If I obtain neither support nor justice, and if my name comes to be pronounced, the photograph, which is today in a secure place, will immediately be published'. The 'veiled lady' had thus provided him with a 'liberating document'. A new legend was put into circulation, and the government had no choice but to take it seriously. Esterhazy's collusion with the General Staff had begun.

However, despite these moves, the Dreyfusards learned his name a few days later. About 7 November, a banker, M. de Castro, recognized his handwriting on one of the facsimiles of the *bordereau* on sale on the boulevards. Esterhazy was a former client of his. Hurrying home, he was able to compare the writing of the *bordereau* with letters he had had from Esterhazy: they were identical. He consequently offered to show these letters to Mathieu Dreyfus.

'I was immediately struck by the extraordinary resemblance in the handwritings,' Mathieu recalled. 'They were completely identical. It was the culprit's handwriting.' Now at last, after so much lost effort, he knew who the real culprit was. One question still disturbed him though. Supposing it was not the person whose name Scheurer had been given by Leblois? He rushed to see Scheurer. 'I will tell you the name of the traitor!' he exclaimed. 'It is Esterhazy.'

'Indeed,' replied Scheurer, 'he's the man.' Mathieu had thus been able to discover the culprit's name independently. He could now denounce him.

On 12 November, at a meeting between Mathieu, Scheurer, Leblois and Emmanuel Arène – a deputy and journalist on *Le Figaro* – Leblois suggested to Mathieu that he could make the denunciation solely on the basis of handwriting. In this way, Picquart would not be compromised.

It was also decided that, before Scheurer made his request for a review, Arène should begin a gradual week-long campaign of revelations in *Le Figaro*. To prepare the public, Scheurer published an open letter to Ranc in *Le Temps* on 15 November, in which he referred to the documents proving Dreyfus's innocence which he had shown to Billot and said he was waiting in vain for the enquiry Billot had promised him. He still, however, did not produce any evidence.

Meanwhile, Arène decided he should divulge the essence of Scheurer's case in an article in *Le Figaro*, which he signed 'Vidi': he asserted that Dreyfus was innocent and that the real writer of the *bordereau* was an officer 'garrisoned in the provinces in a town not far from Paris'. This officer 'was, moreover, very well-known and very widespread in his activities in Paris'. This was enough to identify Esterhazy to those in the know. Arène also cited the 'scoundrel D.' document.

Scheurer was caught unprepared, and the antisemite Drumont in the *Libre Parole* immediately retorted with an article signed 'Dixi' inspired by the General Staff, which presented the public with a long string of accusations against 'XY, a high civil servant in the War Ministry', seen as the 'moving spirit in the plot'. This was a veiled attack on Picquart: the article included all the charges being prepared against him by the General Staff.

The pace of events now began to quicken. Mathieu had to move immediately to the denunciation of Esterhazy, as the newspaper *La Liberté* had named a respectable officer, M. de Rougemont, as the one Arène had been pointing to. He declared in a letter to the War Minister that the *bordereau* was the sole basis for the charge against his brother, named Esterhazy as the writer, and demanded justice without delay.

The government now had no other option but to accept Billot's proposal to open an enquiry about Esterhazy. General Pellieux was put in charge. It was in this way that, by mid-November, the essence of the Dreyfusard position and the name of Esterhazy had been put before the French public.

ZOLA AND CLEMENCEAU

At the same point, too, Zola and Clemenceau entered the fray. The great novelist, who was by now wealthy and world-renowned, had finished the *Rougon-Macquart* cycle, and *Paris*, the third of his *Cities* trilogy. Zola had had his doubts on the day of the degradation ceremony, having been struck, Reinach noted, by how ferocious the crowds were, how worked up against one single man, 'were he guilty a hundred times over'. He sketched out a novel, the story of an innocent soldier who sacrificed himself to peace for the sake of his country. But then he thought nothing more about Dreyfus. Early in November 1897, he received information in turn from Bernard-Lazare and from Leblois, who revealed the whole of the Picquart file. The story appeared 'extraordinary' and 'fascinating'. A decisive luncheon-party took place on 13 November, at which Scheurer tried to persuade him to intervene, and, after hesitating for ten days, he made his mind up on 24 November and offered his support to *Le Figaro*, which had just entered the campaign with the 'Vidi' article.

In his first article of 25 November, Zola took up the defence of Scheurer against the nationalists, praising his life which was 'as pure as crystal': as a novelist, he was still at the stage of admiring the characters in the drama. But he ended his article with these prophetic words: 'Truth is on the march, and nothing can stop it.'

Georges Clemenceau, now 56, was 'short, powerfully built, meticulously dressed', and 'cut a strange figure with his round Mongolian skull, his sleek-skinned face, coal-black eyes and droopy moustache . . . He was feared as much for his marksmanship with the pistol and his skill with the sword as for the sarcastic words with which he attacked his opponents.' Fighting, he said, was his *raison d'être*. He had all his life been a fighter for justice. He had parted company with the moderate Republicans in 1881 to become the vigorous spokesman of a nationalistic radicalism, which reproached Jules Ferry company with wasting French gold and French blood on colonial expeditions, instead of concentrating on defending France against Germany. He had made his political reputation as a fierce debater and a man to topple governments by the way he dispatched Ferry in the Chamber of Deputies after the defeat of the Tonkin expedition in 1885, but he had been forced out of politics after the Panama scandal in 1893. For the time being, he was reduced to mere writing. On 19 October, he joined the new daily *L'Aurore*, which had been founded by Vaughan. But he was impatient to return to action and to struggle. For him, writing was only acting by halves. The Dreyfus Affair could therefore not have come at a more opportune moment.

In 1894, it will be recalled, he had seen Dreyfus as a monster (*see* above, p. 29). But at the end of October 1897 he met Ranc, who happened to mention the name of Bernard-Lazare.

'Oh, that man!' exclaimed Clemenceau. 'We all like him for his talent, but we have insisted he should leave us alone with his Dreyfus Affair.'

'I beg your pardon? Don't you know Dreyfus is innocent?'

'What are you saying?'

'It's true. Scheurer-Kestner has evidence. Go and see him, he'll show you.'

'If it is true, then it is the greatest crime of the century.'

So Clemenceau went to see Scheurer: he became convinced, not that Dreyfus was innocent, but that there had been irregularities in the trial. From 2 November, in *L'Aurore*, he began demanding the truth from the government.

The little band of Dreyfusards, followed cautiously so far by Jaurès, Zola and Clemenceau, was growing larger. Dreyfus's very first supporters, it should be noted, all believed in his innocence. Those who followed them simply started by asking certain questions. They were soon to be joined by the revisionists, those who called for a review of the case without, however, committing themselves as to Dreyfus's innocence.

DE PELLIEUX'S TWO ENQUIRIES

De Pellieux, who was an intelligent but impetuous young general, immediately began his enquiry on 17 November. He first saw Mathieu Dreyfus, who submitted the facsimile of the *bordereau* and specimens of Esterhazy's handwriting to him. Scheurer, without producing any evidence, persuaded him of his 'sincere conviction' and told him that Leblois would explain everything. The latter did indeed tell him about the identity of the handwritings and about Gonse's letters to Picquart. Esterhazy on the other hand repeated the story, made up of the General Staff's charges against Picquart, which the article 'Dixi' had already made familiar to the public.

Esterhazy, it will be recalled, had been in collusion with the General Staff since October, with a view to damning Picquart: Henry had provided him with the information needed to compose the 'veiled lady' letter. Acting together, Esterhazy and Henry had also sent two telegrams to Picquart in Tunisia, signed 'Blanche' and 'Speranza', which were designed to be intercepted and to compromise him. The one signed 'Blanche' said that the *bleu*, i.e. the *petit bleu*, had been fabricated by 'Georges'. This was later to make it possible for Henry to 'scratch out' the name, so as to claim that that of Picquart had been replaced by that of Esterhazy.

Pellieux did have one moment of doubt. But he consulted General de Boisdeffre, who 'enlightened him about the question concerning Picquart'. He concluded in his report that Mathieu had not produced anything, nor had Scheurer-Kestner. As for Leblois, 'in what he had been willing to pass on' there was nothing more substantial than in the Mathieu Dreyfus file. Esterhazy was admittedly an unsound officer, but this was a long way from saying he was guilty of the treason he was accused of. Esterhazy 'seemed to be cleared', whereas Picquart was guilty, 'having handed over official letters, probably secret documents, to a third party'.

On 21 November, the government decided to give the Pellieux enquiry official status, since it was necessary for Picquart to be heard. Pellieux consulted Henry, who told him that Picquart had received Leblois frequently in his office at the Ministry. He then showed him his forgery, and this finally convinced Pellieux of Dreyfus's guilt and therefore of Esterhazy's innocence.

Pellieux's second enquiry was centred essentially on his interrogation of Picquart on 26 and 27 November: the latter clearly explained his 1896 enquiry, and Esterhazy's machinations. This called imperatively for a response.

Meanwhile, Esterhazy was becoming alarmed at the situation, which seemed about to turn catastrophic on the 28th, when *Le Figaro* published his letters to Madame de Boulancy, which dated from the period 1881 to 1884. When they read the 'uhlan' letter, the French public realized exactly what to make of Esterhazy's patriotism and his personality. About the French, he had written:

> I am absolutely convinced that this people is not worth the cartridges you would need to kill them . . . I know of only one human quality, and it is completely lacking in this people; and if I was told tonight that I would be killed tomorrow as a captain of uhlans cutting down Frenchmen with my sword, I should certainly be completely happy . . . At the present time, exasperated, embittered and furious, and in an absolutely atrocious situation, I feel capable of great deeds, if I had the chance, or of crimes, if I could be avenged.
>
> I would not harm a little dog, but I would have a hundred thousand Frenchmen killed with pleasure.

The Dreyfusards were exultant.

Esterhazy thought all was now lost, but his lawyer, Maître Tézenas, recommended that he should ask to be tried by court-martial. This plan appealed to the General Staff; it would save them from the civil libel suit Esterhazy was planning to bring against Mathieu Dreyfus and Scheurer. Despite therefore Pellieux's conclusion that there was 'no evidence' against Esterhazy, and despite the latter's demand for an official investigation of Picquart, General Saussier signed the order to begin proceedings against Esterhazy on 4 December.

'THERE IS NO DREYFUS AFFAIR!'

In Parliament, the nationalist Castelin, pursuing his campaign of harassment against the government, asked the Prime Minister Méline for a statement to reassure the army, public opinion and the Chamber. Méline, clinging to the official line which went back to 1894, then gave an answer which has gone down in history: 'I hope the honourable deputy will allow me what will be the essential word in this debate. There is no Dreyfus Affair. At the present moment, there is not, nor can there be any Dreyfus Affair.' Billot then confirmed the previous government statements to the effect that Dreyfus had been 'tried, properly tried, convicted unanimously . . . regularly and correctly tried . . . For me, in all conscience, as a soldier and as head of the army, I consider that the judgment was properly delivered and that Dreyfus is guilty.' The principle of *res judicata* had, since 1894, constantly implied this denial that there was any such thing as a

Dreyfus Affair. And from now on, the infallibility of the seven judges would be covered by the authority of the Prime Minister and the War Minister. It was further confirmed by a vote in the Chamber.

However, on 7 December, Scheurer attempted to transfer the debate to the Senate. His speech was a much-awaited event, Joseph Reinach noted. People from Belgium, Switzerland and England travelled to hear him. The public galleries were full. But he was still handicapped by Leblois's scruples: as we have seen, the latter had forbidden him to compromise Picquart. He appeared therefore to be bereft of weapons, and to be reduced to asserting that it was untrue that he had not submitted any documents to the government. He had indeed shown documents to Billot and Méline. It was the government's duty to initiate the review of the case. And in the Esterhazy trial, it would be illogical not to arrange for expert reports on the *bordereau*, since the question of the *bordereau* took priority over everything else. 'Otherwise,' he told the government, 'you have to maintain that an accused person has been convicted in France on the basis of documents he has not been called upon to discuss, and which have not been shown to the defence'. He was listened to politely, but in silence.

Billot replied that the *bordereau* was not everything. The War Minister had carried out 'researches and comparisons over a long period of months'. But he did not breathe a word about the secret file. Méline still confined himself to the *res judicata*: 'At the present time, there is only an Esterhazy trial.'

The Senate was reassured and proceeded to vote next business.

THE FAILURE OF THE ATTEMPT TO OBTAIN A REVIEW

This first attempt to obtain a review of the Dreyfus case had thus failed, and the nationalists immediately went over to the offensive in the press. Scheurer was again treated to insults. 'That blackguard is no more than a wet blanket, a human rag sullied by his every shame. The impudent senator and his Jewish crew must be punished.' According to them, the whole of the Dreyfus family was implicated in the treason. The antisemites had been saying for months that the entire Jewish people had formed a 'syndicate' to defend Dreyfus. The Jews were plotting, spending millions to save their co-religionist.

Zola protested in *Le Figaro* that the only people to stand up and defend Dreyfus had been men of goodwill, men wedded to truth and equity, who had come from all corners of the horizon, and had now joined hands. 'Oh yes! I am a member of that syndicate, and I hope that all the decent folk of France are too!'

But *Le Figaro* now abandoned its Dreyfusard campaign in mid-December, after losing several hundred subscribers; and so Zola was deprived of a platform. Finally, on 13 December, Rochefort had the audacity to admit that Dreyfus had been 'convicted on the basis of a secret document, indeed several . . .' And he added: 'One of these celebrated secret documents is a letter from the German Emperor himself . . . Throughout this letter he refers to Captain Dreyfus by name.'

And so another myth was born, which was given ever wider circulation until the day came, in 1899, when the nationalists asserted that the *bordereau* itself had been annotated by Whilhelm II (*see* below, p. 159).

With an atmosphere of violence growing in the streets, and faced with the indifference of the parliamentarians, Lucien Herr now hit on the idea of launching the first petition by intellectuals calling for a review of the case. Eminent professors signed, after Gabriel Monod, then caricaturists like Steinlen. Two young members of the literary avant-garde, Léon Blum and Daniel Halévy, collected the signatures. It was Blum who decided to approach Maurice Barrès, who, though ten years older, was someone he considered as his friend.

BARRÈS AND PÉGUY

Barrès, born in 1862, had begun his literary career at 22, by publishing a little review, *Les Taches d'Encre*. Having thrown himself into the Boulangist venture from 1887, he became at one and the same time an opponent of the Republican regime – which for him lay in ruins, having been undermined by corruption – and the exponent of a 'cult of the Self'. In a world of decline, the Self was the only solid point of reference. He called therefore for the affirmation of the Self against the oppression of the Barbarians. The Self, entirely emotional in *Sous l'œil des Barbares*, became tempered by reason and analysis in *L'Homme libre* (1889), where the watchword was 'one must feel to the utmost whilst analysing as much as possible'. Barrès became the prince of French youth, a literary cult-figure and the inspiration of an entire generation. In the years from 1890 to 1894, after the collapse of the Boulangist cause, he attempted to steer what was left of the movement in the direction of socialism. He even flirted wth anarchism, in *L'Ennemi des lois* (1892). 'For me, just as for most of my friends,' wrote Blum, 'he was not only our master, but also our guide: we formed a school around him, almost a retinue of followers . . . Since he was our chieftain, well then, he would follow us.'

But Barrès would say neither yes nor no to Blum. 'He did not disguise his embarrassment. Was Dreyfus the villain? Or was he a Stoic and a martyr?' asked Barrès. 'I really don't know any more about the business . . . I shall think it over again. I'll write to you.'

A few days later, the letter arrived. Barrès said that as he was in doubt, he would come down on the side of national instinct. The Dreyfus Affair had already settled, for him, the course of the rest of his life: he was to become one of the intellectual leaders of anti-Dreyfusism and of the nationalist movement.

The Latin Quarter was still silent and hesitant: but Herr's office at the Ecole Normale Supérieure was becoming the 'meeting-place for all those who wanted to get to the bottom of the matter'. Herr's first convert among the Ecole Normale students was Charles Péguy. At 24, this short, intense-looking young man with square shoulders and cross-cropped hair had already come far from his modest peasant beginnings in Orléans, and he was the talk of his fellow-students. He was fiercely moralistic, intransigent and demanding, constantly collecting for strikers, and for his *True Newspaper*, which was to be the means to convert the rising generation to socialism. He had entered the Ecole Normale in 1894 and announced in 1895 that he was a socialist. There would for him be no need for a violent revolution; the young would instantly recognize the self-evidence of socialism as presented in his newspaper, and, generation by generation, the whole world would eventually be converted. His socialism looked forward to a situation 'in which all men would play their part in carrying out necessary material tasks, but where all men would enjoy a great deal of leisure for the true life of man'. Though he had lost his Christian beliefs by the age of sixteen, he remained preoccupied by the task of saving mankind from evil on earth, from hunger and war. The heroine of the drama he had just completed was Joan of Arc, 'the war-leader against evil'. After being converted to Dreyfusism by Herr, Péguy set out to carry the Ecole Normale students with him.

In December 1897, the Dreyfusards still numbered only 2–300, according to Daniel Halévy: they were mainly professors and intellectuals; beyond the trio of personalities we have already met, the only political groups who had gone into action were extreme-left revolutionaries: on 15 December, the anarchists Sébastien Faure and Louise Michel organized the first revisionist meeting at the Tivoli-Vaux-Hall. Two days later, Edouard Vaillant and the Blanquist socialists of the Comité Révolutionnaire Central published a manifesto in which, while declaring that they were 'as much enemies of antisemitism as they are of the Jews', and that they 'loathed militarism more than anything else', they denounced 'the attempts by the army and government chiefs to hush up the enquiry into army scandals and acts of treason', and called on all citizens to bring the truth to light. This was the first socialist manifesto during the Dreyfus Affair. On 9 December, these revolutionaries were joined by Marguerite Durand and the feminists who had just launched the newspaper *La Fronde*; they were already Dreyfusards, showing sympathy with someone who, like women, they saw as a victim of oppression.

Battle was joined, but the tiny band of Dreyfusards and revisionists, made up essentially of intellectuals and students, feminists, extra-parliamentary socialists and a handful of anarchists around Sébastien Faure, only represented a minute force as they faced the huge body of their opponents: the General Staff, with its endless manoeuvrings and forgeries, directed both against Dreyfus and against Picquart; the government, which stood firm on its position – though it had conceded the trial of Esterhazy – and was followed by the mass of parliamentarians and the bourgeoisie; the Church, which declared, in the person of Cardinal Richard, archbishop of Paris, that the Dreyfus Affair was entirely 'a matter for the French courts'; and finally the nationalists and the antisemites, strongly supported by the antisemitic Assumptionist order, which was blackening the highly respectable Scheurer-Kestner and encouraging street violence.

Zola launched an appeal to the young men demonstrating against Scheurer. 'Young men! Where are you heading? Students! Where are you going, roaming the streets in bands?' At one time, he said, students used to demonstrate in favour of great causes; now they were jeering at an old man. 'Young people, young people!' he cried, 'Always take the side of justice . . . be humane, be generous!'

Since *Le Figaro* had deserted the cause, Zola had been reduced to expressing himself through pamphlets. He addressed the whole of France on 6 January 1898: 'France, it is you who have come to this: you have arrived at a conviction based on the most self-evident falsehoods.' The press was to blame: 'How could you hope to desire truth and justice?' And in a prophetic passage, he denounced the danger of reaction which was appearing on the horizon: 'And France! Do you know where you are heading? You are heading for the Church, you are returning to the past.' Antisemitism was paving the way for a return to the intolerant Christianity of the Middle Ages. 'People have the audacity to deny the existence of clerical reaction. But it is everywhere.' Together with certain revolutionaries, Zola was one of the first to scent the danger of political reaction in anti-Dreyfusism; he was also one of the first supporters of Dreyfus to turn to anticlericalism.

But Zola could not yet swim against the tide single-handed. Reinach, for his part, persuaded Mathieu that the 1894 bill of indictment, the d'Ormescheville report, must be published. It will be remembered that this document referred only to the resemblance in the handwritings, and to some vague 'indiscretions' on Dreyfus's part. It appeared in *Le Siècle* on 7 January 1898. 'The amazement and indignation caused on the one side were as great as the anger on the other', said Reinach. 'The absurdity, the emptiness of the charge, brought about more conversions, in a few hours, than any speeches could have done.' The public now learned at last that, contrary to what Billot had asserted in Parliament on 4 December, the only charge against Dreyfus had been the *bordereau*.

THE RAVARY INVESTIGATION

In the matter of the Esterhazy trial, Major Ravary, a retired officer who did not understand anything about the Dreyfus Affair, according to Reinach, had been carrying on his preliminary investigation since 8 December. It was largely a repeat of the Pellieux enquiry, with the same witnesses. But now finally it was necessary to call expert witnesses on the *bordereau*. The experts appointed were Couard, who was a paleographer and an antisemite, and Varinard and Belhomme, who tried to avoid becoming involved and had to be persuaded to do so by a magistrate. They concluded that the *bordereau* was not the work of Esterhazy, and that it had 'all the appearance of a forgery, with some parts in the form of tracings'; their astonishing argument was that as Esterhazy had not disguised his handwriting, the *bordereau* could not be by him, since spies always did disguise their handwriting! As to the 'uhlan' letter, it was the 'work of a forger'. On the basis of this evidence, Ravary concluded that the case should be dismissed: his report was full of praise for Esterhazy, but constituted an indictment of Picquart. Esterhazy again asked to be tried by court-martial. To quieten public opinion, on 2 January Saussier signed the order to commit him for trial.

The Dreyfusards remained optimistic until the last minute, despite the hostile climate that prevailed. They supposed Esterhazy would confess, or that he would take to flight. 'The idea never entered our head for a single moment,' wrote Blum, 'that Esterhazy's acquittal might be possible.' Scheurer and Zola refused to believe the tenor of the three experts' reports. Reinach had to disabuse them. From then on, they had no doubt there would be an acquittal. The officers on the court-martial would have no need of a formal order to acquit. The War Minister had solemnly asserted in Parliament that Dreyfus was guilty. That would be enough.

THE ESTERHAZY TRIAL

The trial opened on 10 January, in the rue du Cherche-Midi, in the same courtroom in which Dreyfus had been tried in 1894. The military witnesses avoided Esterhazy, who kept to himself beside the window. Under interrogation by General Luxer, presiding over the court-martial, Esterhazy retold his fable of the 'veiled lady' for the hundredth time 'in a perfectly offhand manner', but refused to identify the 'liberating document' which would clear him. He became confused in his own testimony over burglaries at his home on behalf of Mathieu Dreyfus, which had allegedly taken place one year before the latter even knew his name! But the president of the court let this pass. Esterhazy spoke 'with his usual eloquence, playing very well the part of the ruffianly soldier who had been slandered' (Reinach). The courtroom was on his side, whereas the testimony of Mathieu and Scheurer was met with ironical laughter and murmurs of disapproval. When some officers sneered, on hearing Scheurer say that Dreyfus was innocent, he retorted: 'Oh! So you think that's amusing, do you?' Never had officers with decorations made such a disagreeable impression on him.

Picquart was heard in camera, and thereupon the trial turned into a trial of Picquart. However, the latter refused to accept the role of the accused: to the surprise of the courtroom, he expounded his indictment of Esterhazy. 'All the time he was speaking,' wrote Reinach, 'Esterhazy, his eyes dark and glowering, and making frequent agitated movements, resembled a snake whose tail had been trodden on, and was turning round to bite but dared not do so.'

Gonse, Henry and Lauth testified against Picquart in violent terms. Recalled to the stand, he asked Henry: 'When did you see me consulting the liberating document together with Leblois?' Henry gave a date when Picquart had not been in Paris. 'But it was Henry and his comrades from the Statistical Department who were believed. The liar was Picquart' (Reinach).

Tézenas, Esterhazy's counsel, spoke for five hours in his defence, affirming the existence of the veiled lady and insisting on the suspect nature of Picquart's practices. Before the end of the trial, the courtroom learned from one of Tézenas's secretaries that Picquart would be arrested after the hearing.

The officers prided themselves on the fact that they were making their decision quite freely: but they acquitted Esterhazy in three minutes, after a trial that had lasted two days. The verdict was met by thunderous applause. Cries broke out: 'Long live France! Down with the syndicate!'

The next day, Picquart was taken to Mont-Valérien. The Dreyfusard campaign seemed to have come to a standstill: Scheurer had failed to bring about a review; Esterhazy was triumphant. His acquittal was in fact tantamount to a second conviction of Dreyfus, since the Dreyfusards could now no longer hope to have the case reviewed on the basis of the evidence they held; nor could they now count on the testimony of Picquart. The case for a review, said Blum, 'would from now on come up against a closed, complete, perfect scheme of resistance'. 'There we remained, aghast and desperate, facing the remnants of our work, which had come to pieces in our hands.' There seemed no way out for the Dreyfusards.

But it was at this very moment, when all seemed lost, that one man's intervention completely transformed the situation.

Zola, whose recent pamphlets had fallen flat, immediately took charge of the affair, putting his enormous world-wide reputation at stake in a challenge to French justice, the French state and French society. He had foreseen that Esterhazy would be acquitted, and he had told Leblois, Reinach and Clemenceau that the Dreyfus case must now be brought before civil judges and exposed to full public view.

He realized that to do this it was essential to make a break with the legality to which Mathieu was so attached. It was necessary, too, to override Scheurer's scruples, for the latter was now without weapons: he had been overtaken by events. Moderate methods could offer nothing more. Zola must first therefore bring legal proceedings on himself, so that the whole truth could come out in court. And to prepare the ground for this, he would have to make the truth known, to codify the entire Dreyfusard version of events, thereby abandoning the drop-by-drop technique which had been used so far. Finally, he must challenge the innumerable falsehoods of the nationalists and antisemites, which had never been denied by a government that still continued officially to proclaim Dreyfus's guilt.

He had prepared his pamphlet in outline a few days before the Esterhazy trial. Then, in two and a half days of frenzy, he produced the definitive version of it, in the form of an open letter to the

President of the Republic.[6] Towards evening on the second day, he took it to *L'Aurore*. Clemenceau found the title: *J'Accuse . . .!*

J'ACCUSE . . .!

The letter covered the whole affair, seen through the eyes of a writer expressing himself with great spirit and passion. It was as a novelist that Zola seized on the character of du Paty, 'who had a woolly mind': he became the person mainly responsible. This 'iniquitous' man 'had carried out the whole thing, done it all'. Henry was not even mentioned. Zola's picture did not altogether correspond to reality, but it was striking and dramatic.

In the 1894 trial, 'measures of silence and mystery' had covered up 'the most preposterous of serial stories'.

He denounced the d'Ormescheville report:

> Oh! the emptiness of that bill of indictment! That a man could have been convicted on that document is an unparalleled piece of wickedness . . . Dreyfus speaks several languages: that is a crime; no compromising documents are found at his home: that is a crime; he sometimes goes to his country of origin: that is a crime; he works hard, and endeavours to get to know about everything: that is a crime; he feels disturbed: a crime; he does not feel disturbed: a crime. We are told of fourteen counts, and in the end we can only discover one: the *bordereau*. We even learn that the experts were not in agreement.

He then referred to the secret file, the 'secret document'. 'I deny there was such a document, I deny it with all my strength. A ridiculous document, yes, perhaps the one mentioning some little women, and a certain D., who is becoming too demanding . . . But a document dealing with national defence, which could not be produced without war being declared tomorrow, never, never! That is a lie!'

He gave details of Picquart's discoveries and his disgrace, then finally came to the Esterhazy trial.

> When the War Minister, the top man in charge, has established the authority of the *res judicata*, to the acclaim of the nation's representatives, could a court-martial be expected to give him a categorical denial? In terms of hierarchy, such a thing is impossible. General Billot influenced the judges by his statement, and they delivered judgment as they would go into battle, without discussion . . . The first court-martial may have been unintelligent, the second was bound to be criminal . . .

6 Alain Pagès, *Emile Zola, un intellectuel dans l'affaire Dreyfus* (Paris, 1991), pp. 117–21.

Such then, is the plain truth, Mr President, and it is horrifying . . .
It is only today that this affair is beginning, since it is only today that
the two standpoints have become clear: on the one hand, that of the
guilty men who do not want the truth to come to light; on the other,
that of the righters of injustice who will lay down their lives for it. I
have said elsewhere and I say again, when truth is buried underground,
it collects, it gathers such explosive force that the day it bursts forth, it
carries everything away in the explosion. We shall soon see whether we
have not paved the way for the most resounding of disasters.

But this letter is a long one, Mr President, and it is time for me to
conclude.

I accuse Lieutenant-Colonel du Paty de Clam of having been the
diabolical agent of the judicial error – unconsciously, as I would prefer
to believe – and then of having defended his iniquitous work for three
years, by means of the most absurd and shameful machinations;

I accuse General Mercier of having made himself an accomplice
to one of the greatest crimes in history, at the very least by weak-
mindedness;

I accuse General Billot of having had decisive evidence of Dreyfus's
innocence in his hands, of having concealed it, and of having made
himself guilty of this crime against humanity and against justice for
political reasons, to save the face of the General Staff;

I accuse General de Boisdeffre and General Gonse of having made
themselves accomplices to the same crime, the former no doubt through
clerical passion, the latter perhaps through the esprit de corps which
turns the offices of the War Ministry into the Holy Ark, totally above
criticism;

I accuse General de Pellieux and Major Ravary of having carried
out a vicious enquiry, that is an enquiry of the most monstrous partiality,
which produced, in the second report, an imperishable monument of
naive effrontery;

I accuse the three handwriting experts, Messrs Belhomme, Varinard
and Couard, of having made lying and fraudulent reports, unless a
medical examination certifies them to be suffering from a malady of their
eyesight and judgment.

I accuse the offices of the War Ministry of having carried on a vile
campaign in the press, particularly in *L'Eclair* and *L'Echo de Paris*, in
order to lead public opinion astray, and cover up their own misconduct;

I accuse, finally, the first court-martial of having infringed the law
by convicting an accused man on the strength of a secret document, and
I accuse the second court-martial of having covered this illegality, by
order, committing in its turn the judicial crime of acquitting a man in
full knowledge of his guilt.

In bringing these charges I am aware that I am rendering myself
liable under articles 30 and 31 of the press law of 29 July 1881, which
cover defamation. And I am laying myself open of my own free will.

As to the men I am accusing, I do not know them, I have never seen
them and I feel neither rancour nor hatred towards them. To me they

are mere entities, spirits of social evil. And the step I am taking here is merely a revolutionary means to hasten the explosion of truth and justice. I have but one passion, and that is the truth, in the name of humanity which has borne so much, and has a right to happiness. My burning protest is merely the cry of my soul. So let them dare to bring me before the assize court, and let the enquiry take place in the full light of day! I am waiting.

May I assure you, Mr President, of my profoundest respect.

3 J'ACCUSE . . .! THE AFFAIR AS NATIONAL CRISIS

J'Accuse . . .! went on sale on 13 January at eight in the morning. 'All day long, in Paris,' Péguy recalled, 'one could hear the news vendors hoarsely crying the name of *L'Aurore*, as they ran with huge bundles of it under their arms, selling it to eager purchasers.' Over 200,000 copies were sold. 'Such was the shock that Paris almost changed sides', he added.

The Dreyfusards, Blum wrote, 'felt their confidence flowing back; it rose again, whilst their opponents showed by their fury that they had suffered a blow'.

Admittedly, those in the initial core of Dreyfusards, true to their persistent attitude of caution, showed some hesitation about Zola's intervention. 'I was not expecting it to be so strong and so energetic,' said Mathieu Dreyfus, despite his admiration. It was a risky business, thought Scheurer and Clemenceau, to place oneself at the mercy of the jury. But for Ranc and Reinach the advantages of Zola's act outweighed the disadvantages.

All in all, for the first Dreyfusards, Zola was 'not so much a hero as an unexpected and invaluable ally', said Blum. But *J'Accuse . . .!* persuaded them to resume the struggle. The battle could begin again. In a single day, by his revolutionary act, Zola had relaunched the Dreyfusard movement and radically extended the scope of the conflict.

For the Dreyfus affair was no longer simply a matter of an essentially legal battle over the guilt or innocence of one man, but a much wider confrontation between those who were demanding truth, justice and respect for the Rights of Man, and the supporters of *res judicata, raison d'Etat* and France for the French. This confrontation was to become social and political. For while Zola had made a clear distinction in *J'Accuse . . .!* between 'the guilty men who do not want the truth to come to light' and the 'righters of injustice who will lay down their lives for it', he had also heralded the emergence of broader issues: by defending the patriotism and love of the army of Dreyfus's supporters, and, precisely, by demanding truth and justice, by denouncing the falsehoods, secrets and mysteries, the denials of justice and the misdeeds committed by the offices of the War Ministry – which were justified by *raison d'Etat* – as well as the dangers of rule by the sword and of a military coup, the perversion of the press, and the threats posed by the revival of antisemitism and clericalism. Throughout the Affair, Dreyfus's supporters would fight on these issues. The initial core of Dreyfusards would be transformed into a veritable party, the revisionist party.

From the day after *J'Accuse...!*, they began to count their strength by signing a petition which ran: 'The undersigned, protesting against the breach of legal conventions in the 1894 trial, persist in demanding a review.'

One of the first to sign was Anatole France. This great figure of French literature, while he had already settled his account with clericalism and militarism, remained in 1898 a very shrewd but elegantly sceptical observer of French society. He was only just starting the publication of his *Histoire contemporaine*, that astonishingly lifelike picture of France before and during the Affair.

But, as he said to Daniel and Elie Halévy, who came to ask for his signature: 'I am appalled. I should be the last person in the world to be surprised at any villainy by the military, for I had my mind made up about them already. And yet I am astounded ... I have never come across such cynicism in the realm of crime.'[1]

Thirty or forty other writers signed, including Maeterlinck, Rostand, Sardou and Mallarmé, followed by practically the whole of the younger generation: Fernand Gregh, Gide, Apollinaire, the two Halévy brothers and Proust – the last three collecting the signatures.

Then came the artists: Monet, Pissarro and Signac the impressionists, the nabis Bonnard and Vuillard, and the philosophers: Lévy-Brühl and Séailles. The main body of the signatories were above all university professors from the Sorbonne or the Ecole Normale: in history, Gabriel Monod, Aulard and Seignobos, together with Paul Meyer, director of the Ecole des Chartes; in literature, Lanson and Larroumet; in sociology, Durkheim and Bouglé; in linguistics, Ferdinand Brunot. The most eminent scientist to sign was Emile Duclaux, director of the Pasteur Institute: he was supported by the chemist Edouard Grimaux and two members of the Medical Academy, Paul Reclus and Henri Monod. In general, however, medicine and law remained hostile. Other petitions followed: in a few days, hundreds joined in to support the movement: the total number of signatures

1 Daniel Halévy, *Regards sur l'Affaire Dreyfus* (Paris, 1994), pp. 58–9.

reached 1482.[2] But this was only a beginning. Even amongst writers, artists and scholars, Dreyfus's active supporters – still less than 2,000 in number in January 1898, and only 10,000 by the autumn – were, and remained, a minority: according to official statistics, there were 44,600 writers and artists in 1901. Among university professors in Paris, no more than 26 per cent were Dreyfusards. And as one of the most eminent of secondary school teachers told Clemenceau: 'You will get no one from the lycées. If I gave you my name, that idiot Rambaud would send me off to rot in the wilds of Brittany.' Only a few score of the 9,000 secondary teachers in France dared to sign.[2]

THE INTELLECTUALS

Those who put their name and their literary, artistic and scholarly reputations at stake in the struggle for justice and truth were now dubbed intellectuals by Clemenceau. The word was not new, any more than the commitment: there had been, for example, the campaigns of Voltaire and Victor Hugo. But from January 1898, Clemenceau gave the word a new and wide currency in a sense which has become familiar in the 20th century. The commitment, formerly individual, had now become collective, precisely through the medium of the petition, which was to take priority as a means of action by the intellectuals. The Affair thus witnessed the birth of the modern idea of the intellectual committed as a member of a group, made up of writers, artists and those living by their intellect, who lend the backing of their reputation to the support of public causes.

Generally speaking, the committed intellectual is placed – willingly or otherwise – outside the power structures of his society, and he gives his opinion in the name of high ethical or intellectual principles, without regard to official truths, and to the constraints and compromises inherent in action carried on within those structures. Thus, during the Affair, the intellectuals insisted that the search for truth must be carried on in a totally independent manner, in accordance with the rigorous principles governing scientific research. Edouard Grimaux made this comment on the official documents and the bill of indictment against Dreyfus:

> No man who was used to thinking rationally, no magistrate, no man of science would ever have agreed to sign such documents. All one finds in them is insinuations without proof, fanciful stories, pieces of gossip, and finally the contradictory reports by the experts. A rigorous examination

2 Christophe Charle, *Naissance des 'intellectuels' 1880–1900* (Paris, 1990), p. 142.

69

of these documents shows us that they are worthless: when they are subjected to a severe degree of criticism, nothing, nothing, nothing remains!

Legal action, too, must conform strictly to legality: 'The guarantees offered by justice cannot be withdrawn from a single person,' declared Clemenceau, 'without threatening the whole fabric of society.'

But, as the figures show, most of the men of letters, most of the artists and scholars remained hostile. Reinach judged them with severity: if some of them shared the base passions of the crowd, 'their commonest fault was a lack of judgement. The absence of any scientific spirit is frequent among men of letters, even among scholars. If you take them away from their usual field of study, their reasoning powers are no better than those of coarse and ignorant members of the crowd.' Some of them, he said, did not take the trouble to judge for themselves, finding it easier to accept ready-made opinions; to others, a layman's intervention – or their own intervention – in a question of military justice 'seemed as out of place as that of a colonel from the gendarmerie' in a literary or scientific matter.

This was also the opinion of the literary critic Brunetière, who ridiculed

> the claim that writers, scholars, philosophers and philologists should be raised to the rank of supermen. Intellectual abilities, which I do not despise of course, are only relative in value. For myself, I would rate firmness of will, strength of character, soundness of judgement and practical experience much more highly in the social sphere. And so I do not hesitate to place a certain farmer or merchant of my acquaintance far above some scholar or biologist I do not care to name . . .

It was of course true that the claims of the intellectuals could sometimes become excessive. As Reinach said, 'the genuine scholars were the most modest'.

Maurice Barrès, who as we have seen, had now chosen to join the anti-Dreyfusard camp, equally mocked those who, being less well-known than the celebrities of literature and learning, had to add the title of *agrégé* or of university graduate to their signature on the petition:

> What a lot of graduates! They are marching in serried ranks behind their professors . . . There is nothing worse than these bands of semi-intellectuals. To be semi-cultured destroys instinct without replacing it by conscience. All these aristocrats of the mind insist on maintaining that they do not think like the vile multitude. One can see that only too well. They no longer spontaneously feel in tune with their natural group

and they have not reached that level of clearsightedness which would restore their thoughtful harmony with the mass of the people.

Barrès was now moving towards a rehabilitation of popular sentiment against the reason of the intellectuals.

Thus all the men of letters did not take on the role of intellectuals – far from it. Academicians and those writers who had arrived shared the general opinion during the Affair: Jules Lemaitre, Paul Bourget, Alphonse Daudet, François Coppée, Heredia, Loti.

But of course the opponents of Dreyfus who become most active after *J'Accuse . . .!* were the nationalists and the antisemites, who were outside the intellectual world. Drumont and his friends replied to Zola in an open letter to Félix Faure which accused . . . Joseph Reinach, and they gathered under the banner of 'France for the French'. There were more and more letters of protest and meetings. On 16 January, the antisemitic agitator Jules Guérin launched a national protest against the 'Jewish syndicate' in the *Libre Parole*. The next day, he attracted 4,000 people to the Tivoli-Vaux-Hall in Paris for a meeting to protest against the 'insulters of the army'. But amidst indescribable uproar, the antisemites were driven off the platform by anarchists. Guérin's antisemitic gangs were already flaunting themselves in the streets of the capital. They were made up, according to Reinach, of 'market-porters and butchers, prowlers and brigands of every kind'. Guérin

> never appeared unless surrounded by a dozen butchers from La Villette, armed with cudgels, iron bars in a wooden sheath, which weighed at least a kilo. They would have died for him . . . His popularity was based on the fear he aroused. People thought he was capable of anything. With his very keen sense of immediate and violent action he combined a certain finesse, and, when it was called for, some caution.

ANTISEMITIC RIOTS

In the provinces, antisemitic riots broke out more or less spontaneously, from the same date. They at first affected some 30 major towns. The antisemites had as yet only the beginnings of an organization in the provinces; the rioters were mostly encouraged or set going by Catholic or royalist clubs. At Nantes, on 17 January, said Reinach,

> 3,000 individuals, young people from the Catholic clubs, and the boat-men from the port, marched round the streets shouting death-threats. After stopping for a time in front of the army corps headquarters and the army club, where the crowd acclaimed the officers and ordinary

soldiers, they rushed at Jewish shops, shattering shop-fronts and windows, and tried to break down the door of the synagogue.

Similar scenes took place throughout the second half of January, notably at Angers and Marseille (4,000 persons), at Rouen (2,000), at Saint-Dié, Bar-le-Duc and Saint-Malo (1,000 and 1,500), and elsewhere.[3] Everywhere, to cries of 'Boo to Zola!', 'Death to the Jews!' and 'Long live the army!', Jewish shops and synagogues were attacked, and army officers acclaimed. Within ten days, the disturbances had affected 50 towns, particularly in areas where Catholicism was still strong: in Lorraine and eastern France, and even in Brittany, where Jews were few and far between. In Marseille, Jewish shops were looted; in Algiers the disturbances took on the dimensions of a pogrom: there were some deaths and the whole Jewish quarter was sacked.

The rioters were young men, mainly students and schoolboys. They came from Catholic faculties: at Lille, according to Reinach, the pupils from the church schools burnt an effigy of Zola. The students were joined by some young workers and artisans, by shop assistants and clerks, and by adult onlookers.

THE PARIS STUDENTS

In Paris, where the majority of the Jewish population was now concentrated, the Jews were not, however, the prime target: the demonstrators mainly attacked Zola and *L'Aurore*. After lectures, for example in the Law faculty, where, as we have seen, the professors themselves were hostile to Zola, crowds of 200 to 400, or even up to 500 students, marched up and down the Latin Quarter. The police looked tolerantly on. There were even cries of 'Long live the police!' In *Le Temps* of 17 January, an article read: 'Never, even during the most critical periods of Boulangism, even after the death of Nuger [at the time of the 1893 incidents], have there been so many policemen on the Boulevard Saint-Michel.'

The students shouted insults at Zola with the connivance of the police. They lit bonfires of *L'Aurore* in the street. And they rode up and down the boulevard on the open-top buses and trams, chanting the same slogans all the time. When they managed to cross the Seine, they headed for the offices of *L'Aurore*, or tried to get as far as Zola's house in the rue de Bruxelles, also guarded by the police.

3 Stephen Wilson, *Ideology and Experience. Antisemitism in France at the Time of the Dreyfus Affair* (East Brunswick, NJ/London/Toronto, 1982), p. 110 and ch. 3.

In contrast to May 1968, it was conservatively-minded middle-class students who were demonstrating in January 1898. They were from the faculties of Law, Medicine and Pharmacy which were the centres of anti-Dreyfusism in the University of Paris. The General Association of Students itself protested against *J'Accuse . . .!* Thus Paris students had no need of any particular encouragement from reactionary circles. The Catholic Luxembourg Club, with its 500 members, almost represented a mass-movement in itself.

The tiny groups of students favourable to Zola, essentially made up of socialist revolutionaries, tried desperately to struggle against the tide, but they hardly managed to organize a single meeting.[4] It was the Ecole Normale which was the headquarters of Dreyfusism in the Latin Quarter. Péguy got most of the arts students in his year to sign the petition of the intellectuals.

Student youth in Paris was thus divided in the same proportion as its professors, that is, the majority were against Zola. In the provinces, wherever there were Catholic faculties, the division was a very clear one, according to Reinach.

Zola's letter had therefore, in less than a week, begun to win over the first intellectuals to the revisionist cause; it had triggered off a mobilization of the antisemites in Paris, accompanied by a violent explosion of antisemitism by young hotheads, particularly in the provinces. After the antisemitic riots of 1898, the Antisemitic League attempted to set up a proper national organization. Guérin had revived the League early in 1897, but despite his efforts at recruitment and organization, its membership never exceeded 1,300 to 1,500 during the Affair, though it claimed far more.[5]

MÉLINE VERSUS ZOLA

How did the government of Méline react? The Prime Minister, like all the political leaders, had taken great care not to study the Dreyfus question. He was ignorant of everything Mercier and the General Staff had done in 1894 to ensure that Dreyfus was convicted, and then later to cover the verdict of the first court-martial. He was

---

4 See Eric Cahm, 'Pour et contre Emile Zola: les étudiants de Paris en janvier 1898', *Bulletin de la Société d'Etudes Jaurèsiennes* 71 (October–December 1978), 12–15.

5 See Bertrand Joly, 'La Ligue antisémitique de Jules Guérin' in Michel Drouin, ed., *L'Affaire Dreyfus de A à Z.* (Paris, 1994), pp. 410–11; M. Joly corrects previous estimates by historians.

therefore most surprised and indignant, on 13 January, to read of Zola's charges against the army chiefs.

He thought at first he could refuse to allow the sensational trial the novelist was demanding. But, at a Cabinet discussion, ministers realized that it would be impossible to avoid it. How could they explain such a climb-down when the nationalists and antisemites were already boiling over with passion? Besides, the radicals in the Chamber were equally agitated; they could already begin to see an opportunity to bring down the government.

The day after Zola's letter, the Catholic Right announced it had called an emergency debate on the measures the government was planning to take. But when the sitting began, only one minister was present. De Mun, the Catholic Right's spokesman, demanded that Méline and Billot should be fetched: 'The army will not wait!' he exclaimed. Méline, when he arrived, declared that the government understood the feeling and indignation in the Chamber at Zola's 'abominable attacks', and announced that the novelist would be prosecuted. Jaurès chided him with only intervening after warnings from the Right, and added: 'You are handing the Republic over to the generals!' The government, however, won its vote of confidence.

The announcement that Zola would be tried gave a new impetus to the revisionists. Petitions were still circulating, the nationalists continued protesting and the students demonstrating. Paris was in a fever of excitement. The Antisemitic League announced there would be a demonstration at the Place de la Concorde on the 23rd of the month. It was banned by the Prefect of Police, but he still sent 4,000 men to occupy the surrounding area and maintain law and order.

It was in this highly-charged atmosphere that the summons against Zola was issued by Billot. To make the best of things, it had been decided that the only charge against him and the manager of *L'Aurore*, Perrenx, would be the passage in his letter in which he had accused Esterhazy's judges of having acquitted him by order. It was impossible to prove, and the debate at his trial would be reduced to a minimum; he would above all be prevented from re-opening the Dreyfus case.

But Zola intended to help bring the truth into the open by citing over 200 witnesses: all the General Staff chiefs and those who worked with them, Demange, Leblois, Casimir-Périer and the ministers of 1894, Lucie Dreyfus, Scheurer, Ranc, Jaurès, as well as intellectuals, scholars and foreign diplomats.

Terrified, de Boisdeffre tried to order all the officers not to appear, but he learned that the law only required professional secrecy from them and that they would be obliged to testify. Billot, however, had himself excused by the Justice Minister.

UPROAR IN PARLIAMENT

Before the trial, on 22 and 24 January, scenes took place in the Palais-Bourbon 'unlike anything seen since the Convention', according to one political commentator. Méline still felt threatened by a coalition between Right and Left to bring him down.

The radical leader Cavaignac first demanded the publication of Lebrun-Renault's report on Dreyfus's alleged confession on the day of his degradation. Méline, though he had never seen it, admitted that such a report did exist, thereby admitting the existence of the confession. Cavaignac then withdrew his demand, to the applause of the Chamber.

Méline then went on to launch into an extremely violent outburst against Zola, who had been 'mowing down everything in his path with a superb lack of awareness and without realizing the harm he was doing his country . . . No one is entitled to bring the army chiefs into contempt. That is what is leading to new versions of the *Débâcle*.' He promised the government would put a stop to disorder in the streets. He then turned on the intellectuals: 'Professors and civil servants must not stir up disorder and make it inevitable by their conduct in signing petitions.' Finally, pointing to the socialist extreme Left, he exclaimed: 'And I am telling you, looking at your newspaper articles, that at the present time you are making the most audacious call for revolution in the streets.'

Jaurès flew into a rage: 'The ones who are paving the way for future débâcles are not those who are pointing out mistakes in good time, but those who made those mistakes in the first place: once, it was court generals protected by the Empire; today it is generals nursed by the Jesuits and protected by the Republic.' It was not the socialists who were letting loose sectarian hatred and religious passion in meetings and in the streets. He went on: 'Do you know what it is we are suffering from? Do you know what it is that is destroying us all? I say this on my own responsibility: what has been destroying us since the beginning of this affair are the half-measures, the non-disclosures, the ambiguities and the acts of cowardice!' He was no longer speaking, but thundering, said Reinach. 'In the first place, it is through falsehood and cowardice that the proceedings against Zola have been restricted. At the very least, a hearing in camera needs the corrective of free discussion outside.'

A deputy from the extreme Right, Count de Bernis, shouted: 'You are from the syndicate!'

'Monsieur de Bernis, you are a contemptible coward!'

A score of socialists leapt on Bernis, but he evaded them and struck Jaurès with his fist. The sitting was adjourned. An hour later, insults and blows were still being exchanged in the corridors.

It was only on 24 January that Jaurès was able to express his opinion on the fundamental issue: he had as yet no certainty about Dreyfus's guilt or innocence: 'I say that if I had any certainty I should give my opinion openly.'

As Zola's trial approached, violence continued to rumble on across Paris. Guérin put his troops through their paces in the streets.

Europe and the world could no longer understand France and looked at her in amazement and distress, as Bjoernson said in a letter to Zola. The certainty that Dreyfus was innocent was growing everywhere, except among reactionaries and antisemites.

The German government was insistent on clearing itself of responsibility. The Foreign Minister, von Bülow, stated 'most officially and categorically' before the budget committee of the Reichstag, 'that there have never been any relationships or links of any sort whatsoever between the former Captain Dreyfus, presently held on the Ile du Diable, and any German agents . . . The affair known as the Dreyfus Affair has admittedly stirred up a great deal of dust, but it has never interfered with the peaceful relations between Germany and France.'

THE ZOLA TRIAL

The nationalist press once again announced that there would be a large demonstration on 7 February, the day the trial was due to open. The night before, a proclamation was posted on the streets of Paris, signed by Drumont and the leaders of the Antisemitic League: it issued threats to 'agents of foreign countries' who were 'seeking to disturb the peace'. 'The honest and patriotic population of Paris would not stand for such acts of provocation. IT WILL DO ITS OWN POLICING. France will never come under offensive pressure from foreign Jews.'

However, although on the morning of the trial Guérin's antisemitic gangs were assembled in the immediate area of the Law Courts, the demonstration did not take place, and when Zola arrived via the Place Dauphine, the reception he received was peaceful. The crowd, confined within the small triangle of the Place, was strictly controlled by the police. It was raining and there was an icy wind. As Zola went up the steps into the Law Courts there were only a few boos from the one side and, from the other, some cries of 'Long live Zola!' and 'Long live the master!'

Inside, there was unprecedented excitement. According to *L'Illustration*,

> the lobby and the passageways had been invaded, several hours before the hearing, by a singularly mixed crowd, hurrying, busy, anxious and impatient: officials, magistrates, police officers, witnesses of every type, representatives of the French press at full strength, a close column of foreign correspondents, a battalion of press illustrators dressed for the field and the company of invitees from outside official ranks.

Mathieu Dreyfus stayed away: 'I was afraid that my presence would only cause disturbances.'

The assize court had been taken by storm and was full to bursting point: the pupil barristers had to sit on the floor. In the dock, Zola could be seen, dressed like a well-to-do bourgeois, 'looking pensive, with his chin resting on his walking-stick', and also Perrenx 'with the air of a workman in his Sunday-best'; then, behind them, their defence counsel: Maître Labori, Maître Albert Clemenceau, and Georges Clemenceau, who had also been given permission to plead. The jury was made up of small traders and businessmen.

The witnesses, intellectuals and officers, were in the corridors and in their waiting-room: Esterhazy prowled about among them in civilian clothes, 'like a lean wolf'. The officers had been ordered not to shake hands with him.

The Advocate-General, Van Cassel, a 'sour-faced and brutal man', opened the trial by denouncing Zola's designs: 'An attempt is being made here, and this has been admitted, to spark off a scandalous debate by revolutionary means.' He demanded, right at the beginning, that discussion should be restricted to Zola's insult to Esterhazy's judges. Zola's young counsel, Fernand Labori, replied that the Dreyfus and Esterhazy trials could not be separated.

Labori had already taken part in some sensational trials, according to Reinach. 'He was ingenious over procedure, but uneven as a speaker. He was high-sounding and vigorous, with broad theatrical gestures and a vibrant tone of voice.' His great quality was his enthusiasm, which he cultivated as a kind of technique. The court rejected his conclusions, but confirmed that the military witnesses must appear.

Labori first called Lucie Dreyfus. She was dressed in black, and was trembling in front of the court audience. Delegorgue, the president, refused to let her testify on the 1894 trial: 'The question will not be put.' Throughout the trial, the same violent words came from the president to choke off debate every time the Dreyfus case was mentioned by the defence. Lucie Dreyfus remained silent.

According to Maurice Paléologue, Zola looked 'nervous, sullen and sheepish'. He rose to demand the same right to defend himself as robbers and murderers. Delegorgue: 'You know article 52 of the law of 1881, don't you?' Zola: 'I don't know the law and don't wish to know it.' Uproar broke out, and Zola had to correct himself.

Leblois then recounted the affair of the forged telegrams sent to Picquart, and du Paty's adventures with the veiled lady who had provided information to Esterhazy. Scheurer-Kestner asked to read out Gonse's letters to Picquart. The president refused.

The scene after the hearing resembled a riot: people were fighting in the corridors. Zola, under the protection of the Prefect of Police, was booed and hissed by a huge menacing crowd. The same scenes recurred every night.

The next day, a stream of military witnesses began to testify. First came Boisdeffre, in uniform, looking 'calm, and with nothing stiff about him'. Under questioning on the 'liberating document' and the veiled lady, he took refuge, as expected, in professional secrecy. To him, Picquart had been 'engrossed in an idea of his own'. He had neglected his duties and had not found any piece of conclusive evidence against Esterhazy. Furthermore, he had not been sent away in disgrace, merely sent on an assignment. Dreyfus's guilt had always been 'absolutely certain', said Boisdeffre.

Gonse also took refuge in professional secrecy: his letters to Picquart only concerned Esterhazy. He would not re-open the Dreyfus case. Esterhazy, still full of *amour-propre*, threatened the General Staff that he would 'spill the beans' if the officers did not shake hands with him the next day. Boisdeffre gave the order, but once the ceremony was over the officers turned away from him.

As from the third day, scraps of truth began to emerge, despite the government's precautions. Labori first tried to force Mercier into an admission that he had made use of the secret file in 1894. According to Paléologue, Mercier was 'haughty, severe, precise, superciliously entrenched in the sense of his own infallibility'. He first stated that the 'scoundrel D.' document was unknown to him. Unfortunately, Labori had quoted it incorrectly. He then denied having repeated to anyone that a secret document had been communicated to the judges. And he refused to answer the direct question as to whether the secret file had in fact been communicated to them. 'I do not have to go back over the Dreyfus case, but if I had to, since I am asked for my word of honour as a soldier, I would say that Dreyfus was a traitor who had been justly and legally condemned.'

Maître Salles followed him in the witness-box. This was a moment of suspense, for it was known that he had learned about the use of the secret document from one of the judges of 1894. Was he going to throw everything into confusion? His lips quivered with nervous trembling. He was undecided. Delegorgue: 'Have you anything to say regarding the Esterhazy affair?' – 'No, regarding the Esterhazy affair, nothing.'

Albert Clemenceau seized the opportunity he had been given: 'We claim that the witness has it from one of the judges of the court-martial that a secret document was communicated to them . . . Let the witness deny this in a single word, the president will not have time to stop him.' And, while the courtroom seemed to be shouting to the old man: 'For goodness' sake, say something!', Delegorgue roared: 'You are not to speak!' To Labori, Zola and the Dreyfusards, Mercier's silence, and Delegorgue's furious attempt to stop Maître Salles from speaking, proved that Dreyfus had been condemned illegally.

Now it was the turn of du Paty de Clam. He looked 'pretentious, with his monocle, his curving waistline, his curt speech and his mechanical gestures' (Paléologue). Since he was prouder than any, and was allied to France's greatest families, he found it hard to be denounced by Zola as a torturer and a ferocious madman. He protested, claiming he still enjoyed the esteem of his superiors, and that he had always behaved 'like a gentleman'.

Henry tried to appear for as short a time as possible. The thick-set giant was flushed, and his eyes were bloodshot. He took the stand with a sick-note in his hand, looking pitiful. He stated that the file Picquart had stolen from his cupboard was not the file of the Dreyfus Affair. That file had been placed under seal since 1895. No one understood what he was saying, and Gonse asked for him to have leave to withdraw.

Now General Pellieux testified, 'splendid in his boldness and swagger,' according to Paléologue, 'superb at verbal fencing, with no shadow of a doubt in his mind about Dreyfus's guilt'. According to him, the evidence of that guilt was abundant. After his enquiry and that of Ravary, which had cleared Esterhazy, he could not understand why that officer had been tried.

Zola became excited, exclaiming that there were different ways to serve France: 'France may be served by the sword and by the pen. General de Pellieux has no doubt won great victories. But so have I. Through my works, the French language has been carried to the ends

79

of the earth. I too have my victories. I bequeath to posterity the name of General de Pellieux and that of Emile Zola: let posterity choose!'

Finally Picquart was brought in. His was a long-awaited appearance. He was already a hero in the eyes of the Dreyfusards. On the General Staff side, he was hated as someone who had betrayed his comrades. He seemed young. 'His eyes were narrow and he had a distant look ... his expression was closed and weary-looking, with a certain melancholy hardness about it which was attractive to sensitive souls. Above all he was quite different from the military men who had appeared with him. He was a meditative person, an artist,' said Reinach.

The court listened to him for an hour with sustained attention: he first recounted, very calmly, his discovery of Esterhazy, and the events that had followed. But since he had retained his religious respect for discipline and professional secrecy, he did not reveal his trials and setbacks, or his interview with Gonse, when the latter had told him to stop showing any interest in Dreyfus. He made no complaint about anyone.

This moderation did him a great deal of damage. Everyone understood that what he had said was not the whole truth. The barristers in robes gave him an ovation: the military men were furious. The officers of the Statistical Department kept on hounding him: Gribelin declared under oath that he had seen him with Leblois, leafing through the secret file.

When confronted with Henry, he confounded the latter over the date when he was alleged to have shown the 'scoundrel D.' note to Leblois. He demonstrated that, from the door to his office, Henry could not have recognized it. Henry: 'As for me, I should have recognized it from ten paces.' Picquart gave a categorical denial to this statement. Then, suddenly, Henry exploded. He reaffirmed everything he had said, and he added: 'Colonel Picquart is lying!'

Picquart, 'terribly pale', could take no more, and now revealed his frightful situation to the jury: 'You have seen men like Colonel Henry, Major Lauth and the archivist Gribelin make vile accusations against me here ... Well, gentlemen of the jury, do you know why all this is happening? You will understand when I tell you that the architects of the previous affair, which is closely bound up with the Esterhazy affair ... received from the late Colonel Sandherr a commission to defend, against all attacks, this affair which was the honour of their department.'

Henry and Gonse were put out of countenance. Recalled to the stand, Henry invented a new story; he explained that the 'scoundrel D.' document had nothing to do with the Dreyfus trial, and that the secret file was a different file, which had never left his cupboard. Picquart did not understand a word of this, but Henry had succeeded in covering his tracks.

The following witness, Demange, repeated three or four times over that the law had been broken, whereupon Albert Clemenceau, using the same maneoeuvre as before, asked him whether his certainty that the judgement of 1894 had not been delivered legally did not stem from the fact that one of the court-martial judges had asserted it to Maître Salles, who had in turn repeated it to him. Demange exclaimed: 'Good Heavens, yes!' As a result, Henry's new story about the secret file collapsed and the idea that the law had been infringed emerged more and more clearly.

After the military witnesses, it was the turn of the character witnesses. Duclaux, Ranc and Anatole France all paid tribute to Zola.

Then came Jaurès, who went one step further than he had in Parliament, demanding why, at the Esterhazy trial, the handwriting reports and the Picquart enquiry had been discussed in camera, and why there had been no enquiry about the veiled lady. Finally, he drove his point home over the Esterhazy trial and the illegality of 1894: 'It appears throughout that the trial was conducted not with a view to truth and justice, but so as to vindicate the top army chiefs . . . There are no finer, greater or more sacred words than those of fatherland, national defence and national honour.' But no one was entitled to do them violence.

And why had the government not held an enquiry about the secret document? 'They are hiding all the time behind the ambiguity of the *legal truth!* But that does not tell us whether the communication, unknown at the time the application for a review was made, whether the communcation of a secret document, contravening every legal safeguard, actually took place or not.' There were not four deputies in the Chamber who doubted that there had been an infringement of the law, but, they said, 'what a pity this affair broke a few months before the elections!'.

Mercier, went on Jaurès, had not even taken the precaution of consulting the rest of the government:

> One man, one single man, without even consulting his friends unof-
> ficially, took it upon himself to tip the scales in the trial with a document
> whose value he alone had presumed to assess. I tell you that that man,
> despite the brilliance of his past services and his rank, and despite the
> arrogance of office, is no more than a man, frail and wretched, a creature

81

of darkness and of pride, of weakness and of error, and I do not understand how, in this Republican country of ours, one man, one single man,
can take it upon himself, on his own conscience, on his own powers of
reasoning, on his own head, to decide the fate of another man: his life,
his liberty and his honour; and I tell you now: if we are going to put up
with customs and habits like these in this country, it will be the end of
any liberty and any justice!'

It had been a bad day for the General Staff. The next day, that
of the academics, was a disaster. The archivists and paleographers
affirmed as one man that the style and handwriting of the *bordereau*
were identical with those of Esterhazy. Mme de Boulancy confirmed
the authenticity of Esterhazy's letters to her.

Pellieux, who had, some days before, put himself in charge of the
military witnesses, now attempted to take the situation in hand.
Giving testimoney, he dismissed Esterhazy's handwriting as a 'secondary' matter, since a regimental officer could not have had any knowledge of the subjects mentioned in the *bordereau;* Dreyfus had had
every opportunity to gain such knowledge. He held out threats to the
jurymen:

> What state do you want the army to be in when the moment of danger
> comes, a moment which is perhaps closer than you think? What state
> do you want the poor unfortunate soldiers to be in, if they are to be led
> into battle by officers whom others have sought to discredit in their eyes?
> They would be leading your sons to the slaughter, gentlemen of the jury!
> But Monsieur Zola would have won another battle, written another
> *Débâcle*, carried the French language to the ends of the earth, the very
> day France was wiped off the map of Europe!

To him and his colleagues a review of the Dreyfus case was of little
consequence. What the 1898 court-martial had tried to avoid was
putting an innocent man in the place of Dreyfus.

Despite these fine words, Paléologue recalled, the jurymen, infuriated by the interminable discussions, in which the truth seemed to be
eluding them, were inclining towards an acquittal, according to police
reports reaching the War Ministry.

It was now that Pellieux, impetuous as ever, and more and more
conscious of his own strength, decided, on his own initiative, to strike
a decisive blow. He had been convinced, as we have seen, by the
Henry forgery. It was time to appeal, once and for all, to this key
document. Making the excuse that he wanted to complete his previous
testimony, he asked to be recalled:

> And so I am asking to speak, not about the Dreyfus case, I shall not

speak about that. But I shall repeat the remark which is so typical of Colonel Henry: 'you want the truth? Here goes!'

At the time of the Castelin debate, there was an occurrence I must bring to your attention. The War Ministry received – and please note that I am not referring to the Dreyfus case – absolute proof of Dreyfus's guilt, absolute proof I tell you! And that proof, I have seen it myself! At the time of that debate, a document arrived at the War Ministry whose origins are beyond dispute, a document which says – I will tell you what is in it: 'There is going to be an emergency debate about the Dreyfus affair. You must never tell anyone about the links we had with the Jew.' And, gentlemen, the document was signed! . . . There has been an attempt to obtain a review by backdoor means; I am giving you these facts; I am stating them on my honour, and I am calling upon General de Boisdeffre to confirm them.

Gonse whispered in Henry's ear: 'What? Did you hear that? What an idiot!' Henry was appalled, and for good reason. The next day, he would say to Paléologue: 'That was crazy, what Pellieux did there! You don't thrust such secret documents into a public debate.' All the other officers were exultant. The courtroom rang with applause.

Labori now realized that Pellieux's intervention could put the General Staff in an awkward position. He immediately asked for the secret document to be produced in court: 'However much I respect General Pellieux's word as a soldier, I cannot attribute the slightest importance to this document. As long as we have no knowledge of it, as long as we have not discussed it, as long as it has not been produced in public, it does not count for anything.' He now thought that a review had become essential: 'If Dreyfus is guilty, if the words of these generals are justified, they will prove it in a fair, regular and open debate.'

Gonse, 'timorous, weak and undecided' as ever, according to Paléologue, pleaded for prudence: it was impossible to produce the evidence in public. Pellieux lost all sense of restraint after receiving this lecture. He called to one of his orderly officers in a resounding voice: 'Major Delcassé, go and fetch General Boisdeffre, by carriage, immediately.' 'Now no one counted but him . . . He was a real force,' said Reinach. 'He had passion and willpower, he could hold sway over crowds.'

In the courtroom and the corridors, the uproar was indescribable. But Boisdeffre did not appear until the next day.

'I shall be brief,' he said. 'I confirm the testimony of General Pellieux in every particular, as to its exactness and its authenticity. I have not one word more to say. I have not the right, gentlemen of the jury, I repeat: I have not the right. And now, gentlemen, allow me to say one thing: you are the jury, you are the nation; if the nation does not have confidence in its army chiefs, in those who are responsible for the national defence, then they are ready to leave this heavy task to others, you have only to say the word.'

In the Law Courts, as the trial came to an end, no one doubted any longer that Zola would be convicted. Van Cassel's final speech was dull and lifeless. According to him, Zola had not produced any evidence to show that the judges had been ordered to acquit Esterhazy.

Zola made his reply to boos from the spectators. He explained to the jurymen that his conviction would not quieten the country. 'Do you not understand that what is destroying this country now is that they are stubbornly leaving us in the dark, that half-truths are putting us on our death-bed?' Then, raising the tone in a final effort, he launched into a poetic crescendo. He had, however, to take the part of the intellectual, leaving the legal arguments to Labori:

> Dreyfus is innocent, I swear it. I swear it on my life, on my honour. At this solemn moment, before this court which represents human justice, before you, gentlemen of the jury who are an emanation of the nation itself, before the whole world, I swear that Dreyfus is innocent! And, by my forty years of work, and the authority those labours have given me, I swear that Dreyfus is innocent! And by all I have won, by the name I have made for myself, by my works, which have aided the spread of French literature, I swear that Dreyfus is innocent! May all of this crumble into dust, may my works perish, if Dreyfus is not innocent! He is innocent!'

But these words from an intellectual did not carry enough weight to counterbalance the threats from the generals, and from the antisemitic press, which, day after day, had published the names and addresses of the jury to intimidate them.

Zola was condemned to one year in prison and a fine of 3,000 francs. The next day, Picquart was cashiered.

The generals seemed to have won. The army had taken over from the courts. The General Staff had thrown its sword into the balance, and its infallibility was to become a dogma for the anti-Dreyfusards.

In fact, however, the trial was a turning-point in the Affair, for a review could now be only a matter of time. In February 1898, the Henry forgery had not been produced. Five months later, however, Cavaignac would bring it into the open in Parliament, thus making a review inevitable.

THE LIGUE DES DROITS DE L'HOMME

An immediate consequence of the threats from the generals and the antisemites in the streets, and of the revelation of the 1894 illegality, was the setting up at the end of the trial, on the initiative of Senator Trarieux, of the Ligue des Droits de l'Homme (League of the Rights of Man). Scheurer-Kestner was out of the battle, Zola had been convicted. It was time for the Dreyfusards to come together, and to acquire the collective strength of an association, not simply to defend Dreyfus, but all those whose rights had been violated.

The fundamental point of reference was the Declaration of the Rights of Man of 1789. Trarieux, a former Justice minister and a political moderate, did not want to go any further than this. On 20 February, he brought together a number of friends and intellectuals at his home: Edouard Grimaux, Emile Duclaux, Paul Meyer and Paul Viollet – the latter two being Catholics. They decided to found the Ligue. It was to become the main national centre of activity among the Dreyfusards, thanks to the local groups it set up throughout the country. It would organize meetings, and publish pamphlets. Its nationwide organization enabled it to recruit, beyond the original nucleus, intellectuals, politicians and teachers, but also trade unionists and non-Guesdist socialists. But with less than 10,000 members in 1898, it never became a mass-movement. At the time of the Affair, the central committee remained dominated by leading intellectuals: it included neither Jaurés nor Clemenceau. Paul Viollet, as will be seen, left the Ligue when it began to show signs of anticlericalism.

In the Latin Quarter, the headquarters of Dreyfusism were the Ecole Normale and Péguy's bookshop at the corner of the rue Victor-Cousin. Lucien Herr led the Dreyfusard troops on the days when there were no battles; Péguy was in command in the street.

> Clashes were frequent in the corridors of the Sorbonne, the entrance of which was only 100 metres away. Péguy kept himself in constant readiness to send his friends in to fight. A voice would cry, 'Durkheim is under attack, Seignobos has been invaded!' 'Assemble!' Péguy would reply. If he was at the Ecole when the call came, he would immediately go round the corridors from study to study, opening the doors. 'Assemble!' he cried, at each doorway. They all seized their sticks and rushed to the Sorbonne.[6]

6 D. Halvévy, *Péguy er les Cahiers de la Quinzaine* (Paris, 1979), p. 135.

MODERATE ANTI-DREYFUSISM

On 24 February, the day after the Zola trial, Méline reaffirmed in Parliament the government's line, which had remained unchanged since 1894: the Dreyfus question had never been anything but a purely legal matter; Dreyfus had been properly tried and there had therefore never been any Dreyfus *affair*. The Prime Minister had affirmed as much on 4 December 1897. In February 1898 he declared: 'There is now no Zola trial, no Esterhazy trial, no Dreyfus trial, no trial at all.' As always, the existence of the Dreyfus Affair was denied, or it was minimized.

The government's stand was based on the strictest adherence to legality; there had never been a Dreyfus affair, and no legal question could arise unless new evidence appeared. Furthermore, according to this governmental line, relayed by the Republican press, to the *res judicata* must now be added complete confidence in the 1894 court-martial, and more generally in all the institutions of the Republic, which were the very embodiment of truth and justice.

For the old argument, according to which 'seven French officers could not be mistaken, particularly if they are unanimous', had expanded a good deal, according to Reinach. The seven officers had become 14, with those who had acquitted Esterhazy, and to them had been added the War Minister, the General Staff, the government and both houses of Parliament. Could all these men, both military and civilian, really be villains or fools? Could the whole of official France be corrupt or stupid? Early in 1898, most of the bourgeoisie and nearly half the press preferred to believe the authorized mouthpieces of the Republic.[7]

And they could not but approve when the government, via Méline, condemned agitation, declaring: 'All this must stop, in the interests of the army, which must take up again, in silent contemplation, its unfinished task; it must stop, too, in the interests of public peace, and of the resumption of work by the nation.'

The Zola trial had been bad for business. Fullerton of *The Times* wrote on 15 February: 'The shops are suffering, timorous foreigners hasten their departure and postpone their arrival . . . foreign orders are falling off from a supposed uncertainty of punctual execution.' And George Barlow, commenting on the statement two months later by the Council of the Haute-Saône department regretting 'the move-

7 Janine Ponty, 'La presse quotidienne et l'Affaire Dreyfus en 1898–1899: essai de typologie', *Revue d'histoire moderne et contemporaine* XXI (April–June 1974), 193–220.

ment of opinion produced by the Zola–Dreyfus affair, which is pro-
foundly disturbing the country both in regard to trade and patriotism',
said this body had 'completely let the cat out of the bag'. What
they said was 'an absolutely true expression of French bourgeois
feeling from first to last in the Dreyfus affair . . . But it was a little
rash of the members to the Council of the Haute-Saône to give such
very plain utterance to their conviction that "business" was the one
thing in this world worthy of consideration – ranking even before
patriotism!'[8]

Méline, it should be noted, condemned the agitation in both
camps, that of the intellectuals and that of the nationalists and antisemites, and he once again promised severe repressive measures. Moderate governmental anti-Dreyfusism was hostile to any kind of
agitation or extremism, to all political and religious hatred, and to
violence, from whatever quarter it came: the government, followed
as ever by the Republican press, refused to lump all Jews together
with the traitor Dreyfus, and both refused to hold the whole race
responsible for one man's crime.

Moderate anti-Dreyfusism finally called for calm and restraint,
and it retained a regard for truth, remaining on the level of courteous,
rational argument, even though truth and reason stemmed from
authority, and were not determined by the critical mind of the individual, as the intellectuals affirmed.

EXTREMIST ANTI-DREYFUSISM

Rochefort's and Drumont's anti-Dreyfusism, on the other hand, far
from minimizing the Dreyfus Affair, had done a great deal to spark it
off in 1894 by its revelations; since then, it had made as much of it as
it possibly could, so as to use it as a weapon *against* the government
and against the Jews. It cared nothing for legality, being ready to push
Mercier into crime in 1894, and afterwards to cover his crime by all
possible means. Extremist anti-Dreyfusism, which clearly extended to
the General Staff, was also ready to use forgery. From September 1898,
it was even willing to contemplate the praise of forgery, justified by
raison d'Etat (*see* below, pp. 122–3). And it had so little respect for the
institutions of the Republic that it was ready to revile a vice-president
of the Senate, libel the judges of the Cour de cassation, have the Dreyfus
case removed from their jurisdiction (*see* pp. 130, etc.) and finally
attempt to overthrow the regime by force.

8 George Barlow, *A History of the Dreyfus Affair* (London, 1899), pp. 182–3.

Far from having any concern for peace and tranquillity, it was hate-ridden and passionate: it encouraged agitation and street violence, and in place of courteous and rational argument, wielded both insult and racial prejudice with gusto. As for concern for truth, it replaced this with crude lies, fanciful stories and legends of all kinds.

Thus there was nothing whatever in common, ideologically or politically, between the extremist anti-Dreyfusism of the nationalists and antisemites and the more moderate governmental anti-Dreyfusism of the bourgeoisie, which cared only for peace and quiet and getting on with business. The only conviction they shared was that of Dreyfus's guilt. Even this they believed for quite different reasons.

There has been a long-standing tendency to identify all anti-Dreyfusism with the extremist version: this only tends to perpetuate the stock image of a France split in two between the Dreyfusards, seen as angels of Republican light, and the anti-Dreyfusards, who are wholly identified with the violence and racialism of the extremists, and with their opposition to the Republic and to the traditions of the Revolution. This confusion completely glosses over the governmental position, which was Republican but *anti*-Dreyfusard, and it fails to take into account the existence of the – deliberately – silent Republican majority.

ARMY OFFICERS

Although there was evidently a high degree of complicity between Henry and the officers of the General Staff on the one hand and the extremist anti-Dreyfusards on the other, it cannot be said that the officer corps as a whole was extremist in its views in 1898. Only 1,700 out of 25,000 on the active list were to join, at the end of the year, the violently antisemitic contributors to the appeal in support of Henry's widow (*see* below, pp. 133). 'Thousands of upright French officers,' wrote George Barlow, 'compelled for the most part to remain silent, regarded the proceedings of the General Staff with honest anger and disgust.'[9] And an antisemitic officer in the hussars, when interviewed, openly expressed his contempt for the General Staff, which had made common cause with Esterhazy. It had 'disorganized the army'. 'It will be enough in future for an officer to be a Catholic and a nobleman for any mere corporal to laugh in his face. Discipline is dead, and it is the General Staff which has killed it,' he said.

The officer corps, apart from the aristocratic elements who were

9 Ibid., p. ix.

hostile to the Republic and the Jews, were largely anti-Dreyfusard out of respect for discipline and for the positions taken up by their superiors, which became dogmas removed from the realms of discussion. As soldiers and men of action, they had no time for debate and discussion; their prime virtue had always been and still remained obedience. 'There was much talk about the Affair in the mess,' said an anonymous captain. But 'if it did not lead to any incidents, this was because everyone was in agreement . . . yes, among the officer corps, that is among those circles which might rightly be thought to belong to the nation's intellectual élite, things had reached such a point that no one would tolerate any contradiction, and no one would listen to any opinion but the one which had been endorsed by authority . . . The few Dreyfusards, if there were any, kept silent, to avoid compromising themselves, or being ostracized. We did know a few, though, who did not keep silent and who met with animosity from many directions.'[10] Two officer cadets at Saint-Maixent, when interviewed, declared they were ardent Dreyfusards. Officers who rose from the ranks via Saint-Maixent were now treated with contempt in the army, they said; they denounced the all-powerful General Staff and called for the army chiefs to be elected.[11]

CATHOLICS

In the same way, both kinds of anti-Dreyfusism were represented amongst Catholics, and even Dreyfusism itself. The attitude of the Church hierarchy, and that of most priests, bound by the obligation of restraint which applied to all French state employees, was parallel to that of France's rulers, and was thus one of moderate anti-Dreyfusism. Monsignor Richard, the archbishop of Paris, replying to some Dreyfusard academics who had approached him in December 1897, declared: 'It is not for the Church to intervene in the debate; it is for the French courts to examine and decide on the question, and we shall bow to their verdict.' The Church, and priests as priests, were not entitled to intervene, even though a priest had the right to be a Dreyfusard in his private capacity. The vast majority of the bishops and the clergy respected this rule of neutrality and non-intervention. It is true that Monsignor Mathieu declared: 'While our

---

10 Capitaine de l'armée active, *L'Officier et la crise française* (Paris, 1900), pp. 87–8, and Jérôme Hélie, 'L'arche sainte fracturée', in Pierre Birnbaum, ed., *La France de l'affaire Dreyfus* (Paris, 1994).

11 Eugène Thibault, 'La voix de la muette', Bibliothèque Nationale, MS Naf 14677.

generals were being insulted, our thoughts went towards the frontier near which we were born, and we sympathized with all our heart with those who cried: "Long live France! Long live the army!" ' But such cases were rare. The attitude of the average priest was closer to that of the average Catholic and the average bourgeois. And after all, in a country like France, where almost everyone was nominally a Catholic, the two were almost one and the same thing.

However, contemporaries and historians have tended to identify all Catholics with anti-Dreyfusism, and because all anti-Dreyfusism has generally tended to be confused with the extremist variety, this has meant that all Catholics have been seen as extremists. There has, admittedly, been some excuse for this view. French Catholicism at the end of the 19th century still bore the mark of the Church's traditional theological anti-Judaism, based on the twin ideas of the Jewish people as deicides and as the embodiment of Evil. In the liturgy, notably the ordinary of the mass for Good Friday, there were still references to the 'blindness' of the Jews and a prayer for the 'faithless Jews'.

Nor did French bishops emerge from their silence to condemn antisemitism. The only gesture of this kind was by the archbishop of Lyon in 1896: he refused to attend the Christian-Democratic congress of that year which openly displayed its antisemitism.

Furthermore, there were Catholic organizations – the Union Nationale of the abbé Garnier, and above all the Assumptionist order – whose social and political views came close to those of the national- ists and antisemites. For them, the defence of Catholic interests involved demanding the return of those official posts of which the Catholics had been deprived by the Republicans when they came to power, and which had in certain cases gone to Jews and Protestants; it involved indeed a commitment to nationalism and antisemitism and the notion of France for the French. For *La Croix*, the organ of the Assumptionists, as we have seen, the Jews were not real Frenchmen.

These, the most politicized elements in French Catholicism, were determined to sabotage the Pope's attempts at reconciliation with the Republic: they were already active in the winter of 1897–98 in the run- up to the legislative elections of 1898, in which they would support royalist candidates and adopt nationalist and antisemitic positions. The Assumptionists were in the vanguard of this electoral battle, with their Justice-Equality committees. Their newspaper, *La Croix*, with its many local editions, had been running a systematic campaign of antisemitism since 1890. *La Croix* was read by 20,000 priests, more than one-third of the parish clergy, and hundreds of thousands of laymen.

In view of the silence of the hierarchy on the antisemitic question, the aggressiveness of *La Croix* – which was of course not an official mouthpiece of the Church – did much to give credence, then and since, to the idea that the Church and Catholics in general were anti-Dreyfusards in the style of Drumont. But it must be remembered that the number of priests who subscribed to his newspaper *La Libre Parole* was only 300 out of the 50,000 in the country.

It is legitimate to conclude therefore, with René Rémond, that the Catholics who were identified with nationalism and violent anti-semitism, and so with anti-Dreyfusard extremism, were in the minority among their co-religionists: the majority, even here, no doubt shared the prevalent opinion out of a sense of conformism; and the traditional antisemitism of the Catholics fell short of the violence of Drumont.

The Catholic Dreyfusards, for their part, were a tiny minority, who passed almost unnoticed at the time of the Affair, so convinced was everyone that Catholic meant anti-Dreyfusard. Less than 200 joined the Comité Catholique pour la Défense du Droit (Catholic Committee for the Defence of Justice), founded by Paul Viollet. Most of these were, like him, linked to the tradition of liberal Catholicism, which demanded the same rights for all, including Catholics, on the basis of the Rights of Man of 1789. As we have seen, Viollet had been one of the founders of the Ligue des Droits de l'Homme, but he had left when it refused members of the religious orders the right to teach. Anticlericalism, which was to become such a marked feature of Dreyfusism, was already emerging among the Dreyfusards at the beginning of 1898. It should be noted that, with the Catholic Dreyfusards, the abbé Brugerette at Lyon and the abbé Frémont denounced antisemitism as contrary to the Gospels.[12]

THE PROTESTANTS

Unlike the Catholics, the Protestants were on the whole identified in the public mind with Dreyfusism, no doubt because a number of the first Dreyfusards, such as Scheurer-Kestner or Gabriel Monod, were Protestants or from a Protestant background: this was true, too, of Louis Leblois, or Francis de Pressensé, who was to become President of the Ligue des Droits de l'Homme. And it is also true that many

---

12 Louis Capéran, *L'anticléricalisme et l'Affaire Dreyfus* (Toulouse, 1948), ch. 7, and René Rémond, 'Les catholiques choisissent leur camp', *L'Histoire* 173 (January 1994), 70–3.

intellectuals, the great majority of ministers and a large number of the ordinary Protestant folk of the Midi were active Dreyfusards.

The Protestants in France had, on the whole, remained faithful to Republicanism throughout the 19th century; like the Jews, they were attached to the French Revolution which had brought them their emancipation. They also shared with the Jews, at the end of the century, the reactions of a minority group some Frenchmen wanted to exclude, a group which sought to affirm strongly through its patriotism that it was an integral part of the national community. At the time of the Affair, Protestants, like the Jews, were subject to attack by Catholics and nationalists. The latter denounced the 'Protestant invasion' just as much as the 'Jewish invasion'.

The memory of past persecutions finally helped to encourage Protestants to sympathize with Dreyfus; and the appeal to the individual conscience which characterized their faith helped to stiffen them against the acceptance of official truths. However, in spite of this, the semi-official newspapers which spoke for Protestant ecclesiastical institutions shared the prevailing moderate anti-Dreyfusism based on respect for the *res judicata*. Only the independent press, or that representing the little Churches, was pro-Dreyfusard. Furthermore, certain Protestants reacted not on the basis of their religious traditions but simply as members of the society around them, in accordance with their political views or their class interests. There were anti-Dreyfusards among the bourgeois Protestants of the Nord, and among bankers and businessmen.[13] Bourgeois Protestants in Paris had already, in 1848, shown fear and hostility towards the Revolution, which had been generally welcomed by French Protestants.

THE JEWS

The Jews, for their part, were, like the Protestants, faithful Republicans, attached to the Republic which had emancipated them and had found them a place in its state structures. They too were ardent patriots, anxious to identify themselves with the Republic and with France, so as to shield themselves from the attacks of those who sought to exclude them.

But, in the eyes of the public, they were of course largely identified with the Dreyfusard campaign; for the antisemites, they formed the

13 See *Histoire des protestants en France* (Toulouse, 1977), pp. 223–5, and A. Encrevé, 'La petite musique huguenote', in Birnbaum, ed., *La France de l'affaire Dreyfus*, pp. 451–504.

'syndicate'. And it was true, too, that the Dreyfus family and Bernard-Lazare had been at the very root of the Dreyfusard campaign, and that Jews were even more numerous than Protestants among the Dreyfusards, and in the Ligue des Droits de l'Homme: Reinach, Lévy-Brühl, Michel Bréal, Emile Durkheim and Victor Basch, not to mention the young literary figures, the Halévy brothers, Proust and Léon Blum. Numerous individuals, and even groups, took part in the campaign, notably in Alsace-Lorraine. But, as Péguy pointed out, Dreyfus-ism was most marked among the less well-off Jews. The only public meeting held to protest against antisemitism at the time of the Dreyfus Affair was organized by immigrant Jewish workers in Montmartre on 16 September 1899: they had just set up the Prolétariat juif de France to remind the French that not all Jews were wealthy financiers. For them, antisemitism was a form of clericalism and 'the socialism of idiots'. They combined Marxist internationalism with their fidelity to the French Revolution.

Among the Jews, as elsewhere, official bodies kept silent: the consistories, the Jewish press, and even the Alliance Israélite Universelle, which had actually been set up to defend Jewish interests, played practically no part in the campaign. They, and most of the upper and middle bourgeoisie, displayed more or less the same anti-Dreyfusism of social conformity as other official bodies and the non-Jewish bourgeoisie. Arthur Meyer, editor of the *Gaulois*, only wanted peace and quiet, just like the authorities.

The Jews in general, according to Léon Blum, had accepted the conviction of Dreyfus in 1894 as just and final. He wrote:

> The mass of the Jews met the beginnings of the campaign for a review with much caution and suspicion. The dominant feeling could be described in the following words: *'This is something the Jews must not become involved in'*. All the elements making up this complex feeling were not of the same quality. Admittedly there was patriotism, even a tetchy form of patriotism, and there was respect for the army, confidence in its leaders and a reluctance to accuse them of partiality or fallibility. But there was also a kind of egoistic and timorous prudence which could be qualified in harsher terms. The Jews did not want it to be thought they were defending Dreyfus as a Jew. They did not want their attitude to be put down to any racial distinction or to racial solidarity. Above all, they did not want, by taking up the defence of another Jew, to fuel the antisemitic passion which was raging with great intensity at that time . . . the Jews who were the same age as Dreyfus, those who belonged to the same social stratum, those who, like him, had passed the most difficult competitive exams, and entered the ranks of the officers on the General Staff or joined the most prestigious branches of the adminis-

tration, were infuriated at the idea that hostile prejudice might hold back their unblemished careers. Wealthy Jews, Jews from the middle bourgeoisie, and Jewish civil servants, were afraid of the struggle which had been launched on behalf of Dreyfus.

The Jews were so much identified with the Republic that even Reinach and the Jewish Dreyfusards themselves were prepared to see only a Republican struggle in the defence of Dreyfus, not a Jewish one. Their Dreyfusism was, even for them, the very expression of their patriotism and their attachment to the Republic. As we have seen, when Bernard-Lazare sought to present the struggle in Jewish terms in 1897 (*see* above, pp. 43–4), they dropped him. Those who raised the call for Jewish defence, the future Zionists, received no attention from the Jewish community.

There were even some Jews who were so wedded to patriotism that they lapsed into anti-Dreyfusard extremism, condemning their co-religionists as enemies of France. This was true of Gaston Pollonnais. He and Meyer, after breaking with the rest of French Jewry, had no choice but to pursue their path to its natural conclusion: they converted to Catholicism. Among the Jews as elsewhere, the official world kept silent, and political or class considerations could lead to a partial or complete disavowal of religious traditions and affiliation.[14]

If France's religious communities were not unanimous, in politics, the dividing line between Dreyfusards and anti-Dreyfusards, in this period early in 1898, when the politicization of the Affair was just beginning, ran through the middle of the parties.

THE PROGRESSISTS

The governmental Republicans, or Progressists, were more divided than most. For if the Prime Minister Méline, remained, as we have seen, the leading spokesman for the moderate anti-Dreyfusism of the whole of official France, if he clung to the *res judicata* and was followed by most of the party notables and deputies, it was nonetheless the case that his party was the one where there had been most Dreyfus sympathizers at the very beginning of the Affair: Reinach, Aynard, Trarieux and Scheurer-Kestner. Waldeck-Rousseau was in favour of a review, and the Dreyfusards were well aware that the young leaders – Poincaré, Barthou, Jonnart and Georges Leygues –

14 In addition to Blum, see Bernard Blumenkranz, ed., *Histoire des juifs en France* (Toulouse, 1972), and Michael R. Marrus, *The Politics of Assimilation. A Study of the French Jewish Community at the Time of the Dreyfus Affair* (Oxford, 1971).

were only waiting for the opportunity to unburden their consciences. And if the President, Félix Faure, was reputed to be working against a review behind the scenes,[15] the former president, Casimir-Périer, was a Dreyfusard, according to Blum, and *Le Siècle* had become an organ of Dreyfusism.

THE RADICALS

Amongst the radicals, Clemenceau was one of the leaders who had been ousted after the Panama scandal. With Ranc, he was the only radical of note in the Dreyfusard camp. The new leaders were all anti-Dreyfusards: Léon Bourgeois, Brisson, Pelletan, and above all Cavaignac, who was the dominant figure in the party at the beginning of 1898. Cavaignac was the son of the general who had, with much bloodshed, crushed the working-class rising of June 1848. Having distinguished himself by his severity in the debates over Panama, he made a great show of his republican virtue. He was also an outspoken patriot. Convinced by the Henry forgery and the legend of Dreyfus's confession, he believed it was now essential that the evidence of Dreyfus's treason should be produced and shown to the country. Already in January, he had asked Méline for confirmation that Dreyfus had confessed. The mass of the party was anti-Dreyfusard almost to a man, and frequently used nationalistic language. Indeed, five of the deputies who would be elected as antisemites in the May elections described themselves as radicals, and antisemitic language was also commonly used by radicals in the spring of 1898. The only radical deputy to come out in favour of Dreyfus, the unfortunate Hubbard, was disowned by Cavaignac and Bourgeois. The great radical news-paper, the *Dépêche de Toulouse*, was to remain hostile to a review right up to the Rennes trial of 1899. *L'Eclair*, the most popular radical paper, had set out to work for the General Staff.

Early in 1898, the radicals' main preoccupation remained the danger of clericalism. But they did not as yet perceive any link between their anticlericalism and the struggle on behalf of Dreyfus; nor did they yet see any clerical threat behind antisemitism.

15 See Thierry Billard, *Félix Faure*, (Paris, 1995). M. Billard contends that Félix Faure was not opposed to a review, but clung, in his statements to his entourage, to his constitutional position of neutrality.

THE WORKING CLASS AND THE SOCIALISTS

The situation as regards the workers and the socialists was much more complex: they were divided, and they were to remain very reticent about the Dreyfus question for a long time. During the spring of 1898, most socialist supporters among the workers refused to take sides. In 1894, they had shared the popular feelings of hatred for a traitor which had made them wish for his death. Just over three years later, they must have been more puzzled than ever by the legalistic complications of the Dreyfus case. To them it was a riddle, said Guesde.

The workers, too, had suffered so much. What were the sufferings of an individual, a class-enemy, to them? They said: 'Leave the bourgeoisie to look after their own kind.' Jaurès heard a worker pronounce this sentence about Dreyfus, which saddened him: 'If he had been a worker, people would have lost interest in him long ago.'

Besides, he was an army officer, and the army had been used to quell working-class agitation. 'Dreyfus would have fired on us too,' said the workers. And he was a Jew: many workers were still responsive to the antisemitic arguments of a Rochefort, who retained a significant following among them.

Finally, the deputies and senators who were the first promoters of Dreyfusism were the very ones who had passed laws to repress anarchism. A pamphlet distributed by the trade unionists of the CGT (Confédération Générale du Travail) in the spring of 1898 declared: 'We the Workers, constantly exploited, have no call to take part in this conflict between Jews and Christians! They are both the same, since they both dominate and exploit us!'[16]

But the CGT itself was divided and some workers thought differently, if one is to judge from the dialogue between the old Communard Fléchier and the joiner Roupart in Anatole France's *M. Bergeret à Paris*. 'It seems to me,' said Roupart, 'that to fight against in injustice is to work for us proletarians, on whom every injustice bears down. To me, everything which is equitable is a step on the road to socialism.'

Within the socialist movement, the Allemanists, who were a fiercely anti-militarist, anti-parliamentary group, were the first to enter the fray in support of Dreyfus. Among the parliamentary leaders, the move towards commitment was slower. Jaurès, who had been con-

16 Confédération Générale du Travail, *Congrès national corporatif, 10, 1898. Rennes – Compte rendu des travaux*, pp. 63–4.

vinced of Dreyfus's innocence by Lucien Herr, was still hesitating to proclaim his belief openly, as we have seen from his speeches in the Chamber in January 1898 and at Zola's trial. He still did not go beyond condemning the illegality of 1894.

He was initially only supported by Guesde, Vaillant, Chauvin and Sembat. But he wanted to carry the whole parliamentary group with him into action on behalf of Dreyfus. To Péguy, who said: 'Let us go forward alone, there is no need for numbers', he replied, referring to the group: 'They are eating me up, they are devouring me, they are all afraid of not being re-elected. They hang on to my coat-tails to stop me from mounting the rostrum.'

When the group met after the publication of *J'Accuse . . .!*, Miller-and, Viviani, Jourde and Lavy declared that they were hostile to any intervention. But Guesde and Vaillant said: 'This is a battle we must fight'. 'Oh!' Jaurès recalled in 1900, 'I remember the admirable tones of Guesde . . . The moderate comrades in the group said: "After all, Zola is a member of the bourgeoisie. Are we going to line the party up behind a bourgeois?" And Guesde got up, as if choking at this sort of language, and opened the window of the room where the group was meeting, saying, "Zola's letter is the greatest revolutionary act of the century." '

At this time, however, the point of view of the moderates prevailed, for the manifesto of the parliamentary group, signed by all the deputies including Jaurès, refused to pronounce on Dreyfus's guilt, and presented the Affair as a competition between the Catholic clericals and the Opportunists as to who could gain the largest share of the Republican spoils. The clericals, avid for jobs, hoped that the sentence against Dreyfus would disqualify all Jews, and that France would be handed back to a 'scrawny, ruined nobility'. To them, 'France for the French' meant all the jobs for them. Their opponents, the Opportunist group, were identified with the Jews: 'On the other hand, the Jewish capitalists, after all the scandals that have discredited them, need to rehabilitate themselves somewhat to guarantee them their share of the booty.' Dreyfus's rehabilitation would mean the 'indirect rehabilitation of the group, with its shades of Judaism and Panama . . . Proletarians, do not join either clan in this bourgeois civil war!' The socialist parliamentary group was still using the anti-Jewish argument to attack its capitalist opponents; Panama had also been recently in the news.

As in other circles, the first Dreyfusards among the socialists came from the young, and from all those who, like the Allemanists, were remote from the temptations of electoralism and the corridors of power. The Allemanists sent Zola a letter of congratulation.

Péguy and his socialist friends at the Ecole Normale used the same arguments as the joiner Roupart and declared: 'Since several parliamentarians calling themselves socialists refuse to follow the right path, we, the young socialists, wish to rescue the socialist ideal from them. Socialists, if they are not to fall into a decline, must go for every form of justice which can be achieved.'

Finally, the anarchists around Sébastien Faure became active very early on, being among the first to scent the danger of reaction from the ex-Boulangists and clericals (*see* below, p. 101). From January 1898, they decided to do all they could, and to take to the streets, so as to halt the new threat which had appeared on the horizon. This explains why they went into the attack physically at the antisemitic meeting of 17 January and drove the speakers from the platform. Without siding with Dreyfus, they wanted to 'join in the movement to promote and set going the libertarian trends within it'. It should be noted, however, that other anarchists, Jean Grave and Emile Pouget, adopted the abstentionist argument.

All in all, the socialists and anarchists were essentially politically motivated in their approach to the Dreyfus Affair at the beginning of 1898. The innocence or otherwise of Dreyfus was not their main concern: if they recommended abstention, it was out of electoral caution; if they called for intervention, it was to hasten the coming of the revolution, to oppose militarism, on which they were all agreed, and to bar the way to clericalism and reaction. It was this latter political argument which would later make them go over unanimously to Dreyfusism, identified with the defence of the Republic.

WOMEN AND FEMINISTS

To contemporaries, what seemed particularly characteristic of feminine reaction to the Affair was feelings of compassion: Daniel Halévy included 'women weeping over the martyr' in his list of Dreyfusard types, and many female supporters of Dreyfus expressed this feeling in their letters to Zola. In March 1898, the feminist paper *La Fronde* launched a petition in support of Lucie Dreyfus's request to be allowed to join her husband on Devil's Island, after several wives of prominent Dreyfusards had written a letter to *Le Siècle* calling for tears for her and seeking signatures in support of her request. The compassion of Dreyfusard women thus centred on Dreyfus and his wife; it also extended to Colonel Picquart.

The feminists of *La Fronde* clearly saw Dreyfus and his wife as victims they should support; but like the pro-Dreyfus socialists, they did not separate their concern for them from their wider concern, in this case for their oppressed sisters as a whole. And *La Fronde* spoke up equally for the Jew as pariah, condemning antisemitism; finally feminist concern for victims of the brutality of war led the paper to take up an anti-militarist and pacifist stance. Its Dreyfusism was thus part and parcel of a general commitment.

La Fronde, written and produced entirely by women, had expressed whole-hearted support for Dreyfus from its beginnings in November 1897, and its feminist journalists were thus among the earliest Dreyfusards; after *J'Accuse . . .!*, the paper saluted Zola's 'act of moral courage'. *La Fronde* gave the Affair extensive coverage. But its general aim was not to define a specifically feminist position, but to treat the Affair in exactly the same way as the rest of the Dreyfusard press. To report on the Affair, and to take up the fight for justice on the same terms as men, was a way of affirming women's equal right to intervene in public affairs, which was still denied to them under the Third Republic. As Maria Pognon put it after the *Siècle* appeal, tears were not enough: what the feminists of *La Fronde* demanded for Dreyfus, exactly like other Dreyfusards, was 'the act of justice'. And she echoed Clemenceau in asserting that justice would be safe for no one if it was denied to one single citizen: 'We ask for it because if today Madame Dreyfus is weeping for her exiled husband, tomorrow we may be forced to weep for our husbands, our sons and our brothers, convicted though they are innocent.'

At the same time, there were anti-Dreyfusard feminists, who expressed themselves in *Le féminisme chrétien*. They attacked *La Fronde* with great violence and adopted nationalist, xenophobic and antisemitic positions. These feminists naturally reserved their compassion for the widow and orphan child of Colonel Henry. Thus the Dreyfus Affair, like the 1848 Revolution and the Paris Commune, was an occasion for feminist mobilization, and for the appearance of a remarkable feminist newspaper, this time *La Fronde*. The Dreyfusard, Republican and secularist commitment of this newspaper reduced for a time the suspicions of socialists and Republicans towards its middle-class feminist journalists, to whom all women remained suspect of being too much under the thumb of the Catholic Church. The first group of socialist women was set up at this time, and three women entered the Central Committee of the Ligue des Droits de l'Homme; in June 1898, the socialist Viviani successfully obtained from Parliament the right for qualified women to practise as barristers. The Affair marked certainly a new stage in the campaign for female emancipation in France, but that it did little in the long term to reduce Republican prejudice against votes for women, seen as a Trojan horse for the Church, is shown by the fact that this reform was not introduced until 1945.[17]

THE RIGHT

How did the Right react to the Affair? From early in 1898, it became threatening in tone, at first in Parliament, where, through the voice of Albert de Mun, it attacked the government for not defending the honour of the army with sufficient firmness. The parliamentary Right, as we have seen, seemed ready to join with the radicals to overturn the government of Méline. 'The Right,' said Léon Blum, 'comprised all those members of the former royalist and Bonapartist parties who had not been brought round to the Republic by the passage of time, the policy of Leo XIII and the failure of Boulanger. The position of the royalists and Bonapartists was a curious one in the sense that they were violently and massively anti-Dreyfusard, whereas their natural leaders, the Princes, the pretenders, and the members of the royal and imperial families, had no doubt that Dreyfus was innocent.' Like the Pope, the latter had learned the truth from Berlin and Rome, via diplomatic channels.

Behind the Right stood members of the former ruling classes, nobles and intransigent Catholics, excluded from power by the triumphant Republicans. But they had also been joined in opposition, and in extremist anti-Dreyfusism, by former Boulangists: this was a combined opposition of the Right and part of the extreme Left. 'They exuded only revenge and an air of wanting to stage a return fight,' said Léon Blum. The Affair brought them new hope.

DÉROULÈDE

One of the former right-wing Boulangists, Paul Déroulède, had returned from five years of retirement, at the request of his supporters,

17 See *Le Siècle* (24 March 1898) and *La Fronde* (26 March 1898). On this question I am greatly indebted to a paper by Máire Cross on *La Fronde* and the Dreyfus Affair, to appear in the proceedings of the Tours conference of November 1994 (*see* p. 193). See also Madeleine Rebérioux, *La République radicale? 1898–1914* (Paris, 1973), p. 41; Julie Sabiani, 'Féminisme et dreyfusisme' in Géraldi Leroy, ed., *Les écrivains et l'affaire Dreyfus* (Paris, 1983), pp. 199–206, and M. Albistur and D. Armogathe, *Histoire du féminisme français du Moyen Age à nos jours* (Paris, 1977), pp. 371–3.

and taken up the fight again at the time of the Zola trial. Born in 1846, Déroulède had enjoyed enormous popular success after the defeat of 1871 as the poet who sounded the clarion call to *la Revanche*, the return fight. He had become the bard of a romantic and declamatory nationalism. Through the Ligue des Patriotes which he founded in 1882, he aimed to lead the masses towards a new society based on military virtues. When he reappeared among the anti-Dreyfusards, he became one of their main leaders, determined to forge an alliance between the people and the army. The former Boulangists, said Blum, 'made themselves the keenest champions of the army so as to make it into their tool ... The army was the necessary means to successful coups'. But there were also men of the extreme Left among the former Boulangists, revolutionary socialists, Blanquists or would-be Blanquists like Rochefort. These former Boulangists had now become antisemitic. They worked side-by-side with the antisemites Guérin was attempting to organize in the Ligue Antisémitique.

TOWARDS NATIONALISM

After the January 1898 riots, one of the former Boulangist leaders, Georges Thiébaud, tried to group together, around the name of Rochefort, 'all the revolutionaries who had in times past gone over to Boulangism'.[18] He was trying to take advantage of the Affair to bring about a repeat of Boulangism.

He even tried to bring them into an alliance with former right-wing Boulangists, by setting up, for the legislative elections, a Republican nationalist committee on which there were ex-Boulangists from the Right, the extreme Left and the antisemites: Millevoye, Guérin, Barrès, Vallié, Bailby and Déroulède. 'In its founder's mind,' according to the police, 'the Republican nationalist committee was to follow a path parallel to that of the Ligue Antisémitique, while remaining distinct from it'.[19] But it was not to be long before the two groups, the ex-Boulangists and the antisemites, merged, to form the nationalist party.

It was Thiébaud who 'invented' the word 'nationalist' to denote the new group, in the spring of 1898. At a meeting in Caen, he proposed the setting up of a Republican nationalist party.[20] A new nationalist and antisemitic extreme Right was emerging which would

18 AN F⁷ 12462 (29 January 1898).
19 AN F⁷ 12719 (1 March 1898).
20 AN F⁷ 12462 (29 January 1898).

soon have no connection with the Left. With what remained of the Old Right, it would take advantage of the Affair to mount an attack on the Republic itself; it was to unite against it all the forces of the Left.

THE LEGISLATIVE ELECTIONS OF 1898

In almost all political circles, the great preoccupation, in February 1898, was the coming legislative elections, which were to take place on 8 and 22 May. As Scheurer-Kestner noted, the Republicans more than ever avoided any direct reference to the Affair:

> People on both sides were 'afraid' of bringing up the question of Dreyfus. Some [i.e. those Republicans favourable to a review] trembled at the thought of having to give their opinion in an electoral college where nationalism had taken a terrible toll; others feared to declare themselves as opponents of a review of the Dreyfus case in a college where people were hesitant about making up their minds. It seemed as if the word had been given to set the Dreyfus Affair on one side.

Or as Reinach said: 'Since both Republicans and reactionaries were united against Dreyfus, the balance was restored; at this lower level, the debate between the parties was embarked upon as if Dreyfus did not exist. The only clash was to be between the old programmes based on ideas or interests.'

Only some of the older generation of Republicans, such as Prosper Allemand, George Barlow reported, spoke out forcefully and courageously. Younger men were too interested in place-hunting, he said, and if they cared about the Dreyfus Affair, it was only insofar as it might embarrass Méline and prevent him from handing out jobs.

That the official silence was meant to work against Dreyfus, however, was shown, according to Barlow, by the fact that government pressure was exerted on the departmental councils to come out with expressions of opinion 'calculated to influence the electors' against a review. At least nine expressed confidence in the army and called on the government to put a stop to attacks on the army.[21]

Also, whilst declaiming against the word 'nationalist', said Reinach, the Republicans made it their own. Méline himself used distinctly nationalistic language to appeal to both the Right and the radicals. 'The nation's army,' he declared at Remiremont, 'is the highest embodiment of the Fatherland in the face of the foreigner, and no

21 Barlow, *A History*, pp. 181–6.

one is entitled to weaken it or detract from its standing.' Here again the anti-Dreyfusard meaning was quite clear.

The radicals, too, said Reinach, were as nationalistic as the nationalists themselves; their use of antisemitic language has already been noted.

Finally, some Blanquist socialists were also swept into the nationalist current as happened in the days of Boulanger.

The main overt issue in the elections was Méline's attempt to attract enough Republican votes from the Right to be able to consolidate his majority without at the same time losing support on the left, where the progress of Catholic extremism could only irritate the radicals. The gates of the Republic, he assured the Right, were wide open to all who sincerely accepted Republicanism; at the same time, Barthou sought to reassure the radicals on the left that Méline's concessions to the Catholics were not a betrayal. But the mutual recriminations between Méline and the radicals on the clerical issue only enlarged the gulf between them during the course of the campaign. Thus there was silence over the Dreyfus Affair among most Republicans, of whom many were infected with a nationalism which worked to the detriment of Dreyfus.

As always, it was amongst the anti-Dreyfusard extremists from the old Boulangist movement, now about to merge into the nationalist party, that the Affair was exploited openly, in the fifteen or so departments where they felt strong enough to do so. Déroulède also launched an appeal to every mayor in France, asking them to demand a commitment from each candidate 'to oppose any review, direct or indirect, of the Dreyfus case'. All those, he said, who refused such a commitment must be 'excluded from serving the Republic'. There were a number of candidates who fought on an antisemitic ticket, notably Drumont, brought over to fight in Algiers.

All-in-all, however, the Affair continued to occupy many people's minds during the campaign. The silence was deliberate: it was a sign not of indifference, but of a government blackout, an attempt to disguise the anti-Dreyfusard message, and electoral calculations based on fear. One only had to lift the lid off the pot to discover seething passions underneath, which were ready to boil over at any moment. Election meetings passed off quietly until the Affair was mentioned; the moment that happened there was complete pandemonium, exactly as in the famous cartoon of the dinner in town, published in *Le Figaro*.

The candidates from the parliamentary parties who referred to the Affair were marginal figures, in a tiny minority in their own group: Reinach – supported in a celebrated letter by Prosper Allemand, the

unfortunate Hubbard, Jaurès, Guesde and a handful of other socialists. Jaurès spoke only cautiously of the Affair; Guesde restricted
himself to denouncing antisemitism.

The result was a predictable one: Reinach, Hubbard, Guesde and
Jaurès, Dreyfusards or suspected of being such, were defeated. The
only example George Barlow gave of an outspoken Dreyfusard being
elected was Fiquet at Amiens, 'a candidate against whom a campaign
of the utmost virulence had been waged'.[22]

On the other hand, Déroulède and Cassagnac, who were violently
anti-Dreyfusard, were elected. Drumont, equally triumphant in Algiers, was among the four new deputies elected there as antisemites.
Apart from them, the other nationalists or antisemites elected numbered about fifteen. Other than this minor shift towards extremism,
the election results showed remarkably little change in the balance
between the parties.

MOBILIZATION OR ABSTENTION

Before considering the consequences of the elections, it is worth looking more closely at the social and increasingly political confrontation
which had been produced by Zola's *J'Accuse...!* This confrontation, and the course of the election campaign, provide a guide to
the understanding of what may be called the sociology of intervention
and abstention during the Affair, to the significance of the mobilization of some elements in French society, and the indifference, or
non-mobilization, of others.

It is doubtful, in the first place, whether provincial France was
deeply affected by the passions of the Affair: the prefects' reports
spoke of widespread indifference. J. E. C. Bodley, the greatest British
student of France at the time of the Affair, had travelled extensively
in the provinces. He gave, in his *France*, a striking picture of the
profound indifference of France's hard-working and serious-minded
provincial population towards scandals and the turmoil of political
life in Paris. He noted the importance of electoral abstention. 'Explore
the French departments; live among the people and observe the most
industrious villager or the most cultivated tradesman in the country
town and question him about the local deputy or the elections, and
his reply will be: "Je ne m'occupe pas de politique." ' The press, with
its reflection of Parisian agitation, gave a false impression of the
opinion of the country at large. 'There is no public opinion in France,'

22 Ibid., p. 191.

he wrote, 'as we understand it in England . . . The spirit of the press of the whole country, excepting in matters of local interest, is regulated by the journalists of Paris. They interpret merely the sentiments, sometimes conflicting, sometimes unanimous, of the Boulevards.'[23]

Thus peasants, as well as most of the workers, reacted very largely with indifference to the Affair, simply because the issues raised by it were basically remote and alien to them. They could see no link between the fate of Dreyfus and their daily concerns – which were, for the peasants, the cultivation of the soil and local affairs, and, for the workers, the struggle against insecurity and against the capitalists. The Affair was a matter for Paris, the towns and the bourgeoisie.

It was only insofar as they could relate the Affair to their own preoccupations that most peasants or workers would take any interest in it. Here and there, in the countryside, Zola was burnt in effigy, but in this way the Affair was integrated into age-old rituals. Elsewhere, it was woven into local quarrels.[24] Those in the country who had any opinion were overwhelmingly anti-Dreyfusard. Thus, Reinach wrote: 'The peasant had read in *Le Petit Journal* that the defenders of Dreyfus were accomplices of the foreigner, paid to start a fresh war with Germany. If anyone had mentioned justice to them, they would have been driven off with a pitchfork.'

As to the majority of the workers, they would only make common cause with Dreyfus when they became aware that the Republic was in danger and began to see that the injustice affecting him was inseparable from the social injustice they met with every day.

The rejection of the Affair by most of the bourgeoisie, the Progressists in the government and all of official France was the result of their desire to continue to enjoy, in peace and tranquillity, the benefits of their economic, political, social and cultural position. They felt that this was threatened by the agitation surrounding the Affair. They were, in short, the contented groups in the French society of the end of the 19th century, the well-off, and those who enjoyed positions of power and influence: in government, Parliament, the civil service, the moderate Republican press, the employer class, finance, the Catholic Church hierarchy, the governing organs of the Protestants and the Jews, the French Academy . . . They formed a deliberately silent majority. Their abstentionism, their silence, their continual

23 John Edward Courtenay Bodley, *France*, new edn. (London, 1907), pp. 330, 108; see also pp. 328–33 passim.
24 Michael Burns, *Rural Society and French Politics. Boulangism and the Dreyfus Affair 1886–1900* (Princeton, NJ, 1984), ch. 6.

insistence that there was no Dreyfus Affair, was the expression of what has been characterized above as moderate anti-Dreyfusism: that the governing politicians' language during the election was calculated to work against Dreyfus has been seen above.

Those who were mobilized, both the extremist anti-Dreyfusards and the Dreyfusards, were essentially the socially and politically discontented. First, the extremist anti-Dreyfusards, the royalists and Bonapartists of the old Right, who represented, as we have seen, members of the former ruling classes and a minority among Catholics: these two groups had been driven from power by the Republicans. They dreamed only of the day they would return. Some of the nobility, it is true, reacted by turning their backs on French society, which had excluded them; they adopted a cosmopolitan culture. There were even a few cases of Dreyfusard nobles: but these were no more than celebrated exceptions to the rule.[25]

The extremist anti-Dreyfusards also included the ex-Boulangists and their petty bourgeois and working-class troops. The petty bourgeois shopkeepers and the workers felt that they had not been invited to join in the Republican feast: they were, in their differing ways, victims of the workings of a commercial and industrial system which could ruin them or put them out of work. Shopkeepers and some of the workers were thus ready to follow the extremist anti-Dreyfusards who blamed the Jews and the government for all their troubles, and denounced the Republic as a sink of corruption.

The intellectuals, and those who fought for a review, were also among France's discontented groups. The intellectuals, as has been shown by Christophe Charle's work, were the victims of growing professional competition in the literary world at the end of the 19th century: it was becoming more and more difficult to make one's name. These intellectuals therefore were demanding their place in the sun.[26]

The extent of the social and increasingly political mobilization in France in 1898–99 can thus be explained not only by the great intellectual and moral issues raised by the Affair – which must not be underestimated of course – but also by the important range of social and political groups who could take advantage of the Affair to press their demands on the governing Progressists and bourgeoisie. They were all keen to dispute the dominance of the powers that be.

On both sides, the discontented groups were made up of all those

25 Claude-Isabelle Brelot, 'Entre nationalisme et cosmopolitisme: les engagements multiples de la noblesse', in Birnbaum, ed. *La France de l'affaire Dreyfus*, pp. 339–61.
26 Charle, *Naissance*, pp. 38–64 and ch. V.

who were outside the economic, political, social and cultural systems – either because of their subject condition, or their youth, or because their revolutionary opposition made them outsiders by choice.

On the Dreyfusard and revisionist side, those who began within the system, either within the state structures – the magistracy, the officer corps or the teaching profession – or within the political parties, soon found themselves excluded and forced on to the outside. They were subjected to intense pressure to conform to the prevailing opinion. The politician, the magistrate, the army officer or the teacher who held Dreyfusard opinions was faced with the choice of remaining silent or being ostracized.

The list of official sanctions against real or supposed Dreyfusards is a long one: Scheurer-Kestner was not re-elected as vice-president of the Senate; Reinach, Jaurès, Guesde and Hubbard were sanctioned by their party or the electors; Leblois was suspended for six months by the Bar council and Demange was threatened with the same penalty; in the army, Picquart was subjected to a prolonged campaign of harassment, Messimy was forced to resign, three generals were sanctioned, and Forzinetti, the director of the Cherche-Midi military prison, was removed from the service; Stapfer, dean of the Arts Faculty at Bordeaux, was suspended for six months, and Grimaux forcibly retired from his chair at Polytechnique. And this is not to mention the student attacks on Sorbonne professors or the pressures on the lycée teachers which have already been noted.

Such then was the structure of social and political mobilization at the time of the Affair: whilst a moderate anti-Dreyfusard majority in the centre of French society held the levers of power, followed the prescriptions of those in power or those of their group, refusing to accept that there was an Affair, and doing everything they could to enforce silence around them by group pressure or official sanctions, two radically opposite poles in that society confronted each other in a conflict in which they sought to intervene as energetically as they could, not only because of the multiple issues raised by the Affair, but so as to assert themselves against all the powers that be. This is the explanation for the degree of social mobilization in 1898–99, which eventually transformed the Affair into a political battle.

The processes by which the Affair was being politicized began to accelerate after the legislative elections. For though, on the surface, very little had changed in Parliament, since the governmental majority was still in place, in fact everything was changing, for Méline had not succeeded in strengthening his majority as he had hoped, and his

government was soon to fall. For the first time, the Affair was to
have a direct effect on parliamentary politics.

THE FALL OF MÉLINE

The fall of Méline's government did not appear at first sight to be
directly linked to the Affair, but, in fact, the spectre of had now begun
to haunt the Chamber of Deputies. The parliamentary session opened,
on 1 June, with a highly symbolic scene: Déroulède, Drumont and
the new nationalist and antisemitic deputies took up their seats on the
extreme right, shouting 'Down with the Jews!' The merger of the ex-
Boulangists and the antisemites was now complete, and the new
nationalist party had deliberately and ostensibly taken up a position
on the extreme right.

As a result, the Left now broke with nationalism and antisemitism. The socialists, whom Rochefort had been attacking since February, launched a campaign to denounce him, and the last traces of
antisemitic language disappeared from their discourse.

From June 1898 to February 1899 a gradual step-by-step clarification of the political scene was to take place: the Left, after breaking
with nationalism and antisemitism, would gradually come to identify
itself with Dreyfusism. And it would be more and more directly
opposed to a Right which was wholly anti-Dreyfusard and nationalist
and which now included, in its extreme wing, the ex-Boulangists and
the antisemites.

But this did not happen overnight. On the surface, the fall of
Méline did not take place as a result of the Affair, but as a consequence
of the unending complaints of the radicals about his compromises
with the Catholic Right. On 13 June, Bourgeois took him to task in
the name of the radicals, denouncing 'the intrusion of papal control
into the temporal, political and electoral sphere in France'.

The shaky nature of Méline's majority became clear at the end
of this debate, when the section of the next day's agenda approving
the government's statement was passed by a majority of only 23 votes.
He then won a majority of only twelve for the entire text, which now
included the threatening phrase, 'with the support of an exclusively
Republican majority', a phrase proposed by radicals in an attempt to
detach some Republicans from Méline and which had itself attracted
a large majority (49).

Méline had reached a dead end: he could not break with the
Right and attract more support on his left flank, since there was
irremediable hostility between him and the socialists, and his quarrels

with the radicals had been embittered by the election campaign. So he had nothing more to expect from the Left, which accused him, not without justification, of having become the prisoner of the Right. Moreover, his own supporters were slipping way. His situation had become untenable and he resigned on 15 June.

Despite appearances, the vote which led to his resignation had been influenced by the Affair, for most of the antisemites and nationalists, despite their gesture of 1 June, had voted against him with the Left, so contributing to the destruction of his majority.

The forces ranged against him still represented a right- and left-wing opposition united against the ruling Centre, since the nationalists had not yet, by their vote, placed themselves irretrievably on the Right. But a new majority was now appearing on the horizon, a majority of the Left. The young Progressist leaders on the left of the party, those precisely whom Blum and his friends now knew to be Dreyfusards not yet willing to come out in public, were growing uneasy about the demonstrations of clericalism on the Right and the emergence of the new nationalism: they were already beginning to think in terms of a left-wing majority, and when the new nationalists shifted so as to situate themselves more obviously on the Right, this move further encouraged them to look towards the Left.

Millerand, too, speaking in Parliament for the socialists, who were now in process of breaking with Rochefort, had, on 12 June, expressed their strong disapproval of the nationalists and antisemites. He quite rightly explained to the parliamentarians what has already been seen here: that nationalism, which had not so far been the monopoly of a single party, was in the process of constituting itself as a political party in its own right.

The fall of Méline thus marked the beginning of the end of the period throughout which the Progressists had governed France from the Centre. According to Reinach, the Affair also hung like a cloud over politics during the ministerial crisis, which lasted twelve days. 'None of the parliamentarians offered power by Félix Faure could disguise from themselves the fact that parliamentary life would remain a trial as long as this nightmare [the Affair] continued to be a burden on people's consciences and to let loose their passions.' He added that in this still confused situation only the nationalists knew exactly what they wanted: they demanded the War Ministry for Cavaignac.

THE BRISSON GOVERNMENT: CAVAIGNAC
BECOMES WAR MINISTER

Brisson, aged 62, was a perfect example of the radical who was doctrinaire in his anticlericalism: he was also an anti-Dreyfusard, but at the same time he felt anxious about the threat of reaction. He finally agreed to form the new government, with Caviagnac at the War Ministry. Practically all the other portfolios went to radicals. The new government was thus essentially radical in composition and this would now offer greater guarantees to the Left.

In his statement of policy on 30 June, Brisson naturally insisted on the question of clericalism: 'We are determined to defend energetically, against any encroachment, the independence of secular society and the supremacy of the civil power.' But Déroulède, speaking for the nationalists, announced that they would support the new Cabinet 'because Cavaignac was at the War Ministry, and this would ensure that the honour of the army and the country would be safeguarded'. The parliamentarians were highly scandalized: the price Brisson had had to pay had been paraded in public. However, Brisson won his vote of confidence by 314 votes to 251. The new majority was already nominally one of the Left, but it still had to call on the nationalists for support. Cavaignac was now in a position to carry out his project of making public the details of the Dreyfus case.

Who was this model of probity who had been imposed on Brisson by the nationalists, and who was to take charge of the Dreyfus case for the next two months? 'He had the long lean head of a greyhound, a touch of whisker, and sad staring eyes.' Reinach thought he was the image of his father (*see* above, p. 95), but

> a poor copy, dried-up and blurred, a man who had never been young, clean-shaven, with physical as well as mental blinkers and a hard look, bereft of passion, that summed him up entirely. He was a very well-educated moron, who took himself completely at his own valuation and was self-absorbed to the point of hallucination. For some years, his state of mind had been almost pathological. His mind had gradually become imbued with a fixation to the effect that occult forces had set out to dishonour the Republic in exchange for money, and that whoever got in his way was corrupt.

He had, said Reinach, 'boundless confidence in himself'. He now thought he could settle the Dreyfus Affair single-handed. He said as much to those around him when he entered the War Ministry. He would get rid of Esterhazy and exhibit the evidence of Dreyfus's guilt to the country. He was already a popular man; now he would triumph. The presidency of the Republic seemed within his grasp.

As soon as he arrived at the rue Saint-Dominique, he spent a week studying the Dreyfus file for himself. He was spoilt for choice: his predecessor Billot had arranged for everything to be filed in order, under Gonse's direction and with the help of Henry. The file now contained no less than 365 items! He saw with his own eyes that the handwriting of the *bordereau* was closer to that of Esterhazy than that of Dreyfus, but he simply deduced from this that the two were accomplices. Unfortunately, his determination to come to his own conclusions by personally examining the Dreyfus file was not enough for him. He continued to be credulous or partial, or both. He continued to believe the assurances of the General Staff about the Henry forgery. Brisson counselled caution, but Cavaignac invited him to the Ministry, together with the Justice Minister, and showed him about 60 documents, including the Henry forgery. Brisson asked if it would not be better to imitate Méline. But Cavaignac, his conscience eased, and feeling fortified by the results of his personal investigation, remained obstinate. At last, he would remove France's running sore.

His speech in Parliament on 7 July was a new turning-point in the Affair, representing a complete change in government policy. The new line was designed to appeal to the radicals. Replying to Castelin's call for an emergency debate, which insisted that the government should put a stop to the Dreyfusard campaign, he abandoned Méline's exclusive reliance on the *res judicata*. 'Gentlemen, we must do all in our power to enlighten men of good faith; we must bring them as much truth as we are able . . . I believe that the national sentiment has been so aroused that France would accept it if we ensured respect for the army by repressive means. But this is not the kind of respect we demand for the army.' The army had no need to shelter behind reasons of public safety.

Without naming Esterhazy, he declared: 'There has been an attempt to put another officer in Dreyfus's place: this man will shortly be subject to the disciplinary penalties he had deserved.' In this way, the bad soldier Esterhazy was 'disposed of'. But to Cavaignac's mind, as we have seen, the two were accomplices. Then, having affirmed his absolute certainty of Dreyfus's guilt, he read three documents aloud from the rostrum: one included the words 'D. has brought me a lot of interesting things', the two others were the 'scoundrel D.' document and the Henry forgery. Of the latter, he declared:

I have weighed the authenticity of this document both materially and psychologically.

Materially, its authenticity derives for me not only from the entire concourse of circumstances of which I have been speaking a moment ago, but also from its striking similarity to another document of no importance written by the same person, a document written in the same way in blue pencil on the same rather special paper which that person used for his usual correspondence, and which, being dated 1894, has not since that time left the War Ministry archives.

Psychologically speaking, its authenticity indubitably derives from the fact that it forms part of an exchange of letters which took place in 1896. The first letter is the one I have just read to you. The reply contains a few words designed to reassure the writer of the first letter. A third letter, finally, which clears away many obscurities, indicates absolutely precisely, so precisely that I must not read a single word of it, the very reason these correspondents were so anxious.

Therefore Dreyfus's guilt is established not only by the judgment which convicted him; it is further established by a document dating from two years later, which finds its natural place in a long correspondence whose authenticity cannot be doubted; it is irrefutably established by this document.

Cavaignac also asserted that Lebrun-Renault had testified to the fact of Dreyfus's confession. His speech was acclaimed, the Chamber – socialists included – voted for its placarding in every commune in France. But whilst still claiming to base himself on the judgment of 1894, he had implicitly abandoned the *bordereau*, and he was now relying on documents from a later date. It was this which was to make him vulnerable.

The new policy constituted a bold attempt to formulate an anti-Dreyfusism of the *Left*. Cavaignac's insistence on publicizing his evidence, and his rejection of *raison d'Etat* and repressive measures, had assured him of the enthusiastic support of the Left. At the same time, his assertion that he was certain of Dreyfus's guilt meant he also won the support of the nationalists. He became a momentary hero. Most of the newspapers shared the parliamentarians' enthusiasm for the man who had laid the irritating Dreyfus Affair to rest. Millerand wrote in *La Lanterne* that he had 'eased the public conscience'.

Only the revisionists were not convinced; but they still only represented one person in a hundred across the country. It was for them, like the moment after the Esterhazy trial, a time of despondency, an 'atrocious time', according to Léon Blum. 'The cause which had been won seemed lost once more.'

What was the use of witnesses' assurances, presumptive evidence or inductions, as compared with direct proof? Besides, Cavaignac still enjoyed an unassailable reputation for honesty; his Republicanism was above suspicion: and he could not be suspected of complicity with the Right. 'The antisemites, and Boulangists' campaign,' said Blum, 'had received an official endorsement. Drumont could breathe again: Cavaignac's evidence was decisive. Rochefort acclaimed him as the new Boulanger.'

FORGERIES

However, Jaurès saw at once – like Picquart – that Cavaignac's documents were forgeries. Coming upon Blum, Lucien Herr and Mathieu Dreyfus looking as if they had just been at a funeral, he exclaimed: 'But don't you see that now, for the first time, we can be certain of victory. Méline was impregnable, because he refused to say anything. Cavaignac has come into the open, and now he is lost.' Cavaignac's documents 'smell of forgery, they stink of forgery. I was certain of it simply from listening to him, and now I shall prove it. The forgers have come out of their den; we have them by the throat.'

Jaurès was right. The Affair was not over. The Dreyfusards bounced back. They produced fresh arguments. After all, Cavaignac had conceded that the Affair must be dealt with by means of justice and not by *raison d'Etat*, and that France must decide in full knowledge of the facts. By his speech, said Clemenceau, he had made a review inevitable, since the documents he had read out had never been shown to the defence.

Jaurès went still further. In an open letter to Cavaignac in the *Petite République*, he declared, as he had done to Blum, Herr and Mathieu Dreyfus:

> Yesterday in the Chamber you did a useful piece of work, but it was a criminal one . . . you did not say, you dared not say, that secret documents had been shown to the judges and not to the defence. Better still, by quoting yourself from the documents which you say form the basis of your conviction, and which do not appear in the indictment, you admit, you actually proclaim, the monstrous iniquity involved in the military proceedings.

He demolished the story of Dreyfus's alleged confession; and he denounced the Henry forgery as 'the crudest, the most blatant forgery, which appeared just at the right moment to save Esterhazy'. He affirmed that Esterhazy alone was the traitor, and he offered to produce the evidence to the socialist groups.

Jaurès was hoping at last to carry the socialists and the working class with him into action on behalf of Dreyfus. The Allemanists had been pleading with him to press ahead as vigorously as possible. But Guesde, Vaillant and the moderates refused to follow his lead. The National Council of Guesde's Parti Ouvrier Français published a manifesto on 24 July which once again advised the workers to abstain:

> If the politicos and writers of the bourgeoisie choose to part company over the guilt or innocence of a captain on the General Staff or a major in the artillery; if they choose to tear each other apart over words like Fatherland, law, justice or any others – words which are meaningless while capitalist society still goes on – that is entirely up to them. The proletarians have nothing to do with that battle, it is not their battle.

Guesde would not go beyond what he later called the struggle against 'the excesses of militarism'; this was because he was determined to restrict the party to a purely socialist line. He and Vaillant were worried that Jaurès would take over the leadership in the socialist movement, whilst stressing a theme which seemed to them to constitute a deviation in regard to the class struggle. But Jaurès was now quite determined to produce his evidence against Cavaignac, and he immediately set to work.

The revisionists thus thought the time had come to act, for if a review now seemed inevitable to them, they still had to find a way of setting it in train.

Picquart, for his part, denounced the forgeries Cavaignac had produced in a letter to the Prime Minister, published in *Le Siècle* on 9 July. And Demange sent the Justice Minister a request that the order of 1894 should be quashed. Cavaignac retorted by having Picquart and Leblois arrested, on charges of having disclosed documents concerning the national defence. And he still had to rid himself of Ester-hazy. But on this score, Judge Bertulus had stolen a march on him: he was already carrying out a preliminary investigation on forgery charges against Esterhazy, which had be laid by Picquart over the 'Blanche' and 'Speranza' forged telegrams. Bertulus learned from Esterhazy's cousin that one of these telegrams emanated from Mlle Pays, Esterhazy's mistress, and that there had been numerous contacts between him, General Pellieux and the General Staff. He then had both Esterhazy and his mistress arrested on charges of forgery and use of forged documents. Cavaignac's great plans were already beginning to crumble.

On 18 July, Zola was summonsed to appear before the assizes at Versailles for a second trial. Maître Mornard, who was a barrister at the Cour de cassation, had succeeded in having the February order against him quashed on 2 April. The judges of 1894 having lodged a complaint, the government had decided that the second Zola trial should be held at Versailles, so as to limit the risks to public order. Labori had pleaded incompetency, since Zola lived in Paris. But the government had kept to its decision to locate the trial at Versailles.

When, at the hearing which took place on 18 July, it became evident that Zola could not rehearse again all the arguments he had produced in *J'Accuse . . .!*, he hurriedly left the courtroom to boos from the crowd. Against his own wishes, he was persuaded by his friends to leave for England. There was in any case no need now for a new version of the February trial. A review was being brought closer by other means.

4   HENRY'S SUICIDE AND THE REVIEW OF THE CASE*

LES PREUVES

On 10 August, Jaurès began the publication of his pamphlet *Les Preuves (The Evidence)* in the *Petite République*. Now, at last, he abandoned his hesitations and proclaimed that Dreyfus was innocent.

With *Les Preuves*, the *Petite République* became totally committed to Dreyfusism. Its circulation was to rise to 100,000. According to Blum, *Les Preuves* stood in the same relationship to Cavaignac's speech as *J'Accuse . . .!* and the Zola trial had done to the acquittal of Esterhazy. The upheaval in public opinion produced by *J'Accuse . . .!* 'was repeated over again, for the shock waves continued, and their effects went on for weeks'.

Jaurès first explained that Cavaignac had admitted, by quoting the *Eclair* article, that the 'scoundrel D.' document had not been shown to the defence in 1894. This was already an admission of the 1894 illegality. As to the other two documents, if they had not been shown to the judges, why did they now possess a value they had not had in 1894? And if they had been shown to the judges, and the bill of indictment only mentioned the *bordereau*, it could also only have been illegally. 'The illegality is thus proven,' concluded Jaurès. And, addressing the socialists who had refused to follow his lead, he declared that there were, side by side with the capitalist laws the socialists fought against, 'others which sum up the meagre progress of humanity, the modest safeguards which have been won through the efforts of many centuries and the long series of revolutions. Now among these laws perhaps the most essential is that which does not allow a man to be convicted without any discussion taking place with him.' Once Dreyfus was convicted, he was no longer an officer and

---

* The Cour de cassation, where the case was reviewed, is not strictly an Appeal Court in the English sense. It is concerned with the legality of court decisions, and has the power, on points of law, to quash a trial judgement and free the prisoner, or order a retrial.

116

a bourgeois; and so socialists, without going against their principles, or abandoning the class struggle, could heed the voice of their pity. For who, he asked, if not the proletariat, 'was most threatened by the arbitrary power of the generals, and by the constantly glorified violence of acts of military repression? . . . Therefore, to protest as we do against the illegality – now demonstrated – of the Dreyfus trial is not only to serve humanity, it is also to serve the working class.'[1]

And, while Jaurès was accumulating the evidence that Dreyfus was innocent, a *coup de théâtre* was approaching. On 13 August, Captain Cuignet, who had been instructed by Cavaignac to examine all the documents in the secret file, discovered, by the light of his lamp, when he examined the letter from Schwartzkoppen to Panizzardi – the Henry forgery, which had been Cavaignac's crushing document against Dreyfus – that the cross-ruling on the upper part of the letter and the lower part bearing the signature, and that in the body of the letter, were in two different colours. This showed that Henry had fabricated the letter, using pieces from two different letters. Thus the letter Henry had produced, and whose contents had been placarded in every commune in France, was a forgery.

Cuignet revealed his discovery to General Roget, then to Cavaignac. The latter now realized that his entire demonstration of 7 July had been based on a forgery. But he was not going to act in the same way as Gonse. France would learn the whole truth. He remained, though, more convinced than ever that Dreyfus was guilty.

He continued to act alone. Already, at a dinner-party on 11 August, he had put a wild plan to the government: it was to haul all the Dreyfusards up before the Senate, constituted as a High Court, on the accusation that they had endangered the security of the state. Brisson, who was stunned at the idea, refused such a procedure. By this time, as Reinach noted, the Senate was in any case favourable to a review.

CAVAIGNAC AND HENRY

Cavaignac now prepared to confront Henry. But the latter was away on leave. His suspicions must not be aroused by a sudden order to report. In the meantime, Cavaignac continued to deal with the question of Esterhazy. The latter had been freed after the preliminary hearing on the affair of the forged telegrams. The court decided that the expert report on the 'Speranza' telegram was not significant

---

1 See Jean Jaurès, *Les Preuves. Affaire Dreyfus* (Paris, 1981).

enough to warrant a charge. Cavaignac could therefore now bring Esterhazy up before a court of inquiry. As usual, Esterhazy became threatening again, but Cavaignac finally 'disposed of' him by having him cashiered.

And at last, on 30 August, he was able to question Henry. Two days earlier, Jaurès, in his *Les Preuves*, and Trarieux, in an open letter, had yet again denounced his forgery; Jaurès even went so far as to say he would reveal the forger's name on 1 September! 'Never,' said Reinach, 'had he come so close to the truth.' Indeed, Jaurès was to claim later that it was he who had triggered off Henry's confession.

Cavaignac still insisted on taking all the responsibility on himself. He carried out the interrogation of Henry in person, in the presence of Boisdeffre, Gonse and Roget. He first ordered the officer to say what he knew about the two documents which made up the letter from Panizzardi to Schwartzkoppen: 'There are pieces of the one inserted into the other.'

The huge, peasant-like figure, knowing nothing of the evidence of his crime which was now in Cavaignac's hands, began, boldly as usual, with a lie. 'I did not fabricate the documents.' But when pressed, he eventually admitted he had 'taken some pieces from the first document and put them into the second'.

CAVAIGNAC: You fabricated the entire document.

HENRY: I swear I did not.

CAVAIGNAC: What gave you the idea of doing what you did?

HENRY: I thought my chiefs were very worried, I wanted to reassure them. I wanted to bring back their peace of mind. Everything was being badly affected by all this. I said to myself: 'Let me add a sentence to calm everyone down. What if war were to break out in the situation we are in! But if I do that, calm will return.'

CAVAIGNAC: Did you do this on your own?

HENRY: Yes.

The interrogation seemed to be over and it seemed as if Henry could withdraw. But Cavaignac revealed his evidence: 'Come on! One of the documents is cross-ruled in pale violet, the other in blue-grey, which already shows that some pieces have been inserted: now your explanation is not possible, because the beginning is complete in itself; and the inserts do not correspond with what you are saying.'

Cavaignac pressed Henry further: 'Do you refuse to tell the truth?'

Henry lost his composure, and mumbled some fresh explanations which did not fit the facts. He protested: 'I was acting for the good of the country.'

118

CAVAIGNAC: But that is not what I am asking you about. What you did can be read from the documents themselves.

Then came the *coup de grâce:* 'This is what happened: in 1896, you received an envelope with a letter inside, an insignificant letter; you then suppressed the real letter and fabricated the other one.'

HENRY: Yes.

This was the decisive confession.

Boisdeffre, Gonse and Roget had not uttered a single word during the interrogation, which had gone on for an hour. Boisdeffre wrote out his resignation on the spot; he had been led astray by his confidence in Colonel Henry. He said so to Cavaignac: anyone could be misled, but not everyone had had, like him, the misfortune to tell a jury he was ready to resign if his word was questioned. 'When you have found yourself in that situation, there is nothing for it but to go.'

Cavaignac did not immediately have Henry arrested. Instead, he had him put in confinement at Mont-Valérien barracks. During the journey, Henry talked to himself in front of his escort Colonel Féry. 'It's unbelievable. What are they after? I shall go mad. Whatever I have done, I am ready to do again; it was for the good of the country and the army. I have never harmed anyone; I have always done my duty. What a misfortune to have run into such scoundrels along the way; it is they who are to blame for my misfortune. My poor wife, my poor little boy! Everything is falling apart in one moment. I shall miss the start of the hunting season. They are all expecting us down there. What will people think?'

At the same moment, Cavaignac was recounting Henry's confession to Brisson. He was aghast. That evening, the government ministers were dining with Delcassé, the Foreign Minister: 'Come on!' said Vallé, 'this means a review!' 'Never!' Cavaignac retorted. The news was sent round the world by telegraph. There was a shudder. Soon there would be drama.

HENRY'S SUICIDE

The next morning, 31 August, Henry asked for some writing paper. He sent a final appeal to Gonse. 'I have the honour to request you to be good enough to come and see me here. It is imperative that I speak to you.' He then wrote to his wife: 'My adored Berthe, I see that everyone has forsaken me but you, and yet *you know in whose interests I acted.* My letter is a copy and there is nothing, absolutely nothing forged in it. It only confirms the verbal information I received

119

several days before. I am absolutely innocent, they know it and every-one will know it later on, *but at the moment I can say nothing.*'

This letter, with its mysterious reference to the person in whose interests Henry claimed to have acted, has never been elucidated by historians. No doubt he believed he was acting in the interests of his superiors on the General Staff.

Soon he gave way to despair. The heat was intense. He emptied half a bottle of rum and his mind became confused. He scribbled another note to his wife: 'My beloved Berthe, I feel as if I am going mad, there is an appalling pain all around my brain, I am going to swim in the Seine . . .' The note remained unfinished. About three in the afternoon, Henry lay down on his bed and slit his own throat with a razor which had been left in his room. At six, an orderly found his corpse already cold, and the room drenched with blood.

The next day, 1 September, at the news of his suicide, public opinion swung round in a few hours. The revisionist press went from 2 per cent to 40 per cent. Republican papers that had not yet made their minds up came out for a review: even the main Catholic and nationalist papers accepted it. For Cassagnac, a review was 'the sole, the unavoidable solution . . . Without a review, there can be no way out of the Affair.' *L'Echo de Paris* wrote: 'Everything has changed. The review is a must. It is desired by a great many officers – we know this – and not ones of modest rank either.'

Indeed, even Pellieux, who had brought up the Henry forgery at the Zola trial, now wanted a review, and said so to the press. As soon as he heard that Henry had confessed, he wrote a furious letter to Cavaignac, which began: 'Having been duped by people without honour . . .' He repeated these words to a monarchist journalist. And he offered to resign. As Reinach said, 'if such a popular officer was so eager to make it known he wished for justice, then the whole army would accept it'. One of the judges of 1894, Gallet, said openly that there must be a review.

A number of deputies, including the socialists Viviani and Miller-and, and the radical Pelletan, changed sides. Several departmental councils were still in session; none issued a statement of their wishes hostile to a review. 'One can see from this what a turn-around there has been, in the provinces just as in Paris,' remarked the *Courrier du Soir* (cf. above, p. 102).

Drumont and Rochefort were caught unawares: the *Libre Parole* could only stammer that 'whether they review the case, or otherwise, it will not worry us, seeing the point we have now reached'. Rochefort went so far as to say that Henry's crime was 'odious and stupid'.

Esterhazy took to flight. He left Paris on foot with no luggage, jumped on the first train from Saint-Denis, arrived in Maubeuge, where he had his moustache cut off, and then travelled via Brussels to London.

For the Dreyfusards, Blum wrote, 'The Affair was over . . . The spell was now broken, because the truth had been established. People could still fight against Dreyfus and the Dreyfusards. But they could not escape the fact that logically and historically, Dreyfus's innocence had been established.'

For two days more, Brisson remained inactive. Cavaignac stuck to his guns, announcing to all and sundry that Henry's suicide and confession had in no way altered his opinion on Dreyfus.

'The mass of army officers,' wrote Reinach, 'though they had been disconcerted and stunned for a moment, now regained their assurance. Pellieux rejected the review he had asked for on the 1st of the month and withdrew his resignation.'

Finally, on the third day, Brisson made his mind up to act. He had a telegram sent to Mathieu Dreyfus expressing surprise that he had not heard from Lucie. Demange put in the application for a review the same evening.

The same day, Bourgeois, returning from a visit to Switzerland, tried to reason with Cavaignac. The latter refused to budge. 'I, on my own, was able to prove that the document was a forgery.' He went back to his plan to arraign all the Dreyfusards before the High Court. Bourgeois looked at him in amazement as though he were a madman.

Cavaignac finally said to him that he would not stay a day longer and that he would take his resignation to Brisson.

Blinkered to the end, Cavaignac, instead of disposing of the Affair singlehanded, had, in two months, achieved exactly the opposite: the author of his crushing document had been revealed as a forger and had committed suicide, Esterhazy was on the run, he himself had had to resign, and the need for a review was now widely accepted by the French public.

But, even at the very moment of his resignation, the anti-Dreyfusard extremists were in process of making a recovery. On 3 September, Judet, in *Le Petit Journal*, came up with the idea that, to avoid a war, Henry had put, 'as it were, banknotes' into circulation, 'whose value was based, in his eyes, on documents that were authentic'. What were these authentic documents? They were letters from the German Emperor, and the *bordereau* annotated by him, the same

121

documents that the extremist anti-Dreyfusards produced, as we have seen, at all the critical moments.

Once again, wrote Reinach, came a time of fear: 'A review meant war,' and 'war with the army in a state of disorganization meant a *débâcle*. This was the rumour that spread among all the poor folk,' he said, 'stifling the cry of their consciences, particularly among the women in the working-class suburbs and in the country, where in 1902, three years later, it could still arouse fear ... If Henry had fabricated an apocryphal document, it was, on his own admission, to avoid producing others whose disclosure would have meant compromising state security.'

DEFENDING A PATRIOTIC FORGERY

The idea of the Henry forgery as a patriotic forgery, as a mere 'public reproduction, the popular edition as it were of an absolute truth', was taken up on 6 and 7 September by Charles Maurras in two sensational articles in the royalist *Gazette de France*.

The young Maurras was beginning at 30 to enjoy a certain reputation as a critic and essayist. He had begun his career by denouncing Romanticism as a form of foreign barbarism being imposed on France, and in the 1890s he had been campaigning for a return to Classicism. While serving as a foreign correspondent in Athens in 1896 to cover the Olympic Games, he became aware of France's poor international standing, and he began to think that national recovery could only be brought about by a return to monarchy. He came out as a royalist in 1897. Now, in his articles on Henry, he laid the foundations of his theory of integral nationalism.

He began with praise for Henry: 'You had strength, decisiveness, finesse, you were lacking in nothing, except a little good fortune on your dying day.' The forger became transformed into a bold hero, characterized by his famous 'Here goes!' 'Your unfortunate "forgery" will count amongst your greatest military feats, the only thing that was deplorable about it, its lack of success, having been paid for, and more than paid for, by your blood.' Of this first blood spilt during the Dreyfus Affair, 'there is not a single drop which is not still fuming wherever the heart of the nation beats. This blood will fume and cry out until the spilling of it has been expiated.'

Also, for Maurras, Henry had taken the national idea to heart, he had been motivated by *raison d'Etat*, by 'special, unwritten laws', a sphere of morality 'both higher, more rigorous and more extensive, for those human consciences which have very general obligations'. So

Maurras justified the patriotic forgery as the enterprise of a soldier, invested with every virtue, who had subscribed to the national idea which was now in the process of being revived. And by his eulogy of *raison d'Etat*, Maurras heralded the new nationalism of the extreme Right; for this nationalism, the very touchstone would be the national interest. He had in this way taken the first steps which were to lead to the creation of the Action Française: his supporters came to feel that the movement had its origins in these two articles. For the extremist anti-Dreyfusards, if Dreyfus's guilt could no longer be justified by the facts, the appeal would have to be to *raison d'Etat* and the national interest. Their view amounted to this, said Péguy in *Notre jeunesse*: 'Whether he is innocent or guilty, one must not ... *compromise*, one must not, for one man, for one single man, risk the life and the safety of a people'.

As a result, extremist anti-Dreyfusism found itself, from the autumn of 1898, unequivocally on the far Right. This naturally explains why Cavaignac went over to the other side of the political spectrum. His left-wing anti-Dreyfusism having failed, he had no alternative but to join the nationalists. And as he had never understood that the facts were against him, he had perforce to join the ranks of those whose slogan was: 'Against the evidence'.

Politically speaking, the anti-Dreyfusard extreme Right would henceforward embrace several trends: the royalists and the Bonapartists, and, now added to them, the nationalists from the old Boulangist camp, and the antisemites.

THE PLOTTING BEGINS

The old Right had already begun plotting against the regime in its salons. But its leaders were divided over what regime should replace the Republic. On the royalist side, the pretender was the duc d'Orléans. He had already intervened once in the Dreyfus Affair, by putting out a manifesto against the enemies of the army on the day Esterhazy's letters to Madame de Boulancy were published. He later joined up with the militarist and antisemitic movement. 'It was antisemitism which most appealed to him,' said Reinach. 'He saw in it the popular force which, once domesticated by him, would raise him to the throne. The young men of rank – who were not all from the old nobility or of genuine noble extraction – together with the few members of the bourgeoisie who made up his political bureau, confirmed him in his opinion.'

The antisemite, Guérin, with his supporters in the Antisemitic

League, now entered his pay. The duke promised him 15,000 to 25,000 francs a month, to be paid in secret. Guérin 'could not contain his joy at passing from Drumont's service to that of the House of France'.

Déroulède, on the other hand, setting himself up as a pretender to plebiscitary power, insisted that he was a Republican. He did not want to rescue 'their prey' – France – from the parliamentarians only for it to become the 'inheritance of princes'. He openly proposed to set up the 'people's Republic', via an army coup. At the end of September 1898, he revived the Ligue des Patriotes and began a series of meetings in Paris at which he fulminated against the Dreyfusards. If Dreyfus were to return to France, he said, he would be lynched.

But the military leaders were not really in the frame of mind to consider a coup. 'The generals held forth,' said Reinach. 'They received emissaries, listened obligingly to them. They assured them their swords were quivering and could hardly wait to be unsheathed. But they remained in the scabbard'. The junior officers 'made up for their moment of weakness at the time of the Henry suicide by a provocative attitude. But here again, their contempt for the Republic trailed away in chatter.' As Raoul Girardet has explained,

> the national army had no doubt inherited sturdy anti-democratic preju-
> dices from the pre-revolutionary army. But it had also taken over the
> quasi-mystical cult of discipline, the imperative of total obedience,
> the principle of submission to the duly established government and to the
> legal authorities. The officer from a conservative background may have
> no love for the regime, he may, at times, refuse to have anything to do
> with it, he may publicly lampoon its institutions and its personnel. But
> it would nonetheless be a fundamental breach of the basic duties of his
> office to conspire against it and work effectively to destroy it.

These amateur plotters of the far Right, weakened by their divisions – royalists against supporters of a plebiscitary system – were not, in the coming months, to be able to find a general ready to topple the Republic.

LEFT-WING ANTICLERICALISM

On the Left, the process of laying the foundations for a defensive coalition went on. Anticlericalism and antinationalism were to be its cement. This coalition represented the form the Dreyfusard camp would finally take on, when it had become completely politicized.

During the summer, an incident had fuelled anticlerical polemics among the Dreyfusards. On 18 July, Father Didon, a Dominican, had pronounced a eulogy of force at a school prize-giving in the presence of the head of the French armed forces, General Jamont. 'Force is a good thing in itself,' he said. 'When persuasion has failed, one must brandish the sword, inspire terror, use severe measures, and strike at the opponent.' Clemenceau and Jaurès had protested that this was a call for a *coup d'Etat*, and Pelletan had denounced the 'holy alliance of the army and the church'. These two paragraphs from Father Didon, wrote Capéran, became part and parcel of the arsenal of anticlerical arguments, as a confirmation of the alliance between clericalism and the military.

After Father Didon's speech, the anticlerical atmosphere became so intense that the radicals became uneasy at the lack of serious measures being taken against militarism and the clerical danger. The Freemasons, at their September assembly, denounced the conspiracy between the clericals and the Caesarists, based on their shared hatred for the 1789 Revolution, for democracy and the Republic.

All through the winter, the anticlerical theme grew more prominent on the Left: Ranc was its chief architect. In November, Yves Guyot launched the idea that the Dreyfus Affair was the work of the Jesuits.

As part of the process of political clarification which was going on, the Left finally broke its last links with nationalism and antisemitism. On 21 December, following the socialists' lead, the radical-socialist group in the Chamber excluded those deputies 'who, pleading nationalism or antisemitism, are pursuing a policy opposed to Republican principles'.

The socialists themselves were now preparing at last to follow Jaurès and join the new pro-Dreyfus coalition. The Guesdists, though they were still unwilling to commit themselves over the fate of Dreyfus as an individual, again denounced nationalism and antisemitism at their Montluçon congress on 17–20 September.

ZURLINDEN AND CHANOINE

Meanwhile, the new War Minister, Zurlinden, who had replaced Cavaignac, had been studying the Dreyfus file: he had insisted, as a condition of taking office, that he would make his mind up for himself. In fact, he was soon convinced by Roget and Cavaignac that Picquart had been guilty of forgery: he was supposed to have 'scratched out' Dreyfus's name on the *petit bleu* and substituted that of Esterhazy. Zurlinden came down against a review at the Cabinet meeting of 12 September: however, no decision was taken. But on 17

September it decided by a large majority, against his opinion, to pass Lucie Dreyfus's application to the review consultative committee. Zurlinden then resigned and was immediately replaced by General Chanoine. Brisson explained to the new Minister that the review was a *fait accompli* and that he could not oppose it.

Nonetheless, Chanoine did all he could to hold it up. Under Brisson's nose, he handed Picquart over to the military authorities. Brisson, now determined at last, after all his hesitations, to bring about a review, had high hopes that Picquart, the main witness favourable to Dreyfus, would be set free by the magistrate's court where he was due to appear on 21 September. But Zurlinden, who had been appointed military governor of Paris after his resignation, opened military proceedings against him, and signed the order to prosecute without informing Brisson; the moment Picquart was freed, he was put in the hands of military justice and charged with forgery. He was detained in the Cherche-Midi prison. In this way, through Chanoine's action, Picquart would be unable to testify on behalf of Dreyfus. But yet again, Brisson did not react.

At the same moment, the consultative committee on the review met. After three days of debate, it divided down the middle, by three votes for a review and three against. In the absence of a majority, the committee was bound to advise against a review.

Basing himself on this, the Justice Minister Sarrien opposed a review in Cabinet: but Brisson declared the committee only an advisory body. On 26 September, by six votes to four, the Cabinet voted to refer the application for a review to the Cour de cassation.

This was a first victory for the revisionists. For the first time, the Dreyfus case would come before a civil court.

THE COUR DE CASSATION ENQUIRY

The Criminal Division of the Cour de cassation immediately began its enquiry.

The revisionists now hoped that justice would take its course. The revisionist camp, said Reinach, now represented an

> impressive minority: almost all the socialists, who were now very keen, the usual radical clientele of Brisson and Bourgeois, the Assembly and the world of the Freemasons, and the elite of liberal Republicans; they were supplemented by former royalists and Catholics who had woken up to the truth and would have been ashamed to return to their slumbers.

The public prosecutor, Manau, requested the handing over of the secret file: Chanoine refused. Once again, Brisson let this pass. The antirevisionist press then began a campaign of threats against the judges who had 'sold out to Germany'. Rochefort went so far as to describe the fate he wished on the judges:

> A torturer would cut through the eyelids of the members of the Cour de cassation, their eyeballs would be eaten up by the most venomous species of spiders, and these hideous blind figures would be led to a pillory where a sign would be hung across their chest with the words: 'This is how France punishes traitors who attempt to betray her to the enemy'.

FASHODA AND THE BUILDING LABOURERS' STRIKE

The climate in Paris now worsened as a result of two problems unconnected with the Affair, the Fashoda crisis and the building labourers' strike. Hanotaux and Delcassé had conceived the idea of cutting off Britain's route from the Cape to Cairo. Captain Marchand, after crossing Africa, had raised the French flag at Fashoda on the Nile on 10 July. But France met with complete intransigence from Britain; there could be no question of any concession over the Nile, which was regarded as a zone of influence which must remain sacrosanct. The acute phase of the crisis lasted from 17 September to 12 October. In England, at Portsmouth and elsewhere, preparations for a naval war were made on such a scale that France, without adequate means of response, had to climb down.

The result was humiliation. Henceforward, the wrath of the nationalists was redirected from Germany towards England. The anti-Dreyfusards and nationalists rediscovered France's traditional enemy, perfidious Albion, and began to propose a rapprochement with Germany! Even the moderate Republican press started to favour such a move. On the other hand, the Dreyfusards, Clemenceau and the socialists continued to favour an alliance with England.

The other problem, concerning the builders' labourers, began on 13 September. Several hundred of them, who were working on the site of the 1900 International Exhibition, went on strike demanding an extra 10 centimes an hour. Strike action began again among the workers, and spread to the railways.

Brisson then sent troops into the railway stations, and Paris found itself surrounded by 60,000 men. This lent credence to the belief that a military coup was imminent. Millerand and Clemenceau went to see him to ask whether these troop movements did not signify that a general was planning a coup. Brisson said he had the situation completely under control.

However, the press talked of nothing but a coup for a whole week. Vaughan, the editor of *L'Aurore*, was informed by a telegraph employee of a telegram which had been dispatched to Zurlinden: 'We are still agreed that it will be Saturday.' On 14 October, by an 'identical note', the newspapers announced to the conspirators that the government had been warned. As we have seen, no general was in fact prepared to make a move. Ranc, Jaurès, Millerand and Mathieu Dreyfus remained sceptical. There was no coup.

But the supposed threats to the Republic hastened the process whereby the Left was coming round to support a policy of Republican defence. By 15 October, the delegates from the various socialist organizations had met at the salle Vantier. They declared that 'in the troubled circumstances the Republic is experiencing, all the socialist and revolutionary forces are united, they are determined, and they are ready to face all eventualities'.

For the moment, all the socialists were reconciled. They set up a standing vigilance committee. This committee decided to hold meetings every night. However, not wishing to seem like agitators, they decided not to respond by force to the big demonstration Déroulède had announced for 25 October, the day Parliament reconvened. But they did decide to call the people out to the Place de la Concorde if the nationalists put in an appearance.

In a parallel move, the revolutionaries launched a manifesto which clearly showed their determination to halt reaction in the street: 'A military coup is on the way', said the manifesto:

> They are few in numbers, but they are bold and ready for anything; they have combined all the reactionary parties into one: clericals, royalists, Caesarists, antisemites, *nationalists*.
> ### FREE MEN!
> If you let them pass, if you let them have their way, soon the nationalist party will throttle Freedom ... All group and party rivalries must disappear ... Let us join forces for action. The hour of decision has come ... Let us be ready. Let us fight the reactionary gangs, who would destroy liberty, and let us gain control of the street, the street which is the home of demands, of barricades and of revolutions.

In the event, when Parliament reassembled, Déroulède's men made no move, and neither did the socialists or the libertarians. When the parliamentarians arrived, they found the Place de la Concorde surrounded by barricades, and the Tuileries gardens occupied by cavalry regiments. Guérin's gangs confined themselves to molesting some Jews.

The parliamentarians felt reassured, but the day was to be far from peaceful, and the Brisson government was to fall, having become a victim of its own contradictions. Eighteen questions had been put down for debate. The radicals, despite their reservations about a review, were still ready to support a radical Cabinet. On the other hand, Barthou proposed to the Centre Republican group, at their meeting, that they should vote against the government, as it no longer enjoyed their confidence. Having supported Cavaignac with the help of the nationalists, it had now made a volte-face and was in favour of a review – it was seeking the support of the Chamber *against* the nationalists.

In the debate, Brisson was only able to claim, in his own defence, that he had 'taken the Affair out of politics'. In fact, as we have seen, after deciding on a review, he had left its opponents, Chanoine and Zurlinden, with a free hand.

Déroulède rose and went violently onto the attack. Brisson's government was one of 'encroachments, of violent strokes of policy and of arbitrary power ... the time has come to speak out with courage', he declared, 'and to rid the country of this extraordinary oppression, even if, no matter what our respect for the army, we are obliged – and this will be my last point – to bespatter General Chanoine with our votes'.

This was an invitation to bring down the government. Chanoine rose at once, and he was in such haste to dissociate himself from the rest of the government that, against all the normal rules, he announced his resignation from the rostrum. He said he held the same view of the Affair as his predecessors. There was thunderous applause from the Right. But he then had to flee the Chamber.

Outside, at the same moment, Guérin was continuing to make a disturbance, but there was no coup, and he and his 500 demonstrators were arrested. Brisson, with dignity, asked the Chamber to support him in his determination to ensure the preponderance of the civil power. During a suspension of the debate, the Republican groups drafted a resolution to this effect which demanded a two-day adjournment. If the motion had been put to the vote without debate, it would have been carried. But a confused debate ensued, Brisson ceased to defend himself, and his government was brought down by 286 votes to 254. The Chamber was adjourned till 4 November.

THE REVIEW

Four days later, while France was still without a government, the Criminal Division of the Cour de cassation, by ten votes to four, pronounced the review application on the Dreyfus case admissible, and declared it would proceed to a further enquiry. The court refused, however, to suspend Dreyfus's sentence.

The revisionists cried victory, but another impediment to justice now appeared on the horizon. When the new Prime Minister Dupuy came before the Chamber on 4 November, a motion was put down to remove the case from the Criminal Division and refer it to all three divisions combined: the other divisions were thought to be hostile to a review. Dupuy declared that justice would be respected. For the time being, it took its course, but only half-heartedly supported by the new government.

The Criminal Division heard the testimony of the five War Ministers: Mercier, Billot, Cavaignac, Zurlinden and Chanoine. Mercier was the only one to defend himself. A new piece of evidence against Esterhazy emerged, a letter written by him on the same paper as that of the *bordereau*.

THE PROSECUTION OF PICQUART

The military enquiry continued on the case of Picquart, charged with forging the *petit bleu*. The officers on the General Staff testified against him to Tavernier, who was in charge of the preliminary investigation. The latter misrepresented the handwriting reports on the *petit bleu*, which had said that the name of Esterhazy had been scratched out and written in again, but that the name was not in Picquart's handwriting: 'We find it hard to accept,' he wrote, 'that the accused had no part in its fabrication.'

Picquart had been kept in solitary confinement, and, in accordance with military law, any contact with his defence counsel, Labori, had been forbidden. But public opinion had been alerted. A majority emerged in Parliament for a measure to make the law on preliminary investigations apply to military courts, which would have resulted in ending the secrecy of the proceedings. The General Staff immediately responded by closing the preliminary investigation, which made any discussions between Picquart and Labori impossible.

The court-martial was due on 12 December. Picquart's supporters began to contend that since he was now a civilian, he was no longer subject to military law: they rallied the public. 'For several days, there

was a surge of opinion against the gate of the Cherche-Midi prison.'
Lists of protesters reappeared in the newspapers: people offered their
support by the thousand.

> The slowest to be roused, the most circumspect, those who had at first
> hesitated to compromise their position but now insisted on suffering for
> the sake of justice, even those who had recently been opponents: all of
> them – whether famous or obscure – signed, side by side with those who
> had fought from the first day. This was the second tally of the army of
> justice . . . Every evening, there were public meetings. In an incandescent
> atmosphere, packed so tight they could hardly breathe, workers and
> members of the bourgeoisie, who were used to this sort of spectacle, but
> also society ladies who found it rather appetizing, applauded sonorous or
> violent speeches expressing what the orators had on their minds.

The greatest favourites were the intellectuals, said Reinach, and 'the
attack was extended to all forms of military tyranny, and to social
iniquity as a whole'.

The agitation against the Picquart trial had also spread to Parliament. Millerand, speaking for the Left, maintained that the military
prosecution of Picquart was *ultra vires*.

This was the moment when Poincaré finally chose to intervene:
'If some of us were to remain silent at the present time, that would
amount to real cowardice.' What was being witnessed, he said, was
a final attempt to prevent the abuses committed by certain offices in
the War Ministry from being fully disclosed. The prosecution of
Picquart, he said, seemed to be a matter of reprisals and of per-
secution.

Regarding the 1894 trial, he declared that his former colleagues
'had never heard any precise charge other than the *bordereau* mentioned against Dreyfus', that they had never had knowledge of any
diplomatic or secret file, and that they had never known of 'a confession by the accused to Lebrun-Renault'. 'I know,' he concluded,
'that by breaking this silence which weighs so heavily upon me, I
shall lay myself open to attack, to insult and to calumny. That does
not matter to me. I am happy to have grasped, at this rostrum, the
opportunity to unburden my conscience.'

Two-thirds of the Chamber applauded. It was a great gust of
truth. But a week went by before the legal problem over Picquart was
resolved. Seeing, however, that he and Leblois both stood accused
before a civil court of disclosing the secret file, there was a risk of
conflicting judgments by the civil court and the court-martial which
was due to try him. He applied for all the charges against him to
be transferred to a civil jurisdiction. On 8 December, the Criminal

Division implicitly ordered a deferment, by instructing the two courts to hand over their files: the court-martial had been due to open on the 12th. For the moment, therefore, Picquart was saved. It was a fresh victory for the revisionists.

THE HENRY APPEAL

While the revisionist movement grew, the anti-Dreyfusards were also counting their strength and organizing. In a series of articles in *Le Siècle*, Joseph Reinach had accused Henry of being Esterhazy's accomplice. *La Libre Parole* thereupon launched an appeal on 14 December, to allow Henry's widow to cover the cost of bringing a court case against him. Drumont draped a banner over the balcony of *La Libre Parole*'s offices with the words: 'For the widow and orphan of Colonel Henry, against the Jew Reinach'.

The success of the appeal was phenomenal: in less than a month, 131,000 francs and 14,000 signatures were collected. The signatures on what came to be called the 'Henry monument' were accompanied by commentaries which reflected all the themes of extremist anti-Dreyfusism: first, of course, antisemitism, a passionate antisemitism full of hatred, which held the Jew responsible for all France's ills, whether collective or individual: 'May God will that our poor unfortunate Fatherland be torn from the grasp of the Jews and the Freemasons.' Or this: 'A small trader ruined by the Jews.' The Jew not being a true Frenchman, he should be excluded, or even exterminated. Among other themes were love of France, her army and her Church, as well as hatred for Protestants, Freemasons, Dreyfusards and intellectuals. The extreme nature of the language used, and the appeals to hatred and calls for assassination (there were 929 against Reinach . . .), bore witness to the violence of extremist anti-Dreyfusism. 'Many Republicans, even the very first among the revisionists, were astounded, they could not believe their eyes,' wrote Reinach, 'when they saw the 18 *red lists*, following one after another. But,' he said, 'no warning could have been more salutory . . . it was clear where the enemy was to be found'.

The subscribers came from the social groups most active in the anti-Dreyfusard camp (*see* above, p. 106): the nobility (7.83 per cent, as against 0.14 per cent in the French population); the Catholic clergy (3.1 per cent as against 0.2 per cent); students and *lycée* pupils (8.6 per cent as against 0.6 per cent); soldiers (28.6 per cent as against 3 per cent); the professions (8. 25 per cent as against 2.6 per cent); and workers and artisans (39.25 per cent as against 20.2 per cent). Only the small traders, from whom Déroulède's troops were drawn, were under-represented (2.1 per cent as against 3 per cent), together with the rural professions and white-collar workers. The antisemitism of the Henry subscription was the antisemitism of large and medium-sized cities in the north and east of France, where there was a popular tradition of antisemitism. The small traders, however, no doubt wished to avoid offending their customers.

And it should again be noted that the priests who subscribed were a small minority among the clergy. So too were the officers – 1,700 out of the 25,000 on the active list at the end of the 19th century.[2]

Even the subscribers from the nobility only represented one family in five among the French peerage. This shows that extremist anti-Dreyfusism represented, certainly, a protest of the discontented classes in French society, but it was only a fraction of these groups that was militant enough to sign the Henry appeal: among the nobles, there were those who simply looked towards other horizons;[3] among priests and army officers, the weight of moderate anti-Dreyfusism based simply on social conformism must have been quite considerable.

THE LIGUE DE LA PATRIE FRANÇAISE

The organizational effort among the anti-Dreyfusards was directed towards the intellectual and university world, with the launching, on 31 December, of the Ligue de la Patrie Française (League of the French Fatherland) by three young academics: Louis Dausset, Gabriel Syveton and Henri Vaugeois. These young men wanted to show that all the intellectuals were not on the side of Dreyfus.

Fortified by the success of their first initiatives, and with the encouragement of Charles Maurras, they approached three major literary figures: François Coppée, Jules Lemaitre and Maurice Barrès, who set about collecting signatures in December. The first manifesto, reproduced in the anti-Dreyfusard press, bore the signatures of 22 Academicians (members of the Académie Française), those of members of the Institut, of the universities, such as Emile Faguet, and of writers and artists: apart from Maurras and Barrès, there were Léon

---

2 Stephen Wilson, *Ideology and Experience. Antisemitism in France at the Time of the Dreyfus Affair* (East Brunswick, NJ/London/Toronto, 1982).
3 'Entre nationalisme et cosmopolitisme: les engagements multiples de la noblesse', in Pierre Birnbaum, ed., *La France de l'affaire Dreyfus* (Paris, 1994), p. 342.

Daudet, the antisemitic female novelist Gyp, Frédéric Mistral, Jules Verne, Degas, Renoir and the caricaturists Caran d'Ache and Forain.

The text, which had deliberately been left somewhat vague, seemed initially to suggest that the object of the Ligue was national reconciliation. The Affair was not mentioned directly, for the new organization was to be placed 'outside and above it'. The text ran as follows:

> The undersigned,
> Being concerned that the present most disastrous agitation is persisting and becoming more serious;
> Being convinced that it could not continue without fatally compromising the vital interests of the French Fatherland, and notably those which are gloriously held in trust by the nation's army;
> Convinced that in so saying they are expressing the opinion of France itself;
> Have resolved:
> To work within the limits of their professional duty to maintain the traditions of the French Fatherland, while reconciling these with the progress of ideas and of social customs;
> To unite and form a group, beyond any sectarian spirit, and to take action to this end by word of mouth, in writing and by their example;
> And to fortify the spirit of solidarity which should unite, through the years, every generation of a great people.

'Many who read it were deceived,' wrote Reinach. Hervé de Kérohant, who had signed the appeal in support of Picquart, sent his signature. It was curtly refused, the organizing committee having decided not to accept the signatures of anyone who had supported the demonstrations in favour of Dreyfus and Picquart. Daniel Halévy signed nonetheless.

The well-informed soon realized from the names of the chief promoters that the Ligue was in fact an anti-Dreyfusard organization. The fact that Cavaignac signed on 5 January should have enlightened them once and for all.

The presence of Henri Vaugeois among those who had launched the Ligue is also worthy of note. He had tried unsuccessfully with Maurice Pujo to launch an Action Française committee for the 1898 elections, 'to support in the electoral struggle all the candidates who were in favour of a truly French Republic'. The expression 'Action Française' had again been used by Pujo in an article in *L'Eclair* on 19 December which called on intellectuals to assist in recreating a Republican France which would be better organized internally and more powerful in foreign relations. Barrès, for his part, was to declare that he would only belong to the Ligue to the extent that it became imbued with the nationalist doctrine. There were thus extremist anti-Dreyfusards among the Ligue's founders.

From the outset in fact, the Ligue's message reflected a contradiction between two aims which were difficult to satisfy at the same time. The first of these was to reconcile Frenchmen of all parties and to bring agitation to an end. This was an enterprise exactly along the lines of what has been characterized above as moderate anti-Dreyfusism. The signatories of the first manifesto were entirely typical of the intellectual elements in official France who were aligned with what was actually the majority opinion.

The second aim was to promote extremist anti-Dreyfusard positions. But it was not possible, without contradiction, to enrol establishment intellectuals in an organization set up with such an aim.

The position of the moderates had long been to affirm that Dreyfus had been convicted legally, and that therefore there was no Dreyfus Affair. Once the review was under way, the only viable legalistic standpoint was to agree to bow to the new decisions of the courts; reconciliation would follow later. This was exactly the position of the government-inspired newspaper *Le Temps*, which now wrote:

> It is absolutely necessary today after the Henry forgery that the question of justice and truth should be talked through clearly; we can only put the Dreyfus and Picquart Affairs behind us when they have been settled in the full light of day and in accordance with the law. Then and only then will it be appropriate to call on all good citizens to bring about the abatement of our quarrels and the union of all Frenchmen in our joint devotion to justice and the flag.

This was not, however, how the Ligue saw the situation. Its anti-Dreyfusard promoters had become convinced that they could obtain a decision against a review by forcing the government to remove the case from the Criminal Division of the Cour de cassation and to refer it to the three combined divisions, an idea which had already emerged in Parliament on 4 November. The extraordinary president of the Civil Division, Quesnay de Beaurepaire, made contact with a number of them, and, in order to discredit his colleagues in the Criminal Division, started a campaign of insults. He also accused them of crimes which he had invented. But he resigned suddenly on 8 January. Thus the intention of the promoters of the Ligue was to campaign for the case to be transferred.

The ideological incoherence of the Ligue appeared at the first general meeting on 19 January, at which Lemaitre gave a major speech to an audience of 1,200. He first explained the exclusion of the

Dreyfusards from the Ligue: '. . . we too may claim to cherish truth and justice, and to be attached to the rights of man . . . we think, just as much as they do, and as just sincerely as they do, that one must not leave an innocent man in a penal colony, even if a great public interest is involved'.

This *material* question had been settled legally, he said, by the court of competent jurisdiction, and he condemned the revisionists for setting up their personal judgement against the decisions of legally competent bodies. This was in fact the standard discourse of moderate anti-Dreyfusism; it had now been overtaken by the review procedure. But Lemaitre then put his cards on the table: the new league would only accept the order of the Cour de cassation 'on the express condition that the case be referred either to the Civil divisions or to the combined divisions'. This was a very new conception of legality.

Lemaitre also asserted that the Jews were French citizens: 'How could we have the effrontery to proscribe 70,000 of our fellow-citizens on account of their blood!' Once again, this was in line with moderate anti-Dreyfusism, but Brunetière had already declared on 3 January: 'the antisemites and supporters of M. Déroulède will be welcome to join us'. The Ligue was thus from the outset a partisan body, and it attempted to combine the incompatible moderate and extremist versions of anti-Dreyfusism.

Despite this ideological ambiguity, or perhaps because of it, the Ligue grew extremely rapidly: 2,000 people per day joined from 5 January, and within a few months, its membership had risen to 40,000, far higher than that of the Ligue des Droits de l'Homme. Its members were drawn mainly from the professions, or from the ranks of civil servants; some were students. According to Jean-Pierre Rioux, the Ligue drew its support from those we have called the contented classes, from place-holders, or those on the way to becoming such: lawyers and doctors, law and medical students, and also journalists and teachers; among the nobility, it recruited Academicians, generals, admirals and landowners. Among the upper bourgeoisie, its members were 'big industrialists, stockbrokers, large traders, big names in the professions, parliamentarians of the Right and the Centre, high civil servants at the Cour de cassation, the Conseil d'Etat or the Finance Ministry, senior army officers and influential university professors'. However, a 'good number of the troops came from the level just below, from the independent, hard-working solid bourgeoisie, whether salaried or with unearned income; these people shared dominant social and ideological values, on account of their income, their life-style and their culture. The "middle classes" [roughly, the petty bourgeoisie] were much less numerous.'[4] The membership of the Ligue was thus entirely representative of the moderate anti-Dreyfusism of the contented classes.

The Ligue was very active in the short term, but it soon withered, and it had disappeared by 1905. Beyond the special circumstances of the Affair, what could in the end be the role of a mass organization wedded to the values which were simply those of the whole of official France?

But this was not all: as we have seen, Vaugeois, Maurras and Barrès were men in the extremist anti-Dreyfusard mould. Soon, the first two would move towards the creation of the Action Française, while Barrès would develop the nationalist doctrine of the Earth and the Dead. It was inevitable that they would not remain for long in the same organization with more moderate establishment figures. The nationalism of Barrès and Maurras was incompatible with the parliamentary Republic and its values: they had perforce to affirm theirs from outside. The extemists departed from the Ligue, and it was left without a role. It failed because, without them, it had no other aim than to reassert established values.

It is also worth noting here that the eventual failure of the Ligue de la Patrie Française clearly demonstrates that the intellectual of the Right, just like the intellectual of the Left, can only flourish *outside* established structures. The intellectual's critical role is quite compat-ible with a position on the Right, but only insofar as he remains outside the system. There can only be a temporary role for him within the system when it is under serious challenge, as happened during the Affair. Normally the 'organic' intellectual has little to contribute to a system which has every opportunity of imposing dominant values by institutional means. The Dreyfus Affair thus shows that intellectuals do not only exist on the Left, but, whether of the Left or the Right, they can only find a critical role as outsiders.

Those who set up the Ligue to show that some intellectuals were opposed to Dreyfus all ended up as external critics of the Third Republic, on the political extreme Right. Vaugeois and his supporters did not take long to conclude that the Ligue was too tame for them, that it was lacking in direction and could not really serve as an instrument of national salvation. As early as January 1899, Vaugeois met Maurras, and the two began to consider ways in which they

---

4 Jean-Pierre Rioux, *Nationalisme et conservatisme. La Ligue de la Patrie Française* (Paris, 1977), pp. 22–30.

could act independently: they failed in their attempt to start a cheap evening paper, but they were soon to establish their own framework, the Action Française.

THE EARTH AND THE DEAD

For his part, Barrès accepted an invitation to give the Ligue's third public lecture on 10 March. He now had at last the opportunity to propose to the Ligue the nationalist doctrine he was elaborating.

How did he define his doctrine? 'A nationalist,' he said, 'is a Frenchman who has become conscious of the forces that moulded him. Nationalism means the acceptance of a certain determinism.'

In contrast to the power of reason favoured by the intellectuals, Barrès, in his lecture, advocated a return to feeling. In the very depth of our being, he said, there is a sensitive nerve.

> Touch it, and there is a shock I could not have suspected, a murmur of my entire being. It is not the sensations of an ephemeral individual that are thus irritated: I find to my dread that it is my whole race that is suddenly being summoned up. And so *the best dialectic* and the fullest demonstrations could not define me.

These moments of emotivity allowed him to reach down towards those reservoirs of his being that were his ancestors. 'While I remain, neither my forbears nor my benefactors will have turned to dust.' He was in a total state of dependence towards his ancestors. 'There is no freedom of thought even. I can only live according to my dead ancestors. They and the earth dictate a certain form of activity.' The traditionalist doctrine of the Earth and the Dead was born.

As for the Dreyfus Affair, for Barrès it was merely 'an orgy of metaphysicians. They judge everything in the abstract. We judge everything by reference to France.' It was the national interest which would become the fundamental touchstone for nationalism.

Unfortunately for Barrès, the Prefect of Police banned the use of the hall, most of the committee of the Ligue refused to support him and he was forced to abandon his lecture; the text was published, sent to every parliamentarian and to the General Staff officers, and was given a wide distribution in eastern France. But the Ligue did not accept it as its official doctrine. For Jean-Pierre Rioux, Barrès was now out of step with the Ligue: he would have to develop his doctrine outside: as will be seen, he moved closer to Déroulède, and by October 1901 he had left the management committee of the Ligue, which had become purely electoralist. He and Maurras were henceforward to provide the intellectual backbone for the new nationalism of the extreme Right.

THE TRANSFER OF THE DREYFUS CASE FROM THE CRIMINAL DIVISION

In the short term, the campaign in favour of a law to remove the Dreyfus case from the jurisdiction of the Criminal Division of the Cour de cassation was to be successful. Dupuy, yielding to pressure, decided to go ahead and bring the law in, despite the fact that he had rejected it when it had been put to Parliament in November.

Lebret, the Justice Minister, had promised the Chamber a new enquiry into the alleged misdeeds of the Criminal Division. The senior president, Mazeau, entrusted with the enquiry together with two other magistrates, cleared the Criminal Division of the charges made by Quesnay de Beaurepaire, but he still recommended the transfer of jurisdiction: 'We fear that having been unsettled by the insults and affronts they have met with, and having been drawn into contrary opinions by the prejudices which unconsciously dominate their minds, they would not have, once the preliminary investigation is over, that tranquillity and moral freedom which are essential if they are to act as judges.'

Dupuy met with vigorous opposition from Leygues, Delombre and Delcassé in Cabinet, but the majority supported him. The bill to transfer jurisdiction was presented to the Chamber by Lebret on 30 January, then sent into committee. The majority on the committee found the proposal scandalous. According to the rapporteur Renault-Morlière, 'such laws are essentially dictatorial and revolutionary in the worst sense of the word'. The government's only argument was the state of public opinion.

A group of Progressists took up the committee's objections in a manifesto presented as a 'final appeal to the government', an appeal signed by Brisson, Bourgeois and, among others, Barthou, Isambert, Jonnart, Sarrien, Viviani, Millerand and Pelletan. In the debate in the Chamber, the only justification Dupuy could offer for the law was that of 'exceptional circumstances'. But only Pelletan and Millerand protested. Pelletan denounced the informers who had been spying on the judges' activities. Never, he said, had there been a scandal of such a kind. However, the remark that decided the vote, the one that went down in history, was made by Lebret: 'Gentlemen, look to your constituencies.' The transfer was carried by 324 votes to 207.

This was politically a decisive moment in the history of the Republic. The Progressist party divided: on the left, Brisson's friends, a few moderates and the signatories of the recent manifesto, voted against, together with the socialists. The vote has been described as a 'turning-point which changed the whole orientation of the Republic.' It ushered in a restructuring of the party system. After the socialists and radicals had each in turn broken with nationalism and antisemitism, the decisive step had now been taken which would lead to the emergence of a majority of the Left, replacing the Centre majority on which Méline's government had rested. The new left-wing majority, comprising the left-wing Progressists, radicals and socialists, which was identified with the Dreyfusard camp in its completely politicized form, was to emerge in June.

THE DEATH OF FÉLIX FAURE

Another dramatic event soon followed the vote on the transfer to the combined divisions. On February 16 M. Le Gall, head of the civil secretariat of the President of the Republic, was sitting in the evening, as was his wont, in an outer salon at the corner of the ground floor of the Elysée Palace, a salon which led to the President's office. After a young woman had gone in to see the President, he heard strange shouts emerging from the elegant boudoir beyond the presidential office, and fearing a mishap, he forced his way in through the door. There, according to the account Casimir-Périer received from his valet, he found the President unconscious, in a most significant state of undress, and the young woman, Madame Steinheil, 'stark naked, screaming in a frenzy, and in a fit of nervous hysterics'. Félix Faure had suffered a sudden brain haemorrhage, and he died at 10 p.m. without regaining consciousness. Madame Steinheil was tidied up and bundled out of the presidential palace by a side entrance.

The news of the President's death was immediately sent everywhere by telegraph. It was a surprise, since at 58 Félix Faure still cut a handsome figure and appeared to be in good health; he was always out hunting and refused to spare himself.

According to Maurice Paléologue, the beautiful Madame Steinheil 'had already for some time been driving the President to distraction by the heady philtre of her skilful ardours. She was young, attractive, lustful and "an expert at ruining members of the opposite sex", as Guy de Maupassant put it.' But Félix's Faure's good health was only apparent. 'His glazed look, his puffy eyelids and his sudden stumbling over his words had several times been noticed,' added Paléologue. It was even claimed he had previously had a congestive problem which boded ill for him. He was therefore past the age to know Madame Steinheil. The day after his death, thanks to the gossip of the domestic servants at the Elysée, rumours began to circulate about his dangerous amorous exploits. Drumont, ever inventive, talked of a murder committed by a certain 'Delilah' who was naturally in the pay of the Jews.

Clemenceau summed up in his acerbic way the situation the President's death had created for France: 'Félix Faure has just died. That does not mean there is one man less in France. However there is now a splendid position to be filled. There will be no shortage of pretenders. It was Félix Faure who set out to scuttle the review of the Dreyfus case . . . I vote for Loubet.' Félix Faure was thought, as we have seen, to be quietly working behind the scenes to prevent a review, but Clemenceau had been unwise to present Loubet, who was President of the Senate, as the candidate of the revisionists. Nonetheless, a current of opinion favourable to him appeared, first in the Senate, then in the Chamber, and he was elected President on 18 February by 483 votes to Méline's 279. Méline had been supported by Progressists in the Chamber and parliamentarians on the Right.

Emile Loubet, aged 60, a man of peasant origins and still very provincial in outlook, was a shrewd politician, said Reinach, a Republican through and through, and he had not, above all, been involved in recent party quarrels. However, as soon as he was elected, the nationalists' anger erupted. On his return from his election at Versailles, the new President was hissed between the Gare Saint-Lazare and the Elysée Palace by the members of Déroulède's Ligue, Guérin's antisemites and the supporters of the duc d'Orléans. 'Resign! Panama!' they shouted. (Loubet had once had a vote of censure passed on him in this connection.) 'The police did not react, they let the hissing and the shouting pass,' noted Jean France, who was accompanying the President. 'The work put in by the reactionary leagues, and by the Ligue des Patriotes in particular, had been so effective that it was public knowledge that nine-tenths of the ordinary policemen, and a large proportion of the senior ranks, led by the inspectors, were sympathetic to the anti-Dreyfusards and made no secret of the fact.'[5] 'That day,' said Reinach, 'the core of the mob – five or six hundred men – were behind Déroulède, who was much better at handling men than Guérin'.

Déroulède led the demonstration. The most hot-headed shouted

5 Jean-Marc Berlière, 'La généalogie d'une double tradition policière', in Birnbaum, ed., *La France de l'affaire Dreyfus*, p. 209.

that they should march on the Elysée but Déroulède asked them to be patient and instead to march in pilgrimage to the statue of Joan of Arc at the Place des Pyramides.

A COUP IS ANNOUNCED IN PUBLIC

Leaning back against the pedestal, Déroulède declared war on Loubet: just as Joan of Arc had 'driven the English out of France', they must drive out a foreign constitution. 'Today's election is a challenge to us ... It is not for a parliamentary aristocracy, but for the people to elect the President of the Republic. Together, we shall have to set universal suffrage free.' He then gave them his promise:

> Let us do nothing this evening: a man who was dear to me is still lying dead at the Elysée. Let us meet together on Thursday, and I promise to do my duty; we shall throw the man who has been elected out of the Elysée – for me he is not the leader of the French nation – and we shall overturn the Republic.

The coup was thus, no doubt imprudently, announced in public for the day of Félix Faure's state funeral.

But there were still two pretenders, or even three, if one counted the Bonapartist Prince Victor, who maintained a maximum of discretion. As soon as Félix Faure died, the duc d'Orléans let himself be persuaded that the long-awaited moment of his return had come. Seeking to secure the support of Déroulède, he asked to see him. Déroulède refused. The royalists continued their plotting: in other words, they drafted a letter to a general, or a proclamation, and imagined straight away that the general was on the march and that the people were ready to acclaim their prince on his return to the kingdom of his fathers. But in the face of Déroulède's refusal to collaborate, they were reduced to allowing him to 'open the breach'; they planned to rush into it with him. 'Being accustomed to taking their own rantings and complainings, those of the nationalists, and the hubbub of the press for the cry of the nation, they were more convinced than ever that the people were with them during that noisy week when, every night, gangs on the boulevards hooted at Loubet,' wrote Reinach. On 19 and 20 February, there was so much agitation that the situation appeared revolutionary, following a meeting attended by 3,000 people, and organized by the plebiscitary groups of the Seine department at the Salle des Mille-Colonnes in the rue de la Gaîté.

On 23 February, Déroulède was preparing to march on the Elysée, by taking advantage of the hostility towards President Loubet of the crowds who would gather for Félix Faure's funeral. His plan for a coup reflected his constant aim: with the support of the people of Paris, the army would force Loubet from the Elysée, and install him there in his place, at the head of a plebiscitary Republic. Once the government had been deposed, Parliament dissolved and the constitution repealed, the people would be 'called to their comitia' [electoral assemblies] to endorse the coup by their vote.

The whole scheme was on the Bonapartist model. To ensure its success, Déroulède needed a general and a brigade of troops. It was General Pellieux who gave him, if not a promise, 'at least some words resembling one, a half-promise', said Reinach. Otherwise he would not have gone ahead.

What was the state of the forces on the ground, on 23 February? Déroulède had advised the 25,000 members of his league; he had sent 4,000 telegram-cards, placed notes in the newspapers and put out a poster. His men were told to be at the Place de la Bastille, a few hundred yards from the Place de la Nation, where the troops were to disperse after the presidential funeral parade, at three o'clock.

During the night of 22/23 February, relations went from bad to worse with the royalists. The duc d'Orléans sent an emissary, Castellane, to see Déroulède: the latter declared that if the duke put in an appearance, he would personally 'take him by the collar' and arrest him.

THE FIASCO AT THE PLACE DE LA NATION

When the day of the coup came, Déroulède took up his position with Barrès in a concierge's lodge near the Place de la Nation, 'wearing his deputy's sash, his pockets stuffed with proclamations, decrees, gold coins and banknotes (about 50,000 francs), so as to be ready to meet initial needs'. According to him, the long road from the old Place du Trône customs barrier to the Hôtel de Ville and the Elysée Palace was lined by his supporters. With him at the Place de la Nation were several hundred of his league members, Prince Victor, and Guérin, busily placing his gangs. 'There were therefore just over a thousand men in the area,' said Reinach, 'some belonging to Déroulède, some to Guérin. They were ready for a coup, provided the army allowed itself to be subverted. There were as many passers-by and spectators.'

Not a single policeman was to be seen, according to all the eyewitnesses. The Prime Minister had insisted on massing the main of the police forces, with the Prefect of Police, at the Elysée Palace and around the Interior Ministry. 'It would have been very late in the day,' Reinach remarked, 'to stop a popular and military riot which had already grown bigger and bigger as it approached from halfway across Paris.' Furthermore, the municipal police were no longer reliable. Thus the insurrectionary forces, though divided, represented a far from negligible threat: everything depended on the support of the army and the country. On this score, Déroulède had miscalculated.

As we have seen (above, p. 124), the automatic reflex of obedience, the reluctance to defy legal authority, the habit of being the very upholders of law and order for half a century, all these made even Pellieux, the most turbulent of the generals, recoil from the unthinkable. 'These military men,' said Reinach, 'even the most audacious and the most lacking in scruples, though they talked of smashing everything up and throwing the lawyers out of the windows, were seized with a sudden timidity as soon as it came to taking any action.' We have already noted that only 1,700 officers out if 25,000 on the active list had supported the Henry appeal. Only two line regiments, the 4th and the 32nd, were ready to follow Déroulède.[6]

And Pellieux was no Bonaparte. On the fateful day of the funeral, after the religious service at Notre-Dame, the general, 'after having seen once again that the people were not stirring, that they were not booing Loubet, the Senate or even the Cour de cassation', decided on his plan of action. He ordered his troops to disperse before they reached the Place de la Nation.

The affair therefore soon ended in ridicule. Neither the army nor the people came forward to support the coup. Herr and Péguy had taken responsibility for the Republican counter-offensive. The Allemanists had supplied troops tried and tested in street battles. At strategic points, Péguy had posted groups of men who had been told to keep their eye on events, give the alarm, and bring the people of the working-class suburbs out with them.[7] But no one made a move.

When, at about 4.30, the troops arrived at the Place de la Nation on their way from the Père-Lachaise cemetery, Déroulède moved over with about 200 of his men towards the Avenue de Taillebourg where the sound of drums and bugles could be heard. Barrès took Guérin

---

6 Zeev Sternhell, *La Droite révolutionnaire 1885–1914. Les origines françaises du fascisme* (Paris, 1978), p. 122.

7 Daniel Lindenberg and Pierre-André Meyer, *Lucien Herr. Le socialisme et son destin* (Paris, 1977), pp. 165–6.

by the arm: 'It's good to be here,' he said. But then Déroulède noticed that the general who was approaching was not Pellieux but Roget.

It was too late to retreat: thinking that it was Roget who had been chosen by destiny, Déroulède seized the bridle of his horse, shouting: 'Follow us, general, take pity on the Fatherland; save France and the Republic; friends are waiting for us; follow us to the Place de la Bastille, to the Hôtel de Ville! To the Elysée, general!'

At first neither Roget nor the crowd understood what was happening: these shouts and yells were mingled with the sound of the brass playing the Marseillaise and cries of 'Long live the army!' and 'Long live the Republic!'. The noise startled Roget's horse. 'Let go of my horse, and let me pass,' he said. He pointed out to his troops the way to the Reuilly barracks, via the Boulevard Diderot.

Déroulède's operation seemed to have misfired; but he continued to try to carry Roget along with him by force, barring with his men the entrance to the rue de Reuilly, which led to the barracks. He had told his second-in-command Habert to bar the street on the right – the entrance to the rue de Reuilly being on the right-hand side of the Boulevard. But in the confusion, Habert thought Déroulède wanted to bar the entrance to the rue du Faubourg Saint-Antoine, which was the way to Paris. 'No, no! let them pass,' he shouted. 'That's the way to the Bastille!'

When they reached the corner of the rue de Reuilly, Déroulède implored Roget: 'General, I beg you, save France! You must not go that way to the barracks – you must go to Paris!' 'I shall go where I choose!' Roget retorted violently. Déroulède, with Habert and about fifteen of his bodyguards, passed through the gate of the barracks and entered the courtyard. Déroulède then declared himself 'a prisoner of the army which had betrayed him'.

Roget announced that he was under arrest; and a few hours later, after Dupuy had had time to decide what course to take, Déroulède and Habert were charged, ignominiously, with 'entering the barracks and refusing to leave, despite the injunctions of the military authorities'. Déroulède's escapade finished humiliatingly for him. He did, however, manage to have an insertion put into the report, to the effect that he had gone to the Place de la Nation 'to take the troops along with him in an insurrectionary movement and overturn the parliamentary Republic'.

Paris smiled, the Republic escaped unscathed and peace and quiet returned to the country. Dupuy continued to treat the opponents of the Republic with contempt. Déroulède was accused only of inciting the military to disobedience, while, for his part, he persisted for

145

two months in accusing himself, before the officer conducting the preliminary investigation, of seeking to overturn the Republic: the judge did his utmost, on the other hand, to minimize the importance of each of his actions at the Place de la Nation. His case was finally referred to the assizes. Déroulède felt in no way discouraged.

The royalists were not prosecuted for plotting against the state either. Dupuy wanted to keep them in order through the mere threat of a trial by the High Court. He was aiming, by a skilful balancing act, at avoiding upsetting either the nationalists or their opponents. But in order not to appear totally inactive in defence of the Republic, he prosecuted all the leagues at once, including the Ligue des Droits de l'Homme. They were fined a symbolic 16 francs each, and went on as before.

On 27 February, the law to transfer the Dreyfus case to the Combined divisions came before the Senate. Here, it met firmer opposition than in the Chamber: a series of respected Republicans protested against 'one of the great shameful deeds of the centuries' (Maxime Lecomte), against procedures 'unworthy of the French character' employed against 'irreproachable judges' (Bérenger), and a law that would 'lead the civilized nations to ostracize us' (Monis).

WALDECK-ROUSSEAU MAKES A COME-BACK

Waldeck-Rousseau, in a much-noted return to politics after a silence of five years, observed that it was a paradox to say that 'a criminal court, after it had sought to make enquiries, to investigate and to seek enlightenment should, for that self-same reason, have the case removed from it and should find that the more its ability, its capacity to judge was increased, the more its power to do so was reduced'.

The mark of the new law seemed to be weakness. 'The day public opinion refers the treatment of defendants and judges to political bodies, the word justice will have lost all its meaning and will have become the poorest of travesties.' The aim of the endless insults to the judges was to weaken the government, to disturb people's minds, and 'to create anarchy, so as to pave the way for reaction. There is one thing that is growing, and growing constantly, in this country and that is the power of threats and calumny.' But instead of offering resistance, the government was avoiding its responsibilities; a kind of resignation seemed to be spreading through the country. Was this the moment to be reducing the authority of justice? The French

have always been a people with a passion for the ideal and for reason, but certain words have now become meaningless: to fear there has been a mistake is no longer to bow to the noblest duty, the noblest feeling of humanity. No, according to a certain nationalist jargon, it is to under-value the Fatherland! To seek to put right the mistake was a crime; and now we are being asked for special, extraordinary courts . . . They have talked of public opinion: let us talk of justice . . . I know only one way not to make mistakes and not to lead justice from her true path, and that is, firstly, to heed the voice of one's conscience, and then to obey it!

Alas! the majority in the Senate was in favour of the law to trans-fer jurisdiction over the case: on 1 March it was passed by 158 votes to 118. However, Waldeck-Rousseau had gained a new authority among the revisionists. And, two days later, the Criminal Division retorted by referring the Picquart–Leblois case to a civil court. Pic-quart was transferred from the Cherche-Midi to the Santé prison. The revisionists had scored another point.

Above all, the review continued to take its course, despite the transfer law. Mazeau, first president of the Combined Divisions, chose Ballot-Beaupré, the president of the Civil Division, as rapporteur, to replace Quesnay de Beaurepaire. Ballot-Beaupré was a man of integ-rity and judgement.

The Criminal Division's enquiry was made available to the other divisions and to the defence. Mathieu Dreyfus learned about it from Mornard, Lucie Dreyfus's counsel.

PUBLICATION OF THE COUR DE CASSATION ENQUIRY

Fearing that political passions and the state of mind of some of the judges would lead to a rejection of the review, Labori, Demange, Mornard and Trarieux agreed with Mathieu, at a meeting at Joseph Reinach's home, that the enquiry should be published. But the ques-tion was: how could this be done without compromising Mornard or Mathieu?

Mathieu arranged for some extracts from the most striking depo-sitions and documents to be taken anonymously to Clemenceau. Struck by these mysterious documents, Clemenceau consulted Rein-ach, who then asked Mathieu to authenticate his own documents! 'I pretended to read "my documents" with care,' Mathieu recalled, 'and I declared: "The documents are authentic!" ' After this piece of play-acting, Clemenceau and Reinach decided to arrange for Victorien Sardou, who agreed to take responsibility, to offer them to *Le Figaro*. The newspaper began to publish the documents on 31 March.

147

Through Bernard-Lazare, Mathieu had obtained the services of five Russian Jews to copy them out, so that the handwriting would not be recognized if there was a prosecution. They worked day and night. Every evening, the copies were taken to *Le Figaro* via a series of picturesque intermediaries.

The effect was considerable. For the first time, the main particulars of the case were made available to the public. Many were converted to the idea of a review. 'The circulation of the paper rose to such an extent,' according to Mathieu, 'that M. de Rodays, the editor, had only one thought in mind, how to maintain it.'

The Combined divisions, after the secret file had been turned over to them, found, like their fellow-judges, that there was nothing in it which could incriminate Dreyfus.

The most important witness to come before them was Freystätter, one of the judges of 1894. When asked whether Henry had referred to the 'scoundrel D.' document at the 1894 trial, he replied that only the *bordereau* had been discussed. This was a crucial point.

The judges of the Combined divisions came to the same conclusions as their fellows. On 29 May, the three divisions met in plenary session at the Law Courts to hear Ballot-Beaupré's report.

5 RETRIAL AND PARDON: THE 1894 JUDGMENT IS QUASHED

The same day a few yards away – could it have been a coincidence? – Déroulède and Habert finally appeared before the assizes. After the court had heard a few extravagant remarks by them and they had praised their 'symbolic act', they were acquitted.

Meanwhile, in the large courtroom normally occupied by the Civil Division, a crowd had gathered. The court was packed with journalists. 'The well-known figures from the Zola trial could be seen, lawyers, intellectuals, and many women,' said Reinach, 'but the air of battle had faded, and an atmosphere of respect, something of a religious feeling, hung over the court.' The room was impressive. *L'Illustration* found the décor 'too sumptuous, and in doubtful taste'. A profusion of gold seemed to flow over the walls, the caissons, the cornices and the ornamental motifs. The allegorical fresco on the ceiling, by Baudry, symbolized the glorification of the law. 'A semi-circular marble balustrade enclosed the court area: within it sat the 46 judges in red robes bordered with ermine.' 'Ballot-Beaupré made a fine figure of a judge: he had a round, strong head, and a well-developed forehead, emphasized by his baldness; he was clean-shaven, beaming, but with nothing vulgar about him, thanks to the firmness and nobility of his features, and the sharp intelligence of his look. In short, his physionomy was open but thoughtful, radiating honesty and wisdom.' There was a deep silence.

Ballot-Beaupré first impartially summarized the case for and against. He then introduced his conclusions: the confession referred to by Cavaignac did not stand up to examination; similarly, the secret file only lent itself to inductions. Only one thing was certain: the military attachés had other agents. From the legal point of view, the only matters outstanding were the handwriting of the *bordereau* and the squared onionskin paper it was written on. He finally posed the half-forgotten question: 'Is the *bordereau*, the main basis for the accusation and the conviction, in Dreyfus's handwriting?' He stopped. All eyes were on him. The entire world was waiting for his reply.

Then it came: 'In the end, after an extensive examination, I have, for my part, become convinced that the *bordereau* was written not by Dreyfus but by Esterhazy.'

'A weight, like that of a rock, fell from every breast,' noted Reinach.

> There were tears in almost every eye. Many of the judges, those of the Criminal Division who had been so insulted, those of the Civil Division who had doubted for so long, could not hold back their tears. These men, almost all of whom were at the end of their careers, and were now old men, had seen so much, so many wretched things, that they thought they were hardened and made of bronze; several of them were; but they were still shaken to the core.

Finally, Ballot-Beaupré said a few words

> on certain dangerous defenders that Dreyfus and the army had had. No, the army's position is not at issue before us; it is not under our jurisdiction; it is, thank Heavens! far above these discussions, which can in no way affect it; its honour, assuredly, does not demand that a condemned man who is innocent should continue to be held on Devil's Island.

He did not ask the court to proclaim Dreyfus's innocence, but since there was new evidence, he said, there was cause to refer the case to a new court-martial. Manau and Mornard concluded in the same sense and called for an annulment and a retrial; this is also what Lucie Dreyfus was asking for, since her husband wanted restitution from his peers.

On 3 June, the court quashed the 1894 judgement and committed Dreyfus for trial before the Rennes court-martial.

A small minority among the judges, having been unable to prevent the annulment, succeeded in having inserted into the court order the handing over of the 'scoundrel D.' document, which had been 'proved both by the deposition of President Casimir-Périer, and that of Generals Mercier and Boisdeffre themselves'. The consequence of this would be that a charge would lie against General Mercier, which would embarrass the judges of the new court-martial.

The reading of the judgment at a formal hearing was greeted, said Reinach, by a great cry of 'Long live justice!'. 'There was that day, throughout the world, a great feeling of joy; hearts were deeply moved.' All eyes were on France. But once again, among the anti-Dreyfusard extremists, there was an explosion of anger. They insulted the judges, and they denounced a 'Jewish victory'.

LOUBET ATTACKED AT AUTEUIL

Street disturbances and salon plotting began again. For the anti-Dreyfusards, the great obstacle was Loubet, who had acquired great popularity since his election. It was decided by the fashionable world of Paris to stifle this by booing him the first time he appeared in public. The event took place at the racecourse at Auteuil on 4 June. Just as in February, the salon plotters wagged their tongues about it everywhere; the government was informed, and, just as in February, Dupuy massed the police 'everywhere except where they were needed'. The President was greeted by 300 demonstrators shouting 'Down with Loubet! Down with Panama! Resign!'. A nobleman, the baron de Christiani, ran up the steps of the presidential stand, which was guarded only by the ushers from the Elysée Palace, and raised his stick twice at Loubet. Loubet parried the blow and it only touched his hat. After a 20-minute scuffle, about 50 aristocrats were arrested.

There was now only one thought on the minds of republicans: the defence of the Republic. Dupuy, who had now sat back for a second time, after the February scenes, knew his days in government were numbered. However he gained a reprieve on 5 June after a debate during which he was questioned by the Right on his attitude towards the prosecution of Mercier, who had been charged as a result of the order by the Cour de cassation. The motion carried condemned the disturbances at Auteuil and approved the government's statement. But the Chamber remained in deep perplexity over Mercier's prosecution: it was decided to defer the matter and give a ruling only after the court-martial.

The same day, on Devil's Island, Dreyfus learned that the 1894 judgment had been quashed, that he had ceased to be a deportee, and that the cruiser *Sfax* was coming out to take him back to France. 'My joy was immense, beyond all words. At last I was to escape from the rack on which I had been tortured for five years . . . The day of justice was dawning for me at last.'

The violence continued in France, and the Republicans became anxious that Dreyfus was to be delivered once again into the hands of the military.

The immediate results of the court order – the return of Zola, the departure of the *Sfax*, sent out to bring Dreyfus back to France, the liberation of Picquart after the case against him had been dismissed – all these would have been triumphs, if only it had not seemed as if the Republic was in danger. Déroulède's acquittal, the welcome given to Marchand, the hero of Fashoda, and the Auteuil incident also led

Clemenceau to talk of 'civil war'; for Jaurès, the triumph of reaction was imminent.

But the people took over the task of reversing the situation: faced with governmental paralysis and parliamentary inaction, they mobilized in response to the insult to Loubet. According to George Barlow, the President had become immensely popular overnight with middle- and working-class Frenchmen, 'outraged by the aggression by relics of feudalism'. 'The thousands of addresses reaching Loubet from the large towns and from the smallest villages told of the shock felt in the provinces. This time the protest in Paris would be that of the whole of the Republic.' The Republican papers called for a demonstration at Longchamp racecourse on 11 June, to avenge Auteuil.

THE PEOPLE'S RESPONSE: LONGCHAMP

Prudently, the royalists kept away. But workers, students and petty bourgeois flocked to the demonstration. 'It was as if all Paris had turned out: an immense, determined crowd, singing and joyful, coming from every direction and using every means of locomotion: buses, cabs, policemen on bicycles, bateaux-mouches on the Seine, full to bursting; there were, too, people on foot, in small groups, little streams which eventually flowed together into a great river.' (Jules Isaac)

Dreyfusism that day was represented by the troops of the Left in their entirety, from those furthest left, the anarchists, to moderate Republicans, all those who were now determined to defend both the President and the Republic itself. This time, Dupuy sent 6,000 policemen, 20,000 troops, the gendarmerie, the Republican guard and even a dozen investigating magistrates, to improvise trials, directly on the race course, for offenders caught *in flagrante delicto*. But there were no serious disturbances, apart from one scuffle at the Armenonville pavilion. Loubet was acclaimed, and Dupuy immediately became the man who had defended the President against his own friends. Unlike the situation at Auteuil, the police showed excessive zeal. There were also a few clashes in the evening. Vaillant questioned the government in the Chamber, bringing overwhelming testimony to the rostrum, said Berlière, about the violence of the police and their nationalist and reactionary sentiments.[1] Dupuy did not stoop to defend his police force. He realized he was finished.

---

1 Jean-Marc Berlière, 'La généalogie d'une double tradition policière', in Pierre Birnbaum, ed., *La France de l'affaire Dreyfus* (Paris, 1994).

THE FALL OF DUPUY

The motion which brought about his downfall began: 'The Chamber, being resolved only to support a government determined to defend Republican institutions with energy and to ensure the maintenance of public order . . .' Dupuy's government was brought down by 321 votes to 175. The day of popular action on 11 June had thus eliminated Dupuy, and brought to an end the semi-complicity of government and police with the anti-Dreyfusard extremists who dreamed of toppling the Republic. The way was now clear for the setting up of a government which would whole-heartedly defend it.

But the task was laborious: setting up a new government took ten days. Loubet first approached Poincaré, 'the leading political figure in his age-group', according to Reinach. But he was not successful, because of the opposition of Sarrien and the radicals. Abandoning his attempt, he recommended to the President the name of Waldeck-Rousseau.

WALDECK-ROUSSEAU

Aged 52, Waldeck-Rousseau appeared cold and distant: 'a cropped head, a short moustache, calm and immobile features gave the impression of great self-containment and perhaps capacity'. He was a provincial figure of complete integrity who had earned himself high standing as a member of the Parisian upper bourgeoisie through the exercise of his profession as a barrister specializing in civil cases. It will be recalled that he was the first to be asked to defend Dreyfus.

A Republican deputy since 1879, he was a determined secularizer; he had also been the promoter of the law on trade unions which bore his name, and thus had acquired the reputation of being an intelligent conservative. But, according to Galliffet, he had a horror of politics. 'He prefers water-colours, at which he is very talented, fishing, shooting, and the position of being the leading barrister in Paris.' He concentrated on his professional work after 1885. He was elected as senator in 1890, but had seldom spoken before his much-noted appeal against the transfer law in February 1899. He was a revisionist, but he had always reserved judgement on the question of Dreyfus's guilt. He was primarily concerned, in the spring of 1899, about the growing threat from the Right and from clericalism.

Waldeck-Rousseau was the one man in the Republican movement with the necessary integrity and authority to head a government of Republican defence. But when Loubet approached him, he still showed some distaste for the difficult task he was being offered. It was practically forced on him, according to his confidant Lépine. And he only accepted on two conditions: that he would be free to choose his own ministers, without reference to the Chamber, and that he would be able to bring Lépine in with him as Prefect of Police. The latter had been sent to Algiers in October 1897 because of antisemitic disturbances, but had later been dismissed. Lépine had had an opportunity, Jean-Marc Berlière has pointed out, to note the havoc that had been wrought among the ranks and the senior officers in the municipal police force by the propaganda of the nationalist leagues. The other great problem was of course to restore order in the army, and to this end Waldeck immediately thought he should call on the marquis de Galliffet, a general who had been a personal friend for many years.

GALLIFFET AND MILLERAND

Galliffet, who had fought with distinction at Sedan, had been known since 1871 as the 'butcher of the Commune', because of the way he had, with particular cruelty, selected Communard prisoners at random for execution. Since then, he had occupied a number of senior military posts: in 1880, he had been military governor of Paris. He was now 69, but 'did not look his age', Reinach said,

> such was the vigour still in his weathered, battle-scarred body; he had the upright carriage of a young man, a high-coloured ruddy bronze face, sharp eyes, deep-set behind a beak like that of a bird of prey, a Bourbon nose, eyes that shone with the same fire as in the old days of battle and feasting, and he still had the look which had done so much for his reputation, that of a fearless chieftain and a great nobleman who did not care a damn for anything.

He was, in short, a cynic and a man who said exactly what his current mood dictated. Halévy called him 'an aristocrat to his finger-tips, though he would not answer to the title', and a 'professed Republican', whereas for the historian Pierre Sorlin he was a royalist. He had a contempt for the behaviour of his own class.

Having defended Picquart, he had the reputation among the nationalists of being a Dreyfusard. Pierre Sorlin has, however, noted the variations in his point of view on the Dreyfus question.[2] The only thing he really took seriously, no doubt, was the army. When Waldeck-

2 On Waldeck-Rousseau, his Cabinet and on Galliffet, see Pierre Sorlin, *Waldeck-Rousseau* (Paris, 1966), ch. 8.

154

Rousseau, thinking to take the War Ministry, offered him the post of head of the minister's private office in that department, Galliffet accepted: he was thoroughly bored in his retirement.

At the same time, Waldeck-Rousseau had also decided to take on the socialist Alexandre Millerand, who had been recommended to him by Reinach: it was essential, according to the latter, to call on representatives of all shades of opinion within the Republican movement.

Millerand had been born in the same year as Jaurès. A lawyer and originally a radical parliamentarian, he had become the leader of the Independent socialists in the 1890s and, with Jaurès, one of the principal figures in French socialism. With his massive head and square shoulders, Caillaux said, he had the air of a docker. He lacked Jaurès's culture and rhetorical gifts, but as a barrister he excelled in close argument. He had been very effective in defending the trade unions during strike periods. Since he had proclaimed, in his 1896 Saint-Mandé speech, that the socialization of the means of production could only be brought about by peaceful means, he had become the figure most representative of the development of French socialism towards parliamentarism. He was a man who thought in terms of practical achievements, and he was only waiting for the kind of opportunity to exercise political power which Waldeck had offered him.

As has been seen, he had been an anti-Dreyfusard opposed to socialist involvement in the Dreyfus case, but had switched to revisionism after Henry's suicide.

Jaurès, who had been warned by him about the offers he had had from Waldeck, decided, after much hesitation, to give his consent. According to Andler, it was Lucien Herr who had taken the responsibility of persuading Jaurès to disregard the objections of Guesde and Vaillant, for whom any governmental participation was pointless before the social revolution. Jaurès realized the ordeal he would have to go through on the issue, but he believed socialist support would allow the Republic to survive, and progress to be made towards a review of the Dreyfus case. On 19 June, he wrote in the *Petite République* that 'socialism, by saving the Republic, would make it its own'.

However, Waldeck's first attempt to put together a government failed, mainly because of the demands of the Progressists, who were preoccupied by questions about personalities. He withdrew, and Loubet approached the radicals, without success. Bourgeois refused to commit himself. Loubet then had no alternative but to call on Waldeck-Rousseau again. He pleaded with him to ward off the storm:

155

the main Republican leaders once again told him that it was his civic duty to accept.

THE GOVERNMENT OF WALDECK-ROUSSEAU

On the evening of 20 June, therefore, at Galliffet's beautiful château at Clairefontaine, in the forest of Rambouillet, Waldeck, Galliffet and Millerand put together the new cabinet, which included representatives of all tendencies in the Republican movement. Galliffet himself now became War Minister and would cover any risk to Waldeck from the army; Millerand would cover any from the socialists.

The following day, before any announcement was made, Millerand, without mentioning Galliffet, informed the socialist deputies of the offers he had received, as if they were already a thing of the past. There was no discussion at the meeting of the socialists' standing opposition to any of their number participating officially in a bourgeois government; the only issue raised was the right of an individual to participate.

One deputy, Cadenat, proposed nonetheless that the group should commit itself by an 'official public vote', but Vaillant objected, and the motion passed merely declared that if a socialist did enter a bourgeois government it would be in his personal capacity and that this would not commit the party. Jaurès, being no longer a deputy, was not at the meeting: he told Millerand that he was ready to give the government his support, but knowing that Galliffet was involved, he implored Millerand not to shake the 'butcher of the Commune' by the hand.

The announcement of the make-up of the new cabinet was met by a chorus of criticism in Paris. For the nationalists, it was a scandal, a 'Dreyfus cabinet'. For men of the Left, Pelletan for example, to entrust the Republic to the butcher of the Commune was an act of infamy. Vaillant, having already heard a 'frightening' remark in the Chamber about Galliffet, wrote to Jaurès to say that that would 'wipe out everything said yesterday at the socialist group meeting'. For parliamentarians in general, it defied all reason, since it took no account of the groups in the Chamber.

But, once appointed, Waldeck acted with determination. Within 24 hours, the Prefect of Police had been replaced by Lépine. The latter recalled: 'My first concern when I entered my office was to take charge of the municipal police. I foresaw that I should need them very soon.' Lépine's return, as Jean-Marc Berlière has pointed out, was an essential step. 'It is clear that his temperament did not incline him to tolerate the disorder and the noisy and violent demonstrations of the anti-Dreyfusards, any more than it did to put up with the passivity of the police. He was to impose silence amid the ranks of the senior officers and a sense of duty on "his" policemen.'[3]

At the same moment, the public prosecutor and the state prosecutor were dismissed, and there were a number of postings in the army. Here too, the order was, according to Galliffet: 'Silence in the ranks!'

Waldeck wanted to be judged on the basis of his actions. But the question was, would he have the means to govern? The support of the Chamber was anything but certain. When he came before it on 26 June, he was greeted by howls and animal cries: such an uproar was unheard of in the annals of the Third Republic. When Galliffet appeared, to shouts of 'Murderer!' and 'Butcher!', he replied 'Murderer, present!' without turning a hair. When Waldeck tried to read his statement, the din was so great that he could hardly make himself heard. He was constantly interrupted. Being unable to present a government programme, he restricted himself to an appeal to all Republicans to unite 'to maintain the integrity of our common heritage' and 'to allow justice to carry out its work in the fullest independence'. He felt surprised and defenceless. The sheets of his statement trembled in his hands.

'You're trembling,' said a deputy.

Another one, Dauzon, replied: 'There is not one of you with the courage to do what M. Waldeck-Rousseau is doing!' The Independent socialist Viviani sprang to his defence, but the insults had begun to fly again and he was forced to stand down from the rostrum.

Would he obtain a majority? Appearances seemed to be against him, but according to Pierre Sorlin, he had received promises from the parliamentary socialists and the radicals which would ensure him 180 votes. Everything depended on the moderates: Waldeck already had his friends working on them in the corridors.

Aynard, said Reinach, 'without mounting the rostrum', talked round his friends, and, one by one, prised more than half the moderates away from Méline. Pelletan declared he would abstain. Brisson, though a sick man, then mounted the rostrum to launch a final appeal: 'The government intends to defend the Republic; I give it my vote; and I ask all those of you over whom I have any influence in this Chamber on the strength of my past career, to vote, not for the government I say, but for the Republic.' 'He raised his arms,' said

---

3 Berlière, 'La généalogie', pp. 209–10.

Reinach, 'in an appeal which the initiated recognized as the Masonic sign of distress.' But there was no need for this: 'His distress, his anxiety for the Republic spoke loudly enough through the sobbing of his voice and his ravaged face.'

The government won its majority by 262 votes to 237. The majority consisted of the mass of radicals who, with the exception of the Pelletan group, had responded to Brisson's appeal, most of the socialists and 61 Progressists, including Aynard, Jonnart and Poincaré.

This vote marked the final break-up of the Progressist group in the Chamber, which had begun with the vote on the transfer law. Faced with the danger of nationalist and clerical reaction, Waldeck-Rousseau and his friends now believed that the main danger lay to the right, and that it was time to return to the policy of concentration, in conjunction with the radicals and socialists.

It was thus to be thanks to the support of this new majority of Republican defence, corresponding to the coalition of popular forces which had been mobilized at Longchamp, that Waldeck would be able to govern France until the Rennes trial and beyond. France would now be governed on the left.

DREYFUSARD LEFT VERSUS ANTI-DREYFUSARD RIGHT

The victorious forces of Dreyfusism had now become completely politicized: and the legal battle they were fighting on behalf of Dreyfus would soon be superseded by a broader and more long-lasting one: for the Republic, and against nationalism and clericalism.

What of the forces now outside the new majority? Twenty-nine of the moderates, including Barthou, Dupy and Ribot, abstained, together with Pelletan and thirteen radicals. The revolutionary socialists – the Guesdists and the former Blanquists – left the socialist group in the Chamber. They later published the celebrated Manifesto for Recovery on 14 July, which justified their breach of socialist unity in the Chamber in these words:

> The aim was to have done with what claimed to be a socialist policy but was actually one of compromises and deviations . . . the socialist party, as a class party, cannot be or become a governmental one, otherwise it will commit suicide as a party. It must not share power with the bourgeoisie, in whose hands the state can only be an instrument of conservatism and social oppression.

Despite the popularity of Millerand among a large section of the working-class and socialist electorate, the quarrel over the principle of participation was for long to hinder the efforts to unite all the socialist groups.

The Right, the Catholics who had gone over to the Republic, the friends of Méline, about 30 radicals, and the nationalists and antisemites voted against Waldeck. From now on, the right-wing opposition would bring together all the anti-Dreyfusard forces, whether moderate or extremist, and would be reinforced by a handful of defectors from radicalism, notably Cavaignac. Nationalism and antisemitism were now firmly on the extreme Right. According to Blum, 'even many who had been among the first Dreyfusards now returned to the camp of reaction as towards their natural territory'.

The anti-Dreyfusard opposition of the Right, mirroring its opponents, would also now merge its struggle against a review into a broader political one which would replace it: a struggle against socialism and a secular society, and, for the most hot-headed, against the Jews and the parliamentary Republic itself.

MERCIER AGAINST DREYFUS

On the legal front, during the summer of 1899, it was Mercier, charged, as we have seen, as a consequence of the order of the combined divisions, who led the attack. 'Throughout the month preceding the trial,' said Reinach, 'he carried out a dual operation, declaring publicly that he would reveal everything to the court-martial, and that, come what may, this would be the decisive revelation; at the same time, he spread the undercover rumour that it would be the annotated *bordereau*.'

This legend of the *bordereau*, personally annotated by the German Emperor, a document of which the *bordereau* on onionskin paper was only a tracing or a copy, had, as we have seen, been circulating for a long time; in nationalist circles, in the salons, in newspaper offices and in officers' clubs, people continued, right up to the Rennes trial, to expect that the 'great secret' would at last be revealed.

The nearer the trial came, the more it began to seem like a duel between Mercier and Dreyfus. On 3 August, in *L'Intransigeant*, the general declared: 'Dreyfus will certainly be convicted again. For in this affair, there is certainly a guilty man. And the guilty man is either him or me.'

TOUJOURS DÉROULÉDE

The incurable romantic Déroulède, encouraged rather than the reverse by his acquittal at the assizes, carried on plotting. He had received offers of help from the Assumptionists through their Justice-Equality committees, and also from the royalists and Bonapartists. He had decided, from 17 June, that the leagues must form a federation. In this way he, Déroulède, would, with Guérin, become part of a triumvirate which would take power after the coup. Although the police were close on his heels, he noisily prepared his violent operation, yet again in broad daylight.

After he had been acclaimed by the crowd at the 14 July review at Longchamp, he imagined yet again that the people were with him, and on the 16th, in a speech at the Ligue de la Patrie Française, he launched a fresh appeal for combined action by the people and the army: 'What is the use of shouting "Down with the ministers! Down with the presidents! Down with the men of Panama! Down with the Dreyfusards! Down with parliamentarians and parliamentarism! The corrupters and the corrupt!" Do not the words: "Long live the army!" say everything that needs to be said?'

But as he was still seeking the support of the military he added:

> Perhaps the army are still hesitating to cross the paltry Rubicon, that line drawn by a constitution which has usurped every power and every right? May our cries of yesterday, your acclamations just now, and my speech today reassure and enlighten them. The People is with them; they are with the People!
>
> I shall not insult them by advising them to march with us to avenge us: I ask the army, I implore them, to avenge the Nation, to serve and save the Republic which is being dishonoured, and France, which is being destroyed.

THE BEGINNINGS OF THE ACTION FRANÇAISE

Among the anti-Dreyfusard intellectuals trying to assert their independence from the Ligue de la Patrie Française, the moment seemed to have come, as the spring ended, to present the Action Française to the public. This was what Henri Vaugeois set out to do in his lecture of 20 June, which was, admittedly, still given under the auspices of the Ligue. The prospectus of the new movement spoke of strengthening the links between the people and the 'men of superior culture' to whom the Ligue owed its expansion. The 'little grey review', called *Revue de l'Action Française*, finally appeared on 10 July.

Apart from the royalist Maurras, all the founders of the Action

Française were still republicans. But already by 1 August Henri Vaugeois's aspiration towards order and authority had led him to opt for a return to the past: 'Reaction comes first.' From the beginning, the Action Française placed itself on its natural home ground, the extreme Right.

How did Waldeck-Rousseau and Galliffet, representing in themselves the essential element, the leadership of the new government, face up to the new situation created by the vote of 26 June? Parliament having risen on 4 July, they were in fact able to exercise what Reinach called a 'three-month dictatorship'. Their action was threefold: they had to see to it that justice acted in full independence and with complete respect for legality; they had to bring the army chiefs under control; and they had to keep watch on Déroulède and the plotters.

DREYFUS RETURNS TO FRANCE

Alfred Dreyfus disembarked from the *Sfax* on 30 June; he was transferred at midnight to the military prison at Rennes. He still knew practically nothing about his own affair and had never heard of Picquart, of Scheurer-Kestner, or of the role of Zola.

'The horrible nightmare was ending,' he recalled. 'I believed that men had recognized their mistake, and I was expecting to see my family, and, behind them, my comrades, waiting to welcome me with open arms.' But as soon as he landed, his illusions were shattered. 'Instead of finding men united in a common aim of justice and truth, desirous that the pain of a terrible judicial error should be forgotten, I saw only anxious faces, minute precautions, and a preposterous landing at dead of night in a stormy sea.'

The next day, he was allowed to see his wife.

> The feelings my wife and I experienced when we saw each other again were too intense for human words. There was a little of everything, joy and pain, as we tried to read the signs of our sufferings on each other's faces; there was so much we felt resentful about, all the feelings we had repressed and stifled over so many years: our words died on our lips. We were content just to look at each other, drawing the strength of our affection and our willpower from the looks we exchanged.

'The revisionists,' wrote Reinach, 'who had always lived by their illusions, succumbed to them even more at this time. They listened to the nationalists' din with only half an ear ... even the most sensible of them were lulled into a false sense of security by an unscientific,

161

mystical faith in the innate justice of things; this was only increased by their successes.'

Waldeck-Rousseau was less sanguine. On taking up office, he had sought to inform himself on the question of Dreyfus's innocence: he became convinced of it on reading the 'clear and concise report' drawn up for him by superintendent Tomps. Since he was used to facing up to difficulties, he was convinced that the accused 'only stood a small chance'. So as to avoid any blunders, he himself drafted Galliffet's instructions to the military prosecutor Carrière. The latter's charges were not to bear on any of the points which fell within the jurisdiction of the Cour de cassation and on which that court had pronounced final judgment; no witness could be cited, no debate could be opened on these established and definitive truths, 'on pain of acting *ultra vires* and of annulment'. Any charge regarding matters other than those cited in the order must be set aside and referred to another trial. Galliffet gave up his right to 'outline any charges to the prosecution in writing'.

He was entirely in agreement with Waldeck-Rousseau that they should not seek to put pressure on the judges. The more strongly the judges attacked Dreyfus, he thought, the greater the chances of him being acquitted. As we have seen, his opinion about Dreyfus's innocence was subject to variation. But, according to Pierre Sorlin, 'whatever his personal convictions may have been, Galliffet considered during the summer of 1899 that it was essential to settle the Affair and that an acquittal would be the best way to lay it to rest and make a new beginning'.

For him, the Dreyfus question was no more than a passing episode. What really mattered was to restore order in the army. He directed his energy against the top army chiefs, whom he despised, unlike the lower-ranking officers who, in his opinion, were only concerned to do their duty. He took severe action against Zurlinden, Négrier, de Pellieux and Roget, and several generals were put on the retirement list.

During this period, du Paty became for a time the scapegoat of the General Staff. He was charged with having forged a number of documents, the 'Blanche' and 'Speranza' telegrams, even the Henry forgery, and of having passed the 'scoundrel D.' document to *L'Eclair* in 1896. Two days later, he was freed after the case had been dismissed.

On 4 August, three days before the trial was due to begin at Rennes, Déroulède informed his own supporters, Guérin and the royalists, that he would 'go into action' either on the day Mercier testified, or, the day of the verdict. The men from the three groups would be posted at strategic points in Paris. According to police reports, undoubtedly exaggerated, 'several generals and numerous officers were ready to make their move that day'. General Négrier, who as we have just seen, had been subject to an official punishment, was to head the march on the Elysée. If the action was successful, a new government composed of the plotters would be set up, to include Generals Hervé and De Pellieux, and also Quesnay de Beaurepaire, Marcel Habert and Georges Thiébaud. The list was staggering.

But in France, and throughout the world, all eyes were fixed on Rennes, where the trial opened on 7 August.

RENNES

In 1899, Rennes, according to Colette Cosnier, was an austere city, 'slumbering in dignified provincial conservatism'. The mansions in the city centre – which had been entirely rebuilt after the fire of 1720 – gave it a faded aristocratic air. It was the seat of a university, a Court of Appeal, the 10th Army Corps and the court-martial which was to judge Dreyfus. There were 'few factories, but about 30 religious communities and associations, few workers but many judges, ecclesiastics, professors and soldiers, and, altogether, 69,937 inhabitants'.

From early summer, the Affair had created a few pockets of unrest amid the deep calm of the city. In July, posters appeared on its walls denouncing the Jewish peril or exclaiming 'Long live Dreyfus! Down with the army!'. On 14 July, much shouting was heard in the streets: 'Long live the police! Long live Picquart! Long live Zola! Long live the Republic! Down with the army! Down with Zola! Down with Loubet! Down with the skullcap brigade! Down with the black cassock brigade! Down with Panama!'

A small group of workers and intellectuals in the local branch of the Ligue des Droits de l'Homme found itself opposed to the judges, the military and the majority of the population in what was a city of political and religious conformism. The hatred of the nationalists centred on Victor Basch, the founder of the Ligue's branch. He represented the Enemy par excellence. The antisemitic group held endless meetings; after the one on 29 July, 150 antisemites and 50 Dreyfusards began a fight. Seven on the nationalist side ended up wounded.

At the beginning of August, the great invasion of the city by the Affair began.

From early morning, there was extraordinary excitement in the area around the station. The travellers – witnesses, journalists and public figures – alighted at dawn after a sleepless night being jolted about in the train: the journey from Paris took seven hours, sometimes more. Thus General Mercier arrived an hour and a half late: General de Saint-Germain's carriage was waiting for him in the station yard, and the passers-by were disappointed only to catch such a brief glimpse of him. By an unfortunate coincidence, Barrès got off the same train as Mathieu Dreyfus . . . and Picquart, who was acclaimed by the crowd.[4]

Distinguished writers, politicians and journalists arrived from all over the world, particularly from England and Germany: they all converged on Rennes. From France, apart from Barrès, they included Jaurès, Viviani, Bernard-Lazare, Octave Mirbeau, Jules Claretie, Maurice Sarraut, Marguerite Durand from the feminist paper *La Fronde*, and the beautiful female journalist Séverine. From England came Fullerton of *The Times*, G. W. Steevens of the *Daily Mail* – whose account one can still read in *The Tragedy of Dreyfus* – Dillon of the *Daily Telegraph* and Knight of the *Morning Post*, and these were followed, towards the end of the trial, by the Lord Chief Justice, Lord Russell of Killowen, who was the personal representative of Queen Victoria. Karl Liebknecht, the German social-democrat, represented a Viennese paper. All fashionable Paris, and the representatives of several crowned heads, made Rennes into the place à la mode.

However, the excitement produced by the invasion remained circumscribed. 'You would seek in vain,' wrote *L'Illustration*, 'for signs of fever like those which shook Paris during the Zola trial.' Most of the city maintained its provincial calm: 'Hardly did a few passers-by stop to line the streets when processions of strangers who had been cited as witnesses hurried past, on their way to the court-martial.' In fact there were 'as it were two cities at Rennes throughout the month of August', Joseph Reinach explained:

> the Breton city, where hostility continued, and could be read everywhere in the tense faces, the sidelong glances and the stubborn silence of everyone who was local, and a new city, which had come in from the outside, a city which was Parisian and cosmopolitan, as noisy as the other was taciturn, in which passions burst forth and fumed away in a final conflagration.

According to Mathieu Dreyfus, Rennes in 1899 'bore all the appearance of a city under siege. The streets were full of soldiers and

4 Colette Cosnier, *Rennes pendant le procès Dreyfus* (Rennes, 1984), passim.

policemen. Patrols on horseback constantly rode up and down the main streets.'

The trial was due to open in the main hall of the lycée, an imposing complex of buildings bordering the Boulevard de la Gare (now Avenue Janvier), opposite the military prison. 'The lycée', wrote Mathieu Dreyfus, 'is under military occupation. No one is allowed in. They are afraid of a bomb. The cellars and every corner of the buildings have been thoroughly combed.'

The school hall, shaped like a long rectangular nave, was 22 metres long, 15 metres wide and 8 metres high,

> with coffee-coloured walls and, along each side, six windows surmounted by bull's eyes, which shed a profusion of light over it. A narrow frieze below the bull's eyes was decorated with the names of Breton celebrities.
>
> At one end, raised by about one metre, was a stage within a frame, surmounted, as was appropriate, by the arms of the city.

THE RENNES TRIAL

Maurice Paléologue had been wondering whether 'there was not a risk, in such an enormous, echoing, theatrical hall, that the trial would turn into a spectacle'. On the morning of 7 August, according to him, it was 'full to bursting, with at least 1,000 people'. When Mathieu Dreyfus arrived, he could see, 'on the stage dominating the hall, a large table and chairs for the members of the court-martial, the deputies, the delegates of the War Ministry and the Foreign Ministry and for a few privileged people'.

'A white Christ on a black cross, hanging on the back wall above the President's chair, proclaimed the place a Court of Justice,' Steevens noted. 'On the right, as you faced the stage, were a small raised table for the defence counsel; on the left a similar erection for the military prosecutor and his assistants. Down each side of the body of the hall was a strip of extemporized matchboard bench-and-desk for the Press. In the broader centre were seats for the witnesses, then, behind a bar, for the favoured public.' According to Reinach, there were

> more than 100 witnesses, the military, all except Chanoine in uniform around Mercier – who sat down in the front row after greeting Henry's widow 'swathed in a long mourning veil' – and the regular public of the great days of the Affair, already trembling at the new sensations they had come to Rennes to experience, particularly writers and artists, more than 400 journalists, officers from the garrison, and a great many women, from every social circle, in light-coloured summer outfits, these women being more passionate, in either camp, than the men.

165

'Behind all this ran another bar lined by a guard of the 41st Infantry. Behind their homely peasant faces and between their fixed bayonets peered the general public, five deep, in the shallowest of strips at the very back of the hall.' (Steevens)

It was seven in the morning. Because of the summer heat, the hearings were to finish at noon each day.

'I looked at the witnesses,' Mathieu recalled. 'I recognized Mercier, so ugly he was sinister-looking, his murky eyes half-hidden by thick, creased eyelids, sitting in an armchair.

'A brief order rang out: "Slope arms!", then came a sound of rifles being briskly handled, and, with a clatter of spurs and swords, the members of the court-martial appeared with their deputies.'

The President, Jouaust, was the director of military engineering; all the other judges were gunners, and so they were in a position to understand the technical aspects of the case, unlike their predecessors of 1894. Colonel Jouaust and the judges saluted, and the hearing was declared open.

There was another command: 'Order arms!' and the sound of rifle-butts on the floor. 'Bring in the accused!' called Jouaust.

There was suddenly a deathly silence. Mathieu had his eyes fixed on the long corridor lined with gendarmes along which his brother would pass as he entered the court. All heads turned in that direction. 'It was my brother's first contact with humanity for five years. Would not his physical weakness and the shock make his willpower fail him? I did not have the courage to look. I shut my eyes. I heard a voice saying: "Sit down." Then I opened my eyes.' Everyone was waiting for the man who had for so long been at the heart of the storm but whom so few had actually seen. And now here he was at last.

> Dreyfus entered, in the uniform of an artillery captain, marching with a firm rapid step, deliberately 'automatic and rhythmical', looking straight through his lorgnette at the hall, where everyone was standing. For one moment he seemed to stop, as if dazzled by the splendid light flowing in from the windows. He had three steps to mount to his place below the barristers' raised table. His legs began to give way; the shock was too great, the blood rushed to his heart, he thought he was going to fall; then he straightened himself up again with a painful effort, his face, the iron casing of his soul of steel, remaining motionless and impenetrable, shut off, as it were by a wall. In military fashion, bearing himself like a soldier under arms, he saluted the court-martial, sat down at the President's invitation, and took off his kepi; he looked as though he might have been a statue ... He was 39, but he could have been any age, he looked both young and old at the same time, with his bleached hair, 'just a crown of grey hair', his very clean-shaven face, the exposed dome

of his skull, huge, 'as if to contain more suffering', the nape of his neck emaciated and dried up by the tropical sun, his withdrawn and tensed look, his 'vitrified' eyes, such a pale blue that they seemed white, his body, which had, so to speak, melted away leaving just a little flesh clinging to bones jutting through, his figure hardly stooping, 'upright against the fates', his energetic chin with its protruding lines, his fine moustache, which was still brown, and his complexion, which coloured artificially as his weakened heart sent a rush of blood to his cheeks at every breath, making him, as Barrès said, 'go as pink as a little pig'. (Reinach)

If the journalists of the *Libre Parole* and *Le Journal* insisted he was in good health, even Barrès felt bound to say that 'they had propelled the wretched remains of a human being into the daylight, a living ball of flesh, fought over by the players on both sides, one who had not enjoyed a moment's respite for six years'. But on Dreyfus's innocence, Barrès's mind was already made up: 'I have no need to be told why Dreyfus committed treason . . . That Dreyfus is capable of treason I conclude from his race. That he committed it I know, since I have read the pages written by Mercier and Roget, which are magnificent works.'

But, as in 1894, Dreyfus refused to make an appeal to pity. An innocent man must appeal only to reason, as he was to say; he tried

to hide, behind the appearance of an unvanquished soldier, the wreck he had been turned into by the prison conditions, the deadly climate and the minister Lebon . . . and, being just in the process of recovering from a violent bout of fever, with his liver congested, and unable to eat anything but milk and eggs, he had stuffed himself with stimulants for fear he should be taken ill, and he seemed to have given himself an artificial strength. (Reinach)

The clerk to the court, Coupois, read a few procedural documents, the Cour de cassation's order, and finally the bill of indictment of 1894. Motionless, Dreyfus heard these, but he was not listening.

Jouaust, the old colonel, 'kindly, but gruff nonetheless', made as if to hustle him and treat him as if he was guilty, but this was a show for the benefit of the audience. Personally he was inclined towards an acquittal. He showed Dreyfus the *bordereau* and asked him if he recognized it. Dismissing it with a mechanical gesture, Dreyfus replied in a low voice that the document had been put to him in 1894, but he did not recognize it. Then he suddenly gave a raucous shout, hardly audible in the hall: 'I affirm once again that I am innocent, I have affirmed it already, I shouted it aloud in 1894. I have borne everything for five years, Colonel, but once again, for the honour of

my name, and that of my children, I tell you I am innocent, Colonel.'
– 'So you deny the charge?' – 'Yes, Colonel.'

Disregarding the handwriting of the *bordereau*, Jouaust now
pressed him on the questions about which he might or might not
have been informed. Each time he replied, in a clear voice, with facts
and denials. He denied he had confessed to Lebrun-Renault.

Then, for four days, from 8 to 11 August, a series of in camera
hearings were devoted to the examination, with cross-questioning, of
the secret files, both military and diplomatic. Dreyfus witnessed this
display impassively; according to Paléologue, who was responsible
for the diplomatic file, there were not so much as 20 lines in it that
could be applied to him. By his attitude, he seemed to be saying:
'How does what you are exhibiting concern me?' General Chamoin,
who was responsible for the military file, made himself guilty of
misconduct by allowing Mercier to persuade him to introduce into it
a forgery, a falsified version of the Panizzardi telegram. Mercier's
audacity was prodigious, said Mathieu Dreyfus.

THE PLOTTERS ARE ARRESTED

The hearing of the witnesses was not due to begin until 12 August. In
the meanwhile, Waldeck-Rousseau decided to move against Déroulède
and the plotters. It will be remembered that the latter had announced
he would 'go into action' on the day of Mercier's deposition, set for
12 August. Despite the fact that the testimony obtained after the Place
de la Nation affair, and the police reports on the intentions of the
federated leagues, were vague and inconsistent, Waldeck painted an
exaggerated picture at a Cabinet meeting held at Rambouillet on 10
August, and he persuaded the government to decide unanimously that
the plotters should be arrested, and charged with conspiracy and an
attack 'aimed at changing the system of government'. However, he
insisted no army officer was to be implicated. For the army, the
warning would suffice.

Déroulède, Buffet and the principal leaders of the nationalists,
royalists and antisemites were arrested at dawn on 12 August.
Thiébaud refused to open his front door and made off over the
rooftops. Habert, who had been warned in advance, drafted a manifesto and disappeared for two months. Guérin, who was not at his
mother's when the police broke in, but with his mistress, went to the
headquarters of the Antisemitic League at 51, rue de Chabrol, near
the Gare du Nord, a building he had fortified. He barricaded himself

in with some of his followers, declaring he would open fire on anyone who tried to force their way in.

The 'siege' of 'Fort Chabrol' went on for over a month, vying for space in the newspapers with the reports on the Rennes trial. Waldeck left the situation to deteriorate without attempting to storm the building. The 'siege' became one of the curiosities of Paris. Some Parisians threw packets of provisions to Guérin and his friends from the roof of the building opposite, which allowed him to survive a little longer. Eventually the water was cut off, and surrender came on 20 September.

Was there any real danger of a coup? Certainly not, but as Pierre Sorlin has said, Waldeck thought the nationalists needed a severe lesson; he was afraid of a fresh outbreak of disorder after the trial verdict if there should be an acquittal: it was preferable to make preventative arrests rather than to appear to be wreaking vengeance on them. He was most concerned about the leagues, behind which he saw royalism at work. Events proved him right on one decisive point: calm was to return to the streets.

In any case, on 12 August, public attention was so completely absorbed by the Rennes trial that the initial brief press reports on the arrests aroused 'little emotion', said Reinach. 'In a single night, the Republic had been delivered, without a single drop of blood being shed, by the mere reawakening of the Law.'

MERCIER'S DEPOSITION

When the court reconvened at Rennes that day, nothing had yet transpired about events in Paris. The day's great event was to be Mercier's deposition. Would he at last unveil the 'great secret'? He appeared at the witness stand in uniform. But, instead of producing the expected bombshell, he gave, in a low voice, an 'interminable' lecture on the entire affair, which went on for four and a half hours. He talked of the cryptographic methods of the Statistical Department, and he expatiated on the secret file. 'The expectation of an event was so great that after a quarter of an hour disappointment could be read on every face. Both adversaries and supporters were equally frustrated.'

Mercier proceeded, said Reinach,

> with consummate art, truncating texts, falsifying dates, distorting the facts, sometimes simply by his improper or obscure use of language or by deliberate inaccuracy, sometimes contradicting himself to the point of absurdity within the space of one sentence, but always in such a way

169

as to lead the judges in the right direction and bring them back by innuendo to the same abominable lie. There was no need to assert publicly the existence of the *bordereau* annotated by the German Emperor. He simply stated that for the German and Italian governments, Dreyfus was 'someone well-known', a 'person known to everyone, about whom there was no need to give any details'.

'You know,' he said, 'that M. Mertian de Müller, happening to be visiting the château at Potsdam on 2nd, 3rd or 4th November 1894 I believe, saw on the desk in the Emperor's office an issue of the *Libre Parole* with the Emperor's office stamp on it, and, written in red pencil, the words: *Capitaine Dreyfus ist gefangen* (Captain Dreyfus has been captured).

He also insisted on the fact that in the Panizzardi telegram Dreyfus was mentioned without any explanation. By giving it to be understood that the German Emperor knew Dreyfus and often dealt in person with exceptional matters of espionage, he insinuated that it was not astonishing that he should have annotated the *bordereau* . . .

He then added an account of the 'tragic night', 'M. Casimir-Périer, in his deposition before the Criminal Division, has spoken of the somewhat unusual approach made to him by the German ambassador'; but he 'did not fully complete his deposition. He did not say that he, the President of the Republic, M. Charles Dupuy, the Prime Minister and I stayed that night in his office at the Elysée from eight o'clock till midnight . . . waiting to see whether peace or war would result from the exchange of notes . . . we were on the very brink of war.' If the Dreyfus Affair was to lead to war one night, Reinach remarked, how could one avoid the conclusion that the Emperor had a personal interest in not becoming compromised in this vulgar question of espionage?

Mercier went still further: he placed the 'tragic night' *before* the trial of 1894, and used it to justify the handing over of the secret file to the judges, because of the risk of war, whereas he had denied handing over any secret file when giving evidence at the Zola trial.

In fact, the diplomatic incident dated from 6 January 1895 (*see* above, p. 31–2). Casimir-Périer, who had recalled its real nature in his deposition earlier the same day, protested twice. 'With a violent gesture, he gave the lie to his former minister. But Mercier impassively continued his story.'

He had kept the question of the handwriting of the *bordereau* to the end, knowing that what he had to say was being eagerly awaited. He based himself on Bertillon's system. 'I continue . . . to believe that the *bordereau* was written by Captain Dreyfus, but I do not attach any great importance to this matter, because even if the *bordereau* was written by someone else, a cryptographic examination will show that it could only have been written at the instigation of Captain Dreyfus.'

Having reached his peroration, Mercier turned for the first time towards Dreyfus: 'If gentlemen, the slightest doubt had crossed my mind, I should have been the first to say to you, and to say to Captain Dreyfus in your presence: "I was sincerely mistaken." '

Dreyfus could contain himself no longer. There was

> a yell, fierce and poignant, the bursting of furious passion tight pent up. Dreyfus was up on his feet, his body bent double, checked in mid-spring by the officer's gentle hand on his arm, his fist pommelling the air, his head and livid face craned forward at Mercier, his teeth bared as thirsty for blood. He looked as though he would have leapt upon him like a panther, but for the touch on his arm. And the voice! 'You should say that' were the words. But the voice! None of us who heard it will ever describe it – or forget it. Men heard it that night in their sleep. It was half shriek, half sob, half despair, half snatching hope, half a fire of consuming rage and half an anguished scream for pity. (Steevens)

But Mercier went relentlessly on: '. . . I should have come here to say to Captain Dreyfus: I was sincerely mistaken and I have come here, equally sincerely, to acknowledge it, and to do all that is humanly possible to put right an appalling error.'

DREYFUS: That is your duty.

MERCIER: Well, gentlemen, not so. Since 1894, my conviction has not wavered in the slightest; it has been strengthened by my fuller and more thorough study of the case and by the futility of the attempts to prove the innocence of the convicted man of 1894, despite the immensity of the accumulated effort and the millions spent with such folly.

Hardly had Mercier left the platform when Casimir-Périer 'leapt to the stand. With eyes blazing, and in a strident voice, he exclaimed: "General Mercier has made statements on my role in 1895, which I will not endorse by my silence, and which furthermore I will not tolerate. I wish to be confronted with him." ' Jouaust decided the confrontation would take place on the Monday morning, 14 August.

But that day came yet another *coup de théâtre*. As soon as the hearing opened, a high-pitched shout went up from the hall: 'They have just assassinated Labori!' 'There was uproar, clamouring, alter-cation', said Paléologue. On the banks of the river Villaine, a young man had shot Labori in the lower part of his back; he found himself

171

on the ground, unable to move his legs. The would-be assassin fled shouting: 'I've just killed *the* Dreyfus' or 'I've just killed *a* Dreyfus.' A doctor was fetched, Labori was given treatment, and it was announced the next day that the bullet had not touched any vital organ and that he would resume his place at the trial within a week.

When finally confronted with Mercier that morning of 14 August, Casimir-Périer 'imperiously gave him the lie'. 'Lebrun-Renault never spoke in my presence . . . of any confession.' His anger grew:

> *I* never spoke of any evening, and it was not for General Mercier to accept what I said about any evening . . . General Mercier, whom I had appointed as War Minister, was not called upon to intervene in diplomatic matters. During the evening [of 6 January] I was not disturbed: I do not know who was . . . if the incident was as tragic as it has been portrayed, the ambassador would certainly have referred back to Berlin before arranging to meet the Prime Minister the next day.

Mercier 'persisted in his assertions with the dogged mumble of a schoolboy detected in a lie': 'I do not have any precise memory as to the date.' 'I assent that my memory is perfectly accurate . . . I will not have my words distorted five minutes after I have spoken them', retorted Casimir-Périer.

Mercier still remained unruffled. As soon as he was shifted from one date, he fell back on another: when Demange asked him how events dating from 6 January could have made him decide to hand over the secret file on 22 December, he replied that what happened on 6 January was 'the epilogue of a crisis which had been going on for a long time'!

Mercier escaped unscathed: Labori's friends declared things would have gone differently if he had been able to interrogate Mercier, as he had intended. Labori was a fighter, Steevens remarked. Now he was out of action, 'the devil seemed to have gone out of everybody'.

MERCIER DOMINATES THE TRIAL

By the arrogance of his inventions, by the calmness of his conviction that he had constantly been in the right against all comers, Mercier was the central figure of the trial. He was still as obstinate as ever, still just as proud of the fact that he had never changed his mind. For

Galliffet, he was a man 'suffering from hallucinations', convinced he was the incarnation of France.

He spoke, wrote Steevens, 'in a slow, passionless monotone ... As he sat and strove to wind the toils of treason round the prisoner, he seemed as unmoved by hate as by pity; he accused him dully, as if reading a lesson.' He remained for the rest of the trial 'sitting all the time in his armchair, continually twiddling his thumbs', said Mathieu Dreyfus.

> He paid close attention to every incident and every deposition; he dominated the band of false witnesses by his intelligence, his composure, and his tireless activity – for he was ever-ready to intervene and to pay dearly for doing so; he was in charge of all the forces of falsehood in their assault against truth. His ceaseless activity went on everywhere: his numerous emissaries of all ranks were given the task of haunting officers' messes, their clubs and military circles of all kinds. They spread the good word in all these places.

From 14 August to 7 September, morning after morning in the summer heat, an endless procession of witnesses followed, 75 for the prosecution and 45 for the defence. The testimony for the prosecution was all in line with that of Mercier: first came the former War Ministers, including Cavaignac. Then came the chiefs and the other officers on the General Staff. Most continued to play the same part they had been playing for a long time now; they simply added a few variations. Only General Roget, exuding hate, argued systematically that Dreyfus could have acquired the information referred to in the *bordereau*, while Esterhazy could not. There were few revelations: the trial was beginning to turn into a spectacle, as Paléologue had feared, but it was a predictable one. It had even become a trifle boring.

The military prosecutor did not respect the limits which had been laid down in Galliffet's instructions. This allowed Cavaignac to bring up the legend of Dreyfus's confession; the 'scoundrel D.' note surfaced again too, and there were even some new charges. Minor witnesses recounted allegedly suspect conversations: an officer had met Dreyfus on a station platform. The latter asked: 'Is there any news?'

The swindler Cernuschi was the only prosecution witness to cause something of a stir, when he asserted, on the basis of confidences from another adventurer, that Dreyfus was one of four spies in the pay of Germany. Hearsay evidence proliferated, leaving the English journalists aghast.

Lord Russell of Killowen, in particular, was scandalized by the partiality both of the witnesses and the president. 'What an affront to justice it is, this interminable procession of witnesses making accusations from the stand! A witness is not entitled to make accusations; he must say what he has seen and tell what he knows, and nothing else. Why all this complaisance towards the prosecution? Why does the president allow it?' Dreyfus had himself protested after Roget's deposition: 'All through the last few days, I have been listening to speeches for the prosecution. I cannot defend myself.'

However, all the accusations did not stand up against the testimony of the defence. Picquart explained the whole case for seven hours. 'It was a masterpiece of reasoning, the intellectual triumph of the trial,' wrote Steevens. Major Hartmann showed that the author of the *bordereau* could not have been a gunner. Freystätter, one of the judges of 1894 who felt remorse at having been associated with the conviction of an innocent man, testified on the handing over of the secret file. He stated that Maurel had read seven documents aloud while the judges were considered their verdict. Maurel replied that, after reading the first, he had handed the file to his neighbour saying: 'I feel tired.' In this way, Maurel had to admit the manner in which he had had Dreyfus convicted (*see* above, p. 27). Finally, an officer named Fonds-Lamothe showed, on the basis of a circular dated May 1894, that Dreyfus knew he was not going on manoeuvres and so could not have written the last sentence of the *bordereau*.

The handwriting experts were still in disagreement, except that Charavay acknowledged his mistake of 1894. The intellectuals reaffirmed that the *bordereau* was in Esterhazy's handwriting. The latter did not testify in person but sent the officers letters from London full of threats and insults. He admitted he had written the *bordereau*, but said it had been dictated to him by Sandherr; in any case Dreyfus was a 'wretch', someone 'despicable', a man whose guilt emerged from all that Mercier had left unsaid. As ever, the shadow of the imperial forgery hung over the trial.

On 4 September, so as to calm the nation's nerves at the time of the verdict, the government decided to constitute the Senate as a High Court to try Déroulède and the conspirators who had been arrested on 12 August. The High Court was convened for 18 September.

How would the trial end? As a last resort, Waldeck-Rousseau had made an appeal to Berlin to hand over some of the documents referred to in the *bordereau*. He met with a refusal. Labori, on his own initiative, also applied for permission from Germany to interrogate Schwartzkoppen. This was refused too. Tension had by now flared up between the pugnacious Labori, who had returned to the trial on 22 August, and the more cautious Demange.

Seeing that there was no new evidence from Germany, those of the Dreyfusards who had followed the trial were now pessimistic, despite the weight of evidence from the defence. In Paris, the ministers in the government and the leading Dreyfusards were in no doubt that Dreyfus would be convicted again.

It would certainly have been unlikely that officers not versed in the law, with limited critical faculties and confronted with such a contradictory medley of truths and untruths, documents and forgeries, opinions and hearsay, would have doubted the good faith of their superiors. But Carrière's closing speech for the prosecution was completely formless. 'His interventions in the debates,' said Reinach, 'had been infrequent and usually inane. Clearly, he did not understand the proceedings, he was one of those men who are a caricature of themselves, the macrocephalic type, with a forehead receding at 30°, eyes like those of a weasel, a nose like a beak, a chin as receding as the forehead, and a massive body perched high on his legs, like one of those sad, grotesque waders called marabous.'

'For over an hour and a half, there was not an argument, or even an attempt at an argument. What feeble-mindedness, what ignorance of the law!' remarked Lord Russell. 'How could such a grave task have been given to such a grotesque figure? Does France not know that the eyes of the world are watching the Dreyfus Affair?'

Those who wanted a second conviction were filled with amazement; those who favoured Dreyfus regained hope. But who was to make the closing speech for the defence? Labori had irritated the judges; there was a somewhat hesitant attempt by the Dreyfusards to dissuade him from pleading. In the end, he left the field to Demange.

The great barrister spoke for five hours, discussing every invention and every hypothesis with equal vigour, since any one of them might influence the judges. He addressed himself exclusively to them, almost conversationally, without playing on the audience, and without any rhetorical or even stylistic effects. He never gave the impression of questioning their good faith. Sometimes he aroused pity, drawing such a tragic picture of his client that several of the judges could not control their feelings. He read extracts from Dreyfus's journal written on Devil's Island, to illustrate his cult of the Fatherland. He only touched on the guilty men 'with some hesitation'. Esterhazy was 'more of a swindler than a traitor'. Demange refused to give credence to the complicity of Henry and Esterhazy. 'The judges of 1894 were

175

not fully informed, they did not have Esterhazy's handwriting. You do! Go on now!'

At these words, the members of the court-martial felt a great shudder. Demange concluded.

> You are now going to retire to consider your verdict, and what will you ask yourselves at that time? Whether Dreyfus is innocent? No! *I* attest to his innocence, but you have only to ask yourselves whether he is guilty . . . You will say: we do not know. Another man could have been guilty of treason; but not him, no, no: there are things he could not have been guilty of . . . the handwriting is not his . . . There is a man over there, on the other side of the Channel, who could have committed the crime, yes he could. At that moment, I swear to you, there will be a doubt in your conscience. That doubt is enough for me. That doubt means an acquittal.'

This was the whole of Demange's method: to awaken doubt. At the end of the speech, one of the judges, Merle, was weeping great tears. The entire world was waiting for the verdict.

After Carrière had asked the judges to weigh up the pros and cons and Demange had expressed his confidence in them, Dreyfus, looking horribly pale, attempted to proclaim his innocence. His physical weakness was so great that a hoarse murmur was all that could be heard: 'I am innocent . . . the honour of the name borne by my children . . . your honesty.'

THE VERDICT

After more than an hour's deliberation, the judges re-entered the court. In a deathly silence, Jouaust declared: 'In the name of the French people . . . by a majority of five to two, yes, we find the accused guilty.' Jouaust, who had voted 'No' with de Bréon, had insisted the judges vote for extenuating circumstances. The penalty was fixed at ten years' imprisonment.

There was no protest from the hall, 'only a long murmur, like the moaning of the autumn wind'. Demange, in tears, embraced Dreyfus. All the latter said was: 'Console my wife.'

The first reaction of the revisionists, when they heard the news of this incoherent verdict, was utter amazement. How could there be extenuating circumstances in a case of treason? But it was after all a kind of victory. For Clemenceau, iniquity was on the retreat. Zola declared: 'This is a giant step forward for truth.' But to their mind, the battle must go on.

Abroad, there was universal condemnation of France. In a score of cities, from Budapest to Indianapolis, popular demonstrations broke out. There were attacks on French consulates and the French flag. 'From all quarters,' wrote Reinach, 'came the proposal to ostracize France, and to refuse her invitation to the Universal Exhibition which was to open the following spring, or to attend only as if it were a place of ill repute.' The Universal Exhibition was set to open in Paris in April 1900. If for this reason alone, the feeling began to grow that France must make haste to put a stop to the unrest which had been disturbing the country for two years.

There was no triumphalism among the anti-Dreyfusards: once the verdict had been established, they could even, like everyone else, share in the wave of sympathy that developed for Dreyfus's sufferings. The officers of the court-martial asked that he should not be degraded a second time.

There was good reason for all this: when Mathieu saw his brother again in his cell the day after the verdict, on 10 September, 'his brother's face, beneath its apparent calm, showed signs of such deep sadness, such atrocious inner suffering', that he could hardly keep control of his feelings. 'His features were so to speak convulsed, and the painful fixed grin on his mouth was more pronounced than ever.' Mathieu told him the struggle would go on more fiercely, more ardently than ever, and that he must suffer everything stoically, even a fresh degradation. 'When he heard the word "degradation", he started suddenly and protested, in a fit of anger: "I shall never stand for another degradation; I shall never put on my uniform for it to be defiled a second time. They will have to drag me; they will have to carry me there by force: no, not that, never, never." ' When he got back to Paris, Mathieu said to Reinach and Bernard-Lazare: 'If he stays in prison, he will not live another six months.'

MOVES TOWARDS A PARDON

Reinach explained that he was beginning to think of a pardon. 'A cry of horror will go up from the world,' he told Mathieu, 'not only against the criminals who have had your brother convicted, but against this country. We must dissociate France from this crime.' To this end, there must be an immediate pardon. This is what Reinach had declared in his article in *Le Siècle*, published the same day, under the title: 'France's honour must be cleared.' The idea of a pardon was also emerging in *Le Petit Parisien* and even in *Le Temps*.

But Clemenceau and Jaurès refused to accept Reinach's proposal; for Clemenceau, 'now, after a whole people has been roused to fight for Justice, they are supposed to be satisfied with a pardon for one individual. Dreyfus is to return comfortably home, the pro-Dreyfus troops are to disperse, and that will be the end of the Affair. What an end!' Clemenceau the fighter would not give up the struggle; he continued his press campaign, as did Jaurès. But what way out was there for the government? It could find none. Waldeck-Rousseau soon discovered there was no legal solution; he had thought of an annulment, but that would mean a third court-martial. Galliffet had made this clear in a letter, just before the verdict.

> It will be a battle between two courts-martial and two military appeal courts. It will be a battle against the entire army, standing shoulder to shoulder and resisting mentally . . . we must not forget that in France the great majority are antisemites. We should therefore find ourselves in the following position: on the other side, the entire army, the majority of Frenchmen (not to mention the deputies and senators), and on the other the government, the Dreyfusards and foreigners.

A third court-martial would convict Dreyfus by six votes to one, wrote the cynic Galliffet to Princess Radziwill, a fourth one would convict him unanimously.

Mornard, when consulted by Waldeck, said that the only possible way out was a pardon. Waldeck agreed to it. Reinach went to see him. At the first mention of a pardon, Reinach's face brightened. Waldeck declared that his mind was made up but that he foresaw difficulties. The President of the Republic was worried: the army would have to be prepared for this repudiation of the Rennes judgment. Reinach insisted the pardon must be immediate: in a month's time it would look like a mere act of pity. Waldeck allowed himself to be persuaded and said he would go and see Loubet and Millerand.

Meanwhile, Millerand's legal perspicacity uncovered a new obstacle: it seemed likely that Dreyfus's application for a retrial, which he had made simply as a matter of form, without any real conviction, would be allowed because the judges at Rennes had made a legal blunder. They had forgotten to give a ruling on the supervision to which he would be subject after the sentence. If the Rennes judgment were to be overturned on this point alone, it would be a catastrophe. Dreyfus must therefore withdraw his application. 'And what about the Exhibition?' asked Millerand. 'Is not the Exhibition in jeopardy?'

There was a new outcry among the Dreyfusards, at a meeting at the offices of the newspaper *Le Radical*. 'I do not care what they do with Dreyfus,' Clemenceau exclaimed violently, 'let them cut him up and eat him.' Mathieu arrived and immediately exclaimed: 'No! I shall never advise my brother to withdraw his application! He will die in prison, and his death will be on the ministers' consciences.' 'Ah! That's the stuff!' Clemenceau exclaimed again, shaking him warmly by the hand: 'You are a good fellow, I expected nothing less of you.' Reinach remained silent. Then the telephone rang: Millerand asked Mathieu to call at the Ministry. As he sat in Reinach's carriage, Mathieu confessed his anxiety: more prison for his brother would mean certain death. But did honour allow the application to be withdrawn?

At the Ministry, Millerand explained to Mathieu the nature of the new legal impasse and asked him to return to Rennes to confer with his brother in person. Mathieu stood his ground, but Millerand and Reinach both said that if they were Dreyfus's counsel they would advise him to agree to withdraw the application. Mathieu wanted to consult Clemenceau and Jaurès again. He waited for them with Reinach in the Ministry garden. The latter tempted him: in two days' time he could be miles away, with his brother, in a tranquil spot.

When Clemenceau and Jaurès arrived, with the socialist Gérault-Richard, they returned to Millerand's office. There was a grand debate: Clemenceau accused Reinach of diverting the greatest affair of the century from its course and running it into the sands; Reinach replied that Clemenceau's idealism would only keep going the polemics and the discord.

CLEMENCEAU: You are sacrificing the cause of all the oppressed to one man's interests.

REINACH: You are turning a living creature into a mere battering-ram against political and military institutions.

CLEMENCEAU: You are humiliating the Republic before the sword.

In the end, it was Gérault-Richard's common sense which convinced Jaurès: 'The people will simply see that Loubet did not want to keep an innocent man in prison.'

'Mathieu,' said Clemenceau, 'you have a majority.'

'No,' replied Mathieu, 'it is not a question of a majority. If you continue to advise against withdrawing the application, I shall not agree to it.'

CLEMENCEAU (after a long pause): very well, if I were the brother, I should accept.

No one tried to get any more out of him.

JAURES: It is clearly understood that Dreyfus and Mathieu, after the pardon, will carry on the fight.

REINACH: Can you doubt it?

MATHIEU: (forcefully): I ask you yourselves to write, here and now, the statement he will publish when he comes out of prison.

Jaurès sat down at Millerand's desk. He and Reinach wrote:

> The government of the Republic has restored my liberty. But that is nothing to me without honour. As from today, I shall continue to seek redress for the judicial error of which I am still the victim. I wish the whole of France to know, by a final judgment, that I am innocent; my heart will only be at peace when no Frenchman imputes to me the crime which has been committed by another.

On his return to Rennes, Mathieu persuaded Dreyfus to accept, which he did, thinking of his wife and children.

A final stumbling block emerged at the Cabinet meeting. All the ministers demanded an immediate pardon, whereas Loubet thought it would be more politic to wait for a week until the army and public opinion had been prepared for it and the High Court had met. Millerand, however, had given his word of honour: if the pardon was not immediate he would tender his resignation. Waldeck-Rousseau and Galliffet also saw themselves as committed because of their assurances to Millerand. It was necessary therefore to refer to Mathieu: he must release Millerand from his promise and accept that the pardon would not be signed until 19 September. He agreed.

THE COUNTRY RETURNS TO PEACE AND QUIET

The furore subsided, said Reinach.

The High Court met on 18 September: it heard the indictment by the public prosecutor Bernard, and decided by more than 200 votes to refer the file to the preliminary investigation committee. Loubet signed the pardon on 19 September. Two days later, Galliffet issued an order of the day to the army, having obtained Waldeck's agreement that there would be no reprisals against the military:

> The incident is closed! The military judges, enjoying respect on all sides, have pronounced their verdict in complete independence. – We have, without any kind of reservation, bowed to their sentence. – We shall bow in the same way to the act which a deep sense of pity has dictated to the President of the Republic.
>
> There can no longer be any question of reprisals of any sort.
>
> So, I repeat, the incident is closed.
>
> I ask you, and if it were necessary, I should order you, to forget this past and think only of the future.

With all of you, comrades, I cry most heartily: 'Long live the army!', the army which belongs not to any party but only to France.

To Galliffet, had the Affair ever been more than a mere 'incident'? Dreyfus was already at Carpentras to begin his convalescence.

EPILOGUE

THE END OF THE AFFAIR AND ITS AFTERMATH

Was the Affair over? Yes and no. As far as the Waldeck-Rousseau government was concerned, the main legal question had been disposed of, and the turmoil in the country subsided with remarkable rapidity. The plotters' lack of success showed that disaffection in the army had not been extensive, and the limited nature of Galliffet's disciplinary measures was enough to restore calm among the military.

The Prime Minister's political judgement had been sound: the appointment of Galliffet and Millerand, followed by the unconvincing judgment at Rennes and the presidential pardon, had had two positive results: they had satisfied the army, since Dreyfus had after all been found guilty, but there had been no reprisals; at the same time, Dreyfus had been freed, and there was the assurance that he would not return to prison.

The new situation did not unduly offend the anti-Dreyfusard extremists either, as it had the expected result of demobilizing most of the revisionist troops. The country could at last breathe a sigh of relief and get down to preparing for the 1900 International Exhibition. But Dreyfus and his staunchest supporters were determined to carry on their campaign until his innocence had been officially recognized. Some of the Dreyfusards even reproached him for his acceptance of the pardon and his inactivity during his convalescence.

To complete the clearing up of the Affair, it only remained for the government, in the autumn of 1899, to remove any possible sources of disturbance still remaining in the country, and to consign to oblivion the innumerable court cases the Affair had generated.

The trial of Déroulède and his friends by the High Court lasted from 9 November to 4 January. The lack of any real preparations for a coup soon became apparent and, after a series of noisy hearings during which he and the other accused indulged in propaganda for their cause, he and Buffet were exiled for ten years. Habert, who surrendered in December, was later given a sentence of five years in exile. It was the end of Déroulède and Guérin. Drumont, too, lost all his influence. The apogée of political antisemitism fighting under its own banner was now past; it was to find other outlets.

On the legal side, Waldeck-Rousseau put an amnesty law through Parliament covering all crimes and offences connected with the Drey-fus Affair, setting aside murders and civil lawsuits. This law led to howls of protest from diehard Dreyfusards. For Mathieu Dreyfus, it was a 'shameful, wretched law'. It was, he said, a special law to allow men who had for years broken every law to escape their well-deserved punishment. 'It is a strange conception of equity to spare the criminals so as to convict their victims. Dreyfus is to remain the legal traitor and Picquart to be excluded from the army.' But, for the government, the Dreyfus Affair was now no more than a problem calling for purely political measures, so as to bring about a return to peace and quiet.

Ordinary life returns

Politics had indeed returned. As Blum said in his *Souvenirs sur l'Af-faire*, the great period of the Affair was over for the Dreyfusards. Already, with Henry's suicide,

> the spell had been broken ... We began living like everyone else ... Once the cyclone had passed, France found herself in exactly the same state she had been in before. It was a strange spectacle ... What a surprise! For years, people's personal lives, and the life of the community, had been completely absorbed, they had been turned upside down by unparalleled passions! People had felt different; everything around them had felt different. And yet the moment the acute phase ended and the temperature fell, society, the body politic, groups and individuals found themselves exactly as they always had been, as if nothing had ever happened ... We had not succeeded in bringing about the revolutionary renewal.

It is true that the most idealistic Dreyfusards, like Péguy, had seen the fight for justice and truth in the Affair as a prelude to a moral revolution in which these principles would triumph permanently in society. But the moral revolution they looked forward to so eagerly did not take place: Dreyfusism had, step by step, become completely politicized, and political life, with all its half-truths and its moral compromises, once again took over. Péguy, as a man of moral absolutes, became a relentless critic of politics, condemning the re-opening of the case by Jaurès in 1903 as a 'parliamentary political' operation: the condemnation of everyday politics was to become the central theme of *Notre jeunesse*, written in 1910. The degeneration of Dreyfusism into the morass of politics was the illustration, he wrote, of a universal law: everything began with *la mystique*, an absolute ideal, and ended up in politics.

The re-opening of the case and Dreyfus's rehabilitation

What was the nature of Jaurès's re-opening of the case? Mathieu and Alfred Dreyfus had looked in vain for the new evidence which would permit a review of the 1899 trial. For a long time, they tried to discover the famous *bordereau* annotated by the German Emperor. Then, in 1903, Jaurès seized on the opportunity provided by the invalidation of a nationalist deputy Syveton and made a long speech in which he went over the whole history of the case and raised the matter of the annotated *bordereau*. The Chamber showed little interest, but Jaurès's initiative had the positive effect that General André, Galliffet's successor as War Minister, promised a new enquiry into the documents of the case.

Despite Péguy's criticisms, Jaurès's action did set the final review in train. A whole series of documents turned up which seemed to prove Dreyfus's innocence, and, on 25 December 1903, the consultative committee decided on a review. With great deliberation, and amidst public indifference, the Criminal Division and the combined divisions came to their conclusion: according to the final judgment, nothing remained of the original charges against Dreyfus and the conviction of 1894 was quashed without a retrial on 12 July 1906. On 22 July, at a parade at the Ecole Militaire, Dreyfus was decorated with the Legion of Honour. The Affair was now over.

Had it after all been no more than an episode, what Galliffet had called an 'incident'? The answer depended entirely on the point of view of the questioner. To Péguy the moralist, the revolution had failed. But from 1899, if the Affair had not changed French people's lives fundamentally, it had begun to bring about political, social and ideological changes many of whose effects can still be felt nearly a century later.

The fate of the protagonists

By 1906, some of the main actors in the Affair were already dead: Scheurer-Kestner, Waldeck-Rousseau and Cavaignac. Zola had died by carbon monoxide poisoning in 1902: some alleged that this was a suicide. Jaurès was to be assassinated as war broke out in 1914; Péguy was killed at the front, in the first skirmishes of the battle of the Marne.

But Alfred Dreyfus lived on, though he played no further part in French public life: he always insisted he had been 'only an artillery officer' and that the symbol Dreyfus had been the creation of others. He fought in the First World War, commanding a supply column, and was promoted to *officier de la Légion d'Honneur* in 1919. But he always remained a concerned observer of current affairs, and was committed to the centre-left philosophy of solidarism, a middle way between collectivism and unbridled capitalism. Though he disapproved of militant trade unionism, he actually came out publicly in support of the anarchists Sacco and Vanzetti, who were executed in the United States in 1927. He finally died in 1935. (For the various volumes of his memoirs, see the 'Further Reading' section below).

A few months after Dreyfus's rehabilitation, Clemenceau became Prime Minister: he made Picquart, now restored to the army, his War Minister; the latter died in 1914. Clemenceau became the scourge of the revolutionary trade unions, 'the first policeman of France' and the great opponent of Jaurès, before becoming the Tiger of 1917 and finally representing France at the Peace Conference.

Reinach, because of his role in the Affair, only won back his seat at Digne in 1906; he lost it again for good in 1914. He was the only ex-Dreyfusard politician to retain the respect of Charles Péguy, for he 'did not give way to Dreyfusard demagogy'. He completed his great history of the Affair in 1911, and he became military commentator of *Le Figaro* during the First World War, being regarded by British GHQ, said Chapman, as a 'pestilential nuisance'.

Schwartzkoppen retired in 1908 but he returned to fight in the First World War. He died after a fall from his horse in 1915, crying on his deathbed: 'Frenchmen, listen to me! Dreyfus is innocent.' His memoirs, published by Schwertfeger in 1930, caused a minor sensation as the final confirmation of Dreyfus's innocence from the German side.

Meanwhile Esterhazy remained in England, eventually acquiring a house in Harpenden, where he died in 1923 and lies buried in the parish churchyard as the 'Comte de Voilement'. His life in England has been fully chronicled by Marcel Thomas.

THE CONSEQUENCES OF THE AFFAIR

The prime political consequence of the Affair was the coming to power in France, for a decade, of a government of the Left, which enjoyed the support of the majority which had come together during the Affair to defend the Republic: it was made up of Waldeck-

185

Rousseau and the left-wing elements in Progressism, together with the radicals and the socialists. It was the end of the attempt at government by moderate Republicans from the Centre, and of the combined opposition of a Right and an extreme Left tinged with nationalism, an opposition ever-ready to denounce Republican corruption and scandal.

If Waldeck-Rousseau's majority was flimsy in June 1899, it rapidly grew stronger, and it became the solid foundation for the Bloc des Gauches, which was to govern France until 1909. Together with antinationalism, the cement of the coalition was anticlericalism, as we have seen, which increasingly dominated the programme of the triumphant ex-Dreyfusard Left.

A period of stable government began. Waldeck-Rousseau's policy was to take up once again the Republicans' unfinished programme of secularization. He was under intense anticlerical pressure as a result of the campaign which had begun in the autumn of 1898. But it was not only, for him, a matter of responding to pressure, and of taking reprisals against the excesses of the Assumptionist order during the Affair (though the order was indeed dissolved in January 1900) – it was fundamentally a matter of completing the historic secularizing mission of the Left. Waldeck brought in a law on freedom of association (1901) which imposed special restrictions on the religious orders.

After he left office owing to the sweeping successes of the radicals in the 1902 elections this process of secularization accelerated. The extreme anticlericalism of Combes led to the banning of the teaching orders in 1904 and the Separation of Church and State.

The alliance of Jaurès and the socialists with the radicals in the Bloc des Gauches contributed to the same result, since Jaurès considered that it was in the long-term interest of socialism to urge the radicals on to complete their historic task of secularization, which would then leave the road clear for the introduction of socialism.

The coming to power of the Left after the Affair had itself the consequence of bringing about a change in the nature of the political class: from the time of the Affair, ministers and politicians were increasingly drawn from the more modest groups in society: they had too an increasing grasp of the problems of the working class and of capitalism.

Another change which followed hard on the heels of the Affair was the appearance of political parties in France in something approaching their modern form. These were no longer simply electoral committees of notables: the Parti Radical et Radical-Socialiste appeared in 1901, the Alliance Républicaine in 1901 and the Fédération Républicaine in 1903; the socialists united in the SFIO in 1905.

The question of governmental participation, which had emerged among the socialists when Millerand entered the Waldeck-Rousseau government at the end of the Dreyfus crisis, led to a division among them and a great international debate in the movement. On the one hand, the orthodox Marxists opposed any governmental participation; the parliamentary socialists supported it. This split, essentially between revolutionaries and reformists, led to the formation of two separate socialist parties until they united in 1905. But the debate on socialist participation in bourgeois governments was to continue, and it still preoccupied the SFIO at the time when Léon Blum came to power as Prime Minister in 1936.

The development of large-scale capitalism in the years immediately before the Dreyfus Affair had given the workers a new class-consciousness, and their opposition to capitalism, their increasing espousal of socialism, had led them into new and sharp opposition towards the moderate Republicans who ruled France when the Affair began. No longer were the workers simply Republicans and willing adjuncts in the battle to overcome the forces of clericalism. They turned against the moderate Republicans in power, who seemed, after Panama, to be representative of capitalism and corruption. It was also difficult for workers as we have seen, to take up the case of a Jewish army captain whom they saw as a member of the oppressing class and who was first defended by class enemies. It was only when they became convinced that the Republic was in danger that they came round to an alliance with those Republican forces they saw as genuinely determined to defend the Republic. But with the coming to power of a government of the Left, as Jaurès saw, they would begin to have their own say in the Republic through their socialist representatives, and, despite the quarrel over governmental participation, the integration of the workers into the Republic had begun. Their reconcilliation with the Republic, which had seemed to them in the 1890s to be a Republic of exploiters and of corruption, was now possible.

It is true that the most revolutionary elements among the workers, to be found in the revolutionary syndicalist movement, insisted on remaining aloof from politics. They violently opposed Millerand's attempt to introduce an arbitration system to settle strikes. In 1906, at the Amiens congress of the CGT, Millerand was accused of seeking to domesticate the trade unions. And it was in reaction against this attempt that revolutionary syndicalism developed with such vigour in France before 1914. In the Charte d'Amiens of 1906, the French trade union movement laid down its policy of keeping party politics out of the trade unions. This has remained a permanent feature of unionism in France to this day.

At the same time it remains the case that, as in 1914 and in 1936, the overwhelming majority of the French working class has always rallied to the Republic when it seemed to be in real danger.

What remained of the nationalist leagues, which had now lost their leaders, joined up with the only one still active, the Ligue de la Patrie Française, which turned itself into a purely electoral organization. The wave of nationalist feeling in Paris brought it considerable successes in the 1900 municipal elections, but nationalism in the provinces collapsed, and after the 1902 elections, the moderate nationalist Right stagnated. In the end, for the reasons suggested above (p. 137), the Ligue eventually withered, and it disappeared in 1905.

The future of nationalism, and of antisemitism, lay with the new extreme Right which emerged from the Affair. The Action Française was entirely converted within a short time to monarchism by Maurras, who provided it with the doctrine of integral nationalism. Maurice Barrès became the other theorist of traditionalist nationalism. From the time of the Affair, the Action Française, and the extreme Right in general, have also continued to provide a home for antisemitism in French politics, right down to the present day, though since the Holocaust, antisemitism has had to hide its face and proceed by allusion and insinuation.

Antisemitism disappeared entirely from the discourse of the socialist Left after the Affair. In the years between 1906 and 1914 it fell into a decline again but the Action Française did organize antisemitic street action in 1907–8. It re-emerged at the time of the Popular Front and Vichy. Even in 1990, it could still count on a certain antipathy to Jews in France: according to a survey, 18 per cent of French people found Jews 'unpleasant'.

It is worth noting here that Jean-Marc Berlière has pointed out that the creation, at the time of the Dreyfus Affair, of a police force ready to act loyally to defend the Republic had the paradoxical effect of turning the extreme Right against the police. A 'black legend' appeared, and the police were reviled by the extreme Right as having been responsible for every unexplained crime. At the same time, xenophobia among the police persisted up to the time of Vichy.

Finally, a handful of activists on the extreme Right can still be found in France today who are not quite convinced that Dreyfus was innocent.

With the failure of the anti-Republican plotting of 1899, the collapse of the Leagues and, still more, the consolidation of the Republic, the last hope of a return to power by the old ruling classes faded. The petty provincial nobility had to resign themselves to this and it was without much conviction that they subscribed, said Jacques Chastenet, to the first publications of the Action Française.

The intellectuals, first seen as a significant social group during the Affair, have continued to be a feature of French society up to the present day, and have continued to exercise their critical function and to express their group opinion regarding the great intellectual and moral issues of the day, and those concerning human rights, whether it be the use of torture during the Algerian war or the more recent problems of Bosnia. The Ligue des Droits de l'Homme continues the task it began with the Affair.

The extension to the whole range of social injustice of the intellectuals' critique of that done to Dreyfus led a number of them towards socialism after the Affair, notably Anatole France. A number saw education of the workers as a key task for intellectuals, as a contribution to paving the way for socialism. Péguy broke with the socialist party in 1900 with the initial aim of developing his journal *Cahiers de la Quinzaine* to act as a kind of popular university of socialism. Other socialist journals set about a similar task. 'Popular universities' sprang up, and flourished for several years after the Affair, with the aim of bringing the knowledge of university professors to the workers. However, the initial impetus was not sustained. Over much of the 20th century until the fall of the Berlin Wall, this commitment of the intellectuals to social justice was to lead them to a long love affair with Marxism, and to an identification with communism that has thus only recently finally passed into history.

One area where intellectuals of both the Left and the Right made a lasting contribution before 1914 was in the realm of political ideas. The Affair had its impact on critical political ideas of every complexion. Republican idealism inspired by the Affair asserted itself, as we have seen, in Péguy's general criticism of parliamentary politics, but also in his increasingly bitter critique of what he saw as the failings of parliamentary socialism and of Jaurès. In *Notre jeunesse* in 1910 he gave a religious, and indeed a Christian, connotation to the Dreyfusard principles of absolute Truth, Freedom and Justice to which he had, he said, continued to remain faithful. The philosopher Alain also saw the Affair as a reference point in the development of his anti-authoritarian radicalism, and in particular as a lesson in Republican vigilance. Among the ex-anti-Dreyfusards, the essential

189

themes for Maurras and Barrès were authority, tradition and national-ism. Both sets of attitudes, critical, idealistic Republicanism and mon-archist or plebiscitary nationalism, remained outside the parameters of the existing Republic. For Péguy, the Republic was too political; for Alain it was constantly tempted to exceed its powers and must be kept firmly in check. For Maurras and Barrès it was on the other hand too weak and ineffective properly to govern and defend France. As has been indicated, the nature of such political ideas inevitably situates the intellectual who formulates them outside the system. Jean Jaurès expressed his socialist thinking within the framework of parlia-mentary democracy, and so largely ceased to function as an intellectual in the years after the Affair.

The French press, which had found a new campaigning role in the Affair, has paradoxically become less politicized in the 20th century. The *Petit Journal* lost circulation as a result of its anti-Dreyfusard stand, and was replaced as France's leading daily in the years before 1914 by the *Petit Parisien*, which had adopted a very prudent line over the Affair. The long-term trend in the French press since 1918 has been towards depoliticization, and the number and importance of politically committed or party newspapers has steadily declined. The lesson of the Affair was that to take a strong line was to alienate a substantial part of one's readership: the French provincial press now attempts to be all things to all readers: *L'Humanité* survives with difficulty as the last of the party newspapers.

Catholics paid heavily, after the Affair, for the sins of the Assump-tionists. Many were to turn to the Action Française, though that movement was also eventually condemned, for atheism, by the Vati-can in 1926. The attempts of left-wing Catholics to come to terms with the Republic and with the problems of the workers continued: the activities of Marc Sangnier's Sillon spread throughout France from 1903 until it was condemned by the Vatican in 1910. It was only after 1945 that the Church officially accepted the principle of political democracy, and the MRP appeared as a Christian Democratic party; the problems of the worker priests after the Second World War showed, however, that the Church, despite its social concerns, still fought shy of socialism, let alone communism, which was seen as atheistic. It was not until after Vatican II that it moved closer to the political Left. And it was only in 1994 that an official *mea culpa* was pronounced by Mgr Defois regarding the role of Catholics in the Dreyfus Affair.

The Jewish community equally felt the consequences of the Affair. Jews lost their entrée into upper-class society, according to the picture drawn by Proust in his novels; Jewish officers, too, began to find their careers hampered for the first time. The Affair did much to convince Theodore Herzl that the old aim of the Jews in Western society, assimilation, was unattainable. They would always remain pariahs. His answer to the problem, the call for a Jewish state, first made in 1896, led to the Zionist movement, and the establishment of the state of Israel. But the process of integration of the French Jews into French society continued, and Zionism has had a limited impact in France. Jews, such as Léon Blum and Laurent Fabius, to name only two, have reached the highest positions in the state. In a survey conducted in 1994 by the Ligue des Droits de l'Homme, 81 per cent of those questioned declared they would not be uncomfortable if a Jew were elected President of the Republic. However, though there is no evidence of anti-Jewish discrimination in France today, there is clearly still some residue of vague antisemitic feeling affecting about one Frenchman in five. These Frenchmen, who correspond to the other 18 per cent who find Jews 'unpleasant', may provide some sort of an audience for a Le Pen who is reduced by present anti-racialist legislation to making the occasional crypto-antisemitic remark.

Most striking, of course, has been the impact of the Dreyfus Affair on the French army. After the Affair, the old attempt to Republicanize the army was taken up again by General André. He set up a system of recording the political opinions of officers, and this led in 1904 to accusations of snooping. A parliamentary scandal followed, and André was obliged to resign. But if the system of promotion was changed to prevent continuous co-optation of conservatives by conservatives, and if it became in the 20th century advisable, for career reasons, for army officers to at least profess Republican opinions in public, the history of the army's relations with the Republic since the Affair suggests that, underneath, not a great deal has changed in basic attitudes among officers whose fundamental values are those of force and action, and who have little time for parliamentary methods. Between the wars, General Weygand constantly deplored the weakness and instability of parliamentary government. And would it be too mischievous to suggest that the Fifth Republic, set up by a noted general precisely to remedy what he saw as the defects of French parliamentarism, has come to represent the final *revanche* of the military spirit over a parliamentary democracy which set out to bring the army to heel after the Dreyfus Affair?

The army has, however, remained faithful to its basic duty to obey the civil power, albeit with some notable exceptions: General de Gaulle in 1940 (though his rebellion was in the name of the Republic) and the generals who rebelled in Algiers in 1961. Outside these most exceptional of circumstances, the military have remained content to grumble about parliamentary democracy, and to make the occasional public outburst on military policy whenever they feel civilians really do not understand their problems. For the rest, they remain largely true to their fundamental commitment to keeping quiet, submitting to the powers that be and maintaining law and order. In that sense, *plus ça change, plus c'est la même chose.*

Much the same could have been said finally of the army's anti-Dreyfusism, after the celebrated episode early in 1994 when the head of the Service Historique de l'Armée de Terre, Colonel Gaujac, had to be sacked by the Defence Minister for publishing an official note on the Affair which included several errors and the statement that 'the innocence of Dreyfus is the thesis generally admitted by historians'. It is not known how many anti-Dreyfusards still remain in the upper ranks of the French army. The suspicion is there may be some. The Dreyfus Affair has been too great a trauma for the army; it has looked as if it could not quite look the facts in the face. It should be remembered in this connection that Tim's statue of Dreyfus was refused for the Ecole Militaire in the late 1980s by Charles Hernu, the Defence Minister, on the grounds that the location was not open to the public. It was suspected that the Minister was speaking for the army. The statue today stands on a small square along the Boulevard Raspail (the place Pierre-Lafue) after being discreetly hidden for a few years in the Jardin des Tuileries. It is a safe distance from the Ecole Militaire.

One final hesitation: there were objections from the military to the holding of the major 1994 centenary exhibition on the Affair at the Invalides, and there was some doubt as to whether the exhibition would actually go ahead. A century on, the Affair has still seemed an embarrassment to the French army.

However, the official army standpoint was at last clarified in a historic statement by General Mourrut, the new head of the Service Historique de l'Armée de Terre. On 7 September 1995, he appeared in full dress-uniform before an audience of 1700 at a specially convened meeting of the Central Jewish Consistory of France. On behalf of the French army, he officially declared Dreyfus innocent, something which the army had never done in all the century since the trial of 1894. The Dreyfus Affair, he said, 'was a minor legal news item, resulting from a military conspiracy which led, partly on the basis of a falsified document, to a man – an innocent man – being condemned to transportation. This gives us cause to reflect on the flimsy nature of the rule of law'. The French army of a century ago, he added, like the society of that period, fostered both the old-fashioned and the modern prejudices against Jews. But Captain Dreyfus was a modern officer, he was not from the officer caste, nor was he a ranker. 'The modernity of Captain Dreyfus,' he added, 'reveals the modernity of the Affair itself. It is linked to the secular idea, the essential motor of integration . . . It is a sign of the difficult march to the Republic, towards values of truth, freedom and justice, towards the idea that the cause of humanity is superior to any other . . . The rôle of the Affair was to reveal the nature of a period, a society and an army.'

The general concluded with quotations from Péguy's *Notre jeunesse*: 'One single injustice, one single crime, one single illegality . . . one single affront to justice and the law, breaks, and is enough to break, the entire social compact, one single felony, one single disgrace, suffices to dishonour, to ruin the honour, of an entire people.' Péguy declared, he said, 'and may he be heard by our young people: "The Dreyfus Affair was essentially a mystical affair. It lived by its mystique. It died of its politics. Every party lives by its mystique and dies of its politics." ' the fact that in 1995 the French army had finally publicly cleared Dreyfus and come round to using classic Dreyfusard language meant that, 89 years after the 1906 decision of the Cour de Cassation, France had indeed witnessed the very last official act of the Dreyfus Affair. The fact was not lost on outside observers and the *Daily Telegraph* (13 September 1995) even printed the spectacular headline 'Dreyfus innocent – official at last'. (*see* also *Libération* and *le Figaro* (13 September 1995).

But for official France, in 1994, there could be no *celebration* of the centenary: 'One does not celebrate a crime.' But historians must continue to help each generation to remember. That is the first step, but of course only the first step, to avoiding crimes being repeated in the future.

The above brief account of the consequences of the Affair should have sufficed to give a hint of the remarkable breadth and longevity of its impact on contemporary France.

For the historian, there is as much left to write about the aftermath of the Affair as there is to be said on the Affair itself. In history, as in natural science, it remains true that as soon as one territory has been explored, another comes into view on the horizon, perhaps even more extensive than the last. The view that everything has already been said on the Affair is grotesquely mistaken.

NOTE ON CENTENARY CONFERENCES AND PUBLICATIONS

Among the numerous academic conferences on the Affair held in 1994, several were centred on the newest areas of research, notably the reception of the Affair by the various social, political and religious groups in France, and reactions to the Affair throughout the world. (For the proceedings of the Rennes conference, see Michel Denis, Michel Lagrée and Jean-Yves Veillard eds., *L'Affaire Dreyfus et l'opinion publique en France et a l'étranger* (Rennes, 1995); for that at Montreuil, see *Jaurés, les socialistes et L'Affaire Dreyfus. Actes du colloque de Montreuil (3 décembre 1994) organisé par la Société d'Etudes Jaurèsiennes et la Musée de l'Historie Vivante, Jaurès, Cahiers trimestriels* 138 (September–December 1995). The proceedings of the Tours conference will appear in 1996 as *Les representations de L'Affaire Dreyfus dans la presse en France et à l'étranger* (Publications de l'Université de Tours).) Other conferences have been held at Paris, Jerusalem and Tel-Aviv, Potsdam and New York. The aftermath of the centenary has equally been marked by the establishment of the Société Internationale d'Histoire de l'Affaire Dreyfus – details from M. Philippe Oriol, 12 rue de Nice, 75011 Paris, France. The Société hopes to publish information on and reviews of the proceedings of the 1994–95 conferences. For a review of some of the publications of the centenary year not referred to in the 'Further Reading' section of this book, see *Modern and Contemporary France*, NS3, no. 2, 202–5.

A SHORT CHRONOLOGY OF THE AFFAIR

1894

27 September	The *bordereau* arrives at the Statistical Department of the War Ministry.
6 October	At the Ministry, it is attributed to Dreyfus.
15 October	Dreyfus is arrested.
1 November	An article by Drumont in *La Libre Parole* launches the press campaign. The ministers decide to start proceedings against Dreyfus.
c. 8 November	Mercier decides Dreyfus will be convicted thanks to a secret file. Volte-face by Drumont and Rochefort, who become his supporters.
3 December	D'Ormescheville report.
19–22 December	First trial. Secret file shown to judges but not to defence. Dreyfus convicted. He is to be transported for life and degraded.
31 December	Dreyfus's appeal is rejected

1895

5 January	Dreyfus is degraded at the Ecole Militaire. His alleged confession to Lebrun-Renault.
6 January	Approach by Münster to Casimir-Périer.
January	Mathieu Dreyfus is entrusted by the Dreyfus family with a propaganda campaign and the search for the real culprit.
21 February	Dr Gibert learns from Félix Faure that Dreyfus was convicted on the strength of a secret document.
End of February	Mathieu Dreyfus asks Bernard-Lazare to write a pamphlet in defence of his brother
13 April	Dreyfus arrives at the Ile du Diable.

1896

March	Picquart receives the *petit bleu*: he has Esterhazy followed without success.

27 August	Picquart becomes convinced that Dreyfus is innocent.
3 September	A false report of Dreyfus's escape is published in London, then in Paris.
14 September	Article in *L'Eclair*: 'That lout Dreyfus'.
15 September	Picquart to Gonse: 'I shall not let my secret die with me'.
26 October	Picquart, having become an embarrassment, is sent away on an assignment.
2 November	The Henry forgery presented to Gonse. He is delighted.
6 November	Bernard-Lazare publishes his first pamphlet.
10 November	*Le Matin* publishes a facsimile of the *bordereau*.

1897

June	Picquart asks Leblois to act as his lawyer.
14 July	Scheurer-Kestner announces at the Senate that he is convinced Dreyfus is innocent.
Autumn	Herr convinces the first Dreyfusards.
6/7 November	Mathieu Dreyfus discovers the identity of the real culprit.
November	Clemenceau and Zola enter the fray.
15 November	Mathieu Dreyfus denounces Esterhazy.
17 November	Pellieux ordered to hold an enquiry on the latter.
4 December	The preliminary investigation in the Esterhazy trial is entrusted to Ravary. Méline to the Chamber: 'There is no Dreyfus Affair.'
7 December	Scheurer launches a debate at the Senate.
13 December	Rochefort implicates Wilhelm II, the German Emperor, in the Affair.

1898

2 January	Esterhazy committed for trial.
7 January	*Le Siècle* publishes the d'Ormescheville report.
10–11 January	Esterhazy trial: he is acquitted.
13 January	Zola publishes *J'Accuse . . .!*
14 January–late January	Petitions by the intellectuals and emergence of revisionist party; protests by nationalists and antisemites; antisemitic riots in the provinces.
18 January	Abstentionist manifesto of Socialist parliamentary group.
20 January	Zola and Perrenx summonsed to appear before

	the Assizes.
22 January	Fight in the Chamber of Deputies. Jaurès struck by de Bernis.
7 February	Zola trial begins.
17 February	Pellieux quotes the Henry forgery during the Zola trial.
18 February	Boisdeffre and the generals threaten to resign.
20 February	It is decided to found the Ligue des Droits de l'Homme.
23 February	Zola is condemned to one year in prison and a fine of 3,000 francs.
8 and 22 May	Parliamentary elections.
14 June	Fall of Méline.
28 June	Brisson Cabinet: Cavaignac at the War Ministry.
7 July	Cavaignac speech presenting the Henry forgery as a proof of Dreyfus's guilt.
10 August	Jaurès begins publication of *Les Preuves* in which he declares Dreyfus innocent.
13 August	Major Cuignet discovers the Henry forgery.
30 August	Cavaignac interrogates Henry; he confesses.
31 August	Henry commits suicide.
3 September	Lucie Dreyfus applies for a review of the Dreyfus case.
5 September	Zurlinden War Minister.
17 September	Chanoine War Minister.
20 September	Proceedings begin against Picquart.
26 September	The Cabinet decides to refer the application for a review to the Cour de cassation.
October	Labourers' strike in Paris. Rumours of a military coup. France climbs down over Fashoda.
25 October	Parliament reconvenes. Chanoine resigns at the rostrum. Brisson Cabinet resigns.
29 October	The Cour de cassation declares the application for a review admissible and opens an enquiry.
1 November	Dupuy Cabinet.
Autumn	Emergence of the idea of transferring the application for a review to Combined Divisions of the Cour de cassation. Dreyfusism now identified with the anticlerical and antinationalist Left.
14 December	*La Libre Parole* launches an appeal for Henry's widow.
31 December	The Ligue de la Patrie Française is founded.

1899

10 February	The law to transfer application for a review to the combined divisions is passed by the Chamber of Deputies.
16 February	Death of Félix Faure.
18 February	Emile Loubet is elected President.
23 February	State funeral of Félix Faure. Déroulède's march on the Elysée ends in a fiasco.
31 March	*Le Figaro* begins publication of the Cour de cassation's enquiry.
29 May	Ballot-Beaupré at the Cour de cassation recommends that Dreyfus should be retried by court-martial at Rennes.
31 May	Déroulède acquitted at Assizes.
3 June	A retrial ordered. Dreyfus committed for retrial by court-martial at Rennes.
4 June	Aristocratic protest at Auteuil: Loubet struck by Baron Christiani.
11 June	Longchamp: Republican counter-demonstration in defence of Loubet. Scuffles.
12 June	Fall of Dupuy Cabinet.
22 June	Waldeck-Rousseau Cabinet, including Galliffet and Millerand. Control of army and police reasserted.
30 June/1 July	Dreyfus landed and taken to Rennes.
Summer	Mercier against Dreyfus. New Déroulède plot.
7 August	Rennes trial opens.
12 August	Déroulède and the plotters are arrested. Deposition of Mercier. The siege of 'Fort Chabrol' begins.
9 September	Dreyfus found guilty again by five votes to two, with extenuating circumstances. He is sentenced to ten years' imprisonment.
19 September	Dreyfus is pardoned by Loubet.
20 September	Surrender of 'Fort Chabrol'.
21 September	Galliffet: 'The incident is closed.'

1900

27 December	Amnesty law.

1903

6 and 7 April	Jaurès relaunches the Affair in the Chamber.

1904

5 March   The Criminal Division of the Cour de cassation declares admissible the second request for a review.

1906

12 July   Order rehabilitating Dreyfus.

1995

7 September   The French army officially declares Dreyfus innocent.

FURTHER READING

The outstanding general accounts of the Affair available in English are: Guy Chapman, *The Dreyfus Trials* (London, 1972), essential reading on the events and the political context (for the earlier, fuller edition, *see* his *The Dreyfus Case: a Reassessment* (London, 1955)); Nicholas Halasz, *Captain Dreyfus: The Story of a Mass Hysteria* (New York, 1955), a highly readable narrative, excellent on Dreyfus, the other characters and the historical context; and Jean-Denis Bredin, *The Affair: The Case of Alfred Dreyfus* (New York, 1986), a translation of the fullest and most up-to-date survey of the Affair in all its aspects, first published in French in 1983 (reissued as *L'Affaire* (Paris, 1993) with an updated bibliography).

See also:

Leslie Derfler, *The Dreyfus Affair. Tragedy of Errors?* (Boston, MA, 1967). Important analyses by leading French historians in translated extracts.

Douglas Johnson, *France and the Dreyfus Affair* (London, 1966). Extensive discussion of the legal and military issues and of espionage.

Roderick Kedward, *The Dreyfus Affair* (London, 1965). Discussion of political and religious issues as an introduction to documents in French.

Maurice Paléologue, *My Secret Diary of the Dreyfus Affair 1894–1899* (London, 1957). Key source on the trials, diplomacy and public opinion in an excellent translation. (French original: *Journal de l'Affaire Dreyfus 1894–1899. L'Affaire Dreyfus et le Quai d'Orsay* (Paris, 1955).

Louis L. Snyder, *The Dreyfus Case. A Documentary History* (New Brunswick, NJ, 1973). Translations of basic documents including *J'Accuse . . .!*.

Other sources to complement the present work, in order of interest:

Léon Blum, *Souvenirs sur l'Affaire* (Paris, 1981). Essential on the Dreyfusard movement and on politics.

Robert Gauthier, ed., *'Dreyfusards!'* (Paris, 1965). Includes substantial extracts from the memoirs of Mathieu Dreyfus, Bernard-Lazare, Scheurer-Kestner, etc.

Mathieu Dreyfus, *L'Affaire telle que je l'ai vécue* (Paris, 1978).

Alfred Dreyfus, *Cinq années de ma vie (1894–1899)*, introduction by Pierre Vidal-Naquet (Paris, 1982, reissued 1994). (Translation: *Five Years of my Life* (London, 1901).)

A. and P. Dreyfus, *The Dreyfus Case* (New Haven, CT, 1937).

P. Dreyfus, *Dreyfus: His Life and Letters* (London, 1937).

Emile Zola, *L'Affaire Dreyfus. La vérité en marche*, preface by Colette Becker (Paris, 1969). Includes *J'Accuse . . .!* and the other Zola texts. Reissued 1994.

Bernard Schwertfeger, ed., *The Truth about Dreyfus from the Schwartzkoppen Papers* (London/New York, 1931).

Jean Jaurès, *Les Preuves. Affaire Dreyfus* (Paris, 1981).

Charles Péguy, *Notre jeunesse* (Paris, 1993). Includes his celebrated portrait of Bernard-Lazare.

Maurice Barrès, *Scènes et doctrines du nationalisme*, 2 vols (Paris, 1925).

Bernard-Lazare, *Une erreur judiciaire. L'Affaire Dreyfus* (Paris, 1993). Reproduces the second edition of his pamphlet.

Patrice Boussel, *L'Affaire Dreyfus et la presse* (Paris, 1960). Press articles.

Introductory references in French:

Madeleine Rebérioux, *La République radicale? 1898–1914* (Paris, 1975), ch. 1. Translation in Jean-Marie Mayeur and Madeleine Rebérioux, *The Third Republic from its origins to the Great War, 1871–1914* (Cambridge, 1984).

L'Affaire Dreyfus. Vérités et mensonges, L'Histoire 173 (January, 1994).

Janine Ponty, 'La presse quotidienne et l'Affaire Dreyfus en 1898–1899: essai de typologie', *Revue d'histoire moderne et contemporaine* xxi (April–June 1974), 193–220.

Jean-Pierre Peter, 'Dimensions de l'affaire Dreyfus', *Annales ESC* (November–December 1961), 1141–67.

Michel Drouin, ed., *L'Affaire Dreyfus de A à Z.* (Paris, 1994). Encyclopaedia articles on all aspects of the Affair, notably foreign reactions. Major bibliography to 1994 (1128 references).

The starting points for all serious research:

Joseph Reinach, *Histoire de l'Affaire Dreyfus*, 7 vols (Paris, 1901–11). Very useful general index in vol. 7. Despite its inevitable, and well-known, errors – for example on the role of Henry and on the Jesuit plot – this fundamental work remains an inexhaustible source of information on events, characters and the political and social context. Much better informed than some more recent work by historians who have not troubled to read it carefully.

Marcel Thomas, *L'Affaire sans Dreyfus* (Paris, 1961). The definitive work on the spy-story and the role of the General Staff.

Louis Leblois, *L'Affaire Dreyfus. L'Iniquité. La Réparation. Les principaux faits et les principaux documents* (Paris, 1929). Over 1,000 pages of documents, mainly extracts from the trial records. The basic introduction to the sources.

Louis Capéran, *L'anticléricalisme et l'Affaire Dreyfus* (Toulouse, 1948). Another essential but under-used book which offers far more than its title would indicate: on the role of the Catholic Church, but also on the Dreyfusards and on the political context.

Pierre Birnbaum, ed., *La France de l'Affaire Dreyfus* (Paris, 1994). The first attempt at an overview of the long-term social and political dimensions of the Affair. (See my review in *Modern and Contemporary France*, NS3 (1), 58–61.)

On particular aspects, see:

Pierre Albert et al., *Historie générale de la presse française, III: De 1870 à 1940* (Paris, 1972).

Hannah Arendt, *The Origins of Totalitarianism* (New York, 1973).

Maurice Baumont, *Au cœur de l'Affaire* (Paris: 1976).

Pierre Birnbaum, *Les fous de la République. Histoire politique des juifs d'état de Gambetta à Vichy* (Paris, 1992).

Michael Burns, *Dreyfus. A Family Affair 1789–1945* (London, 1992). Outstanding on Dreyfus and his family.

Ibid., *Rural Society and French Politics. Boulangism and the Dreyfus Affair 1886–1900* (Princeton, NJ, 1984).

Robert F. Byrnes, *Antisemitism in modern France. The Prologue to the Dreyfus Affair* (New York, 1969).

Eric Cahm, *Péguy et le nationalisme français* (Paris, 1972).

Christophe Charle, *Naissance des 'intellectuels' 1880–1900* (Paris, 1990).

Adrien Dansette, *Histoire religieuse de la France contemporaine* (Paris, 1965).

Cécile Delhorbe, *L'Affaire Dreyfus et les écrivains français* (Paris, 1932).

Egal Feldman, *The Dreyfus Affair and the American Conscience 1895–1906* (Detroit, MI, 1981).

Laurent Gervereau and Christophe Prochasson, eds, *L'Affaire Dreyfus et le tournant du siècle (1894–1910)* (Paris, 1994). Articles, mainly on cultural, particularly artistic, aspects. A visual history of the period with 600 illustrations. (But *see* Eric Cahm, 'L'Europe au temps de l'Affaire Dreyfus, pp. 267–74).

Raoul Girardet, *La société militaire dans la France contemporaine 1815–1939* (Paris, 1953).

Ibid., *Le nationalisme français. Anthologie 1871–1914* (Paris, 1983).

Nancy L. Green, *The Pletzl of Paris: Jewish Immigrant Workers in the Belle Epoque* (New York, 1986).

Harvey Goldberg, *The Life of Jean Jaurès* (London/Madison, WI, 1962).

Richard Griffiths, *The Use of Abuse. The Polemics of the Dreyfus Affair and its Aftermath* (New York/Oxford, 1991). Covers the main writers.

Daniel Halévy, *Péguy and the Cahiers de la Quinzaine* (London, 1946). French paperback edition: *Péguy et les Cahiers de la Quinzaine*, ed. E. Cahm with 100 pp. of notes (Paris, 1979).

Norman L. Kleelbatt, ed. *The Dreyfus Affair. Art Truth and Justice* (Berkeley and Los Angeles, CA, 1987). Catalogue of New York exhibition. Essential for the iconography of the Affair.

Le R. P. Lecanuet, *Les signes avant-coureurs de la Séparation* (Paris, 1930).

Géraldi Leroy, ed., *Les écrivains et l'affaire Dreyfus* (Paris, 1983).

Daniel Lindenberg and Pierre-André Meyer, *Lucien Herr: Le socialisme et son destin* (Paris, 1977).

Jean Maitron, *Histoire du mouvement anarchiste en France (1880–1914)* (Paris, 1981).

Michael R. Marrus, *The Politics of Assimilation. A Study of the French Jewish Community at the Time of the Dreyfus Affair* (Oxford, 1971).

P. Michel and J.-F. Nivet, *Octave Mirbeau, l'imprécateur au cœur fidèle* (Paris, 1990).

Aaron Noland, *The founding of the French Socialist Party 1893–1905* (Cambridge, MA, 1956).

Pascal Ory and Jean-François Sirinelli, *Les intellectuels en France, de l'Affaire Dreyfus à nos jours* (Paris, 1986).

Alain Pagès, *Emile Zola, un intellectuel dans l'affaire Dreyfus* (Paris, 1991).

Pierre Pierrard, *Juifs et catholiques français* (Paris, 1970).

David R. Ralston, *The Army of the Republic. The Place of the Military in the Political Evolution of France 1871–1914* (Cambridge, MA/ London, 1967).

René Rémond, *The Right Wing in France: From 1815 to De Gaulle* (Philadelphia, PA, 1968).

Jean-Pierre Rioux, *Nationalisme et conservatisme. La Ligue de la Patrie Française* (Paris, 1977).

Shlomo Sand, *L'illusion du politique. Georges Sorel et le débat intellectuel 1900* (Paris, 1985).

Auguste Scheurer-Kestner, *Mémories d'un sénateur dreyfusard* (Strasboug, 1988).

Willa Z. Silverman, *The Notorious Life of Gyp. Right-wing Anarchist in Fin-de-siècle France* (New York/Oxford, 1995).

Pierre Sorlin, *La Croix et les juifs* (Grasset, 1967).

Ibid., *Waldeck-Rousseau* (Paris, 1966.

Zeev Sternhell, *La Droite révolutionnaire 1885–1914. Les origines française du fascisme* (Paris, 1978).

Ibid., *Maurice Barrès et le nationalisme français* (Paris, 1972).

Marcel Thomas, *Esterhazy ou l'envers de l'affaire Dreyfus* (Paris, 1989).

David Robin Watson, *Clemenceau. A Political Biography* (London, 1974).

Eugen Weber, *Action Française. Royalism and Reaction in Twentieth-Century France* (Stanford, CA, 1962).

Claude Willard, *Le mouvement socialiste en France (1893–1905). Les guesdistes* (Paris, 1965).

Nelly Wilson, *Bernard-Lazare. Antisemitism and the Problem of Jewish Identity in Late Nineteenth-Century France* (Cambridge, 1978).

Stephen Wilson, *Ideology and Experience. Antisemitism in France at the Time of the Dreyfus Affair* (East Brunswick, NJ/London/ Toronto, 1982).

Michel Winock, *Edouard Drumont et Cie. Antifascisme et fascisme en France* (Paris, 1982).

Older books in English which remain useful:

George Barlow, *A History of the Dreyfus Affair* (London, 1899). A remarkable chapter on the elections of 1898.

Fred C. Conybeare, *The Dreyfus Case* (London, 1898). Very well-informed for its date.

G. W. Steevens, *The Tragedy of Dreyfus* (London, 1899). Centred on the Rennes trial of which it gives a vivid eye-witness account, one of the fullest available. A remarkable gallery of portraits.

INDEX

206